DIY 86

DIY 86

MARSHALL CAVENDISH
LONDON · SYDNEY · NEW YORK

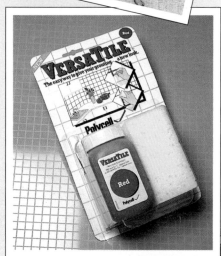

Credits

Editor	Alan Ross
Sub-Editors	Paul Berman Neil Bingham Mark Chivers Mike Crossman David Rosam
Art Editor	Keith Vollans
Designers	Kay Carroll Ray Leaning
Picture Researchers	Irene Lynch Vickie Walters
Project Coordinator	Robert Paulley
Production Controller	Steve Roberts
Editorial Director	Maggi McCormick

PICTURE CREDITS
p2 centre right, Sally and Richard Greenhill; p2 bottom right, British Gas; p3 centre left, John Wyand; p3 bottom left, AGA Thermovision/Science Picture Library; p5 bottom left, Sally and Richard Greenhill; p11 top, Sainsburys; p11 inset, Barnabys; except where otherwise stated all photographs in Product Section p12-p59 by Ray Duns; p13 bottom left, S Barnett-Rodwell PR Projects; p15 centre right, Medite; p15 top left, Sandvik; p18 top, Vencil Resil Home Improvements; p19 right, Butterley Building materials Ltd; p21 left, Polycell Products; p22 right, Wolfcraft; p22 left, Makita Electric (UK); p24 centre, Midway Marketing Ltd; p25 right, Steinel; p25 centre, Spiralux Handtools Ltd; p26 left & centre, Peglars Ltd; p28 right, Bartol Plastics Ltd; p29 left, UNI-tubes Ltd; p29 centre, J Manger & Son Ltd; p33 centre, Philips; p33 right, Thorn EMI; p36 left, Copydex; p37 left, OBO; p37 centre, Polycell Products; p39 centre, ICI Paints Division; p43 left, Cuprinol; p43 right, Hansil Ltd; p44 left, Hansil Ltd; Appliance Co Ltd; p48 right, 3M United Kingdom PLC; p49 centre, Frelen; p49 right, 3M United Kingdom PLC; p50 left, Potterton International Ltd; p54 left, Swish Products Ltd; p54 right, Hansil Ltd; p55 left, Colt International Ltd; p56 right, H Burbridge; p65 Photographers Library; p67 Elizabeth Whiting Associates; p69 Sefton; p74 North Thames Gas; 076 Dynorod; p77 Sally Neal/Greenhill; p78 Ace; p79 John Wyand; p81 Aerofilms; p84 John Wyand; p85 top, Barnabys; p85 bottom, Elizabeth Whiting Associates; p86 bottom, Sefton; p86 right, Elizabeth Whiting Associates; p88 top, Ace; p88 bottom, Design Council; p89 Barry Lewis/Network; p90 top, Sally and Richard Greenhill; p90 middle, Sefton; p91 Sally and Richard Greenhill; p92 Sally and Richard Greenhill; p93 top, John Wyand; p93 bottom, Barnabys; p94 Dynorod; p95 top, John Wyand; p95 bottom, Rentokil; p96 Sally and Richard Greenhill; p98-9 Sally and Richard Greenhill; p100 John Wyand; p101 AGA infrared/Science Photo Library; p102 Hook/Willan Homes- p103 top, Elizabeth Whiting Associates; p103 bottom, Barnabys/Alan Smith; p104 Calor Gas/Chilmark PR; p105 top, Elizabeth Whiting Associates; p105 bottom, Parkray; p106 Thorn EMI; p107 Jesch/Bournville; p109 Rentokil; p110 Rentokil) p111 top, Alpine; p111 bottom, Robin Maclean/Standard Carpets; p112 3M; p115 top, Elizabeth Whiting Associates; p115 bottom, Barnabys; p117 Ray Duns; p118-9 Barnabys; p121 Mothercare; p122 bottom left, Sally and Richard Greenhill; p122 bottom right, Sally and Richard Greenhill; p123 Spectrum Colour Library; p124 Spectrum Colour Library; p125 top, Spectrum Colour Library; p125 centre, Jeremy Butler/RIBA; p126 centre, Sheridan Photo-Library; p126 bottom, John Topham Picture Library; p129 top, Sally and Richard Greenhill; p129 centre left, Barnabys; p129 centre right, Barnabys; p130 John Frost Newspaper Collection; p131 top, Barnabys; p131 bottom left, Elizabeth Whiting Associates; p131 bottom right, Elizabeth Whiting Associates; p132 top, Elizabeth Whiting Associates; p132 mid right, Elizabeth Whiting Associates; p132 top right, Elizabeth Whiting Associates; p133 Sefton.

ARTWORK CREDITS
p17,, 31, 41, 47, 53, 59 Stan North; p66, 68, 70-1 John Hutchinson; p72-3, 74, 75 Stan North; p83, 89 Kuo Kang Chen; p104, 106, 108, 114, 117, 120, 122 Stan North; p127 John Hutchinson.

Published by Marshall Cavendish House
58 Old Compton Street
London W1V 5PA

ISBN 0-86307-453-7

Typesetting by Bookworm, Manchester
Manufactured by New Interlitho, Spa, Italy

READERS' PROJECTS
We are always interested to hear about our readers' own experiences in the DIY field. If you have carried out a particularly successful or unusual DIY project, or even if you have a horror story to tell, why not let us know so that we can consider it for inclusion in the next Yearbook.

Please send any relevant details of your project or experience to The Editor, The Knack Yearbook, Marshall Cavendish, 58 Old Compton St., London W1V 5PA. The Publishers regret that they cannot accept responsibility for loss of or damage to any material sent.

Editor's letter

What's new in DIY . . . ? Well, I hope this completely new yearbook answers all your queries as its sole aim is to present up-to-date information on a range of DIY topics.

If it's DIY products you want to find out about, then turn to the first half of the book which reviews the latest and most interesting of the DIY products on the market. Here, you can get an idea of what kinds of tools and materials are now available for your various projects.

The second half contains background information so vital for every householder. For instance if you want to know whether your planned extension requires planning permission, where to get the most suitable mortgage, which specialist to call in – it's all there in an easy-to-read style.

I hope you find it a practical help and a pleasure to read.

The Editor

Contents

Product Review 1986

Every year there are more and more DIY products flooding on to the market. Great claims are made for all of them but very often they sink without trace. Some of them really do make life easier and are everything that the advertisements say, but other products have drawbacks that only become apparent when you have paid your money and try to use them.

The *Product Review* section of the Yearbook looks at a variety of new inventions and devices designed for the DIY enthusiast. The products in question cover the whole range of DIY activity – some would find a home in any tool kit, like the drill bit that can be adjusted to bore holes of different sizes, while other products could easily pay for themselves in an emergency, like the repair kit for burst water pipes.

The rapid development of electronics has spread into the DIY field. You can now buy an electronic Command Centre which switches on and off a number of appliances around the house at predetermined times. There is also an intercom available which uses the ordinary domestic wiring to enable you to speak from one room to another.

Interior decorating is easier than ever

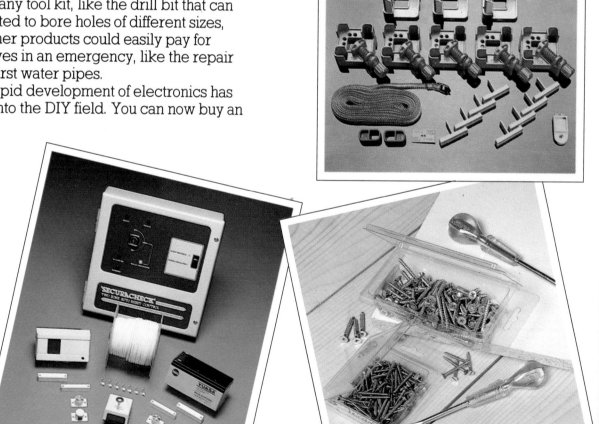

before, whether you are paperhanging with the help of an automatic pasting machine, or painting with a brush supplied with paint by a soda siphon bulb. There is also a product to give tiled surfaces a fresh new look by colouring the grout and a special tape for sealing unsightly cracks in the plaster.

Safety and security products are another growth DIY market sector. We look at a burglar alarm kit you can install yourself, an infra-red alarm system and some easily-fitted locks.

Throughout the *Product Review* section of the Yearbook there are step-by-step *Projects*, featuring an in-depth look at the product, what it does and how easy it is to use. For example, if you want extra heat in your kitchen, there is a new heater on the market which fits under the floor of a kitchen unit and does not take up any valuable space. The *Project* feature tackles the job of fitting the heater. Another new idea highlighted in a *Project* is a window frame which comes in kit form, allowing you to tailor its dimensions to fit the window exactly.

All in all, the *Product Review* section gives unbiased information on new ideas and inventions, so that you can choose the products that are most suitable for your own home and DIY capabilities.

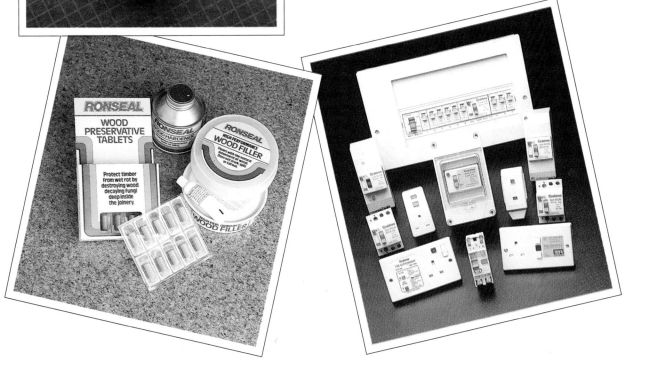

Shop Around

There has never been a wider choice of DIY materials nor has there ever been such a number of retail outlets, large and small, selling them. The fierce competition among sellers means that prices are always competitive and the need to attract customers has made the DIY superstores, in particular, into convenient and interesting places to shop with room sets and plenty of space to browse. However, the specialist supplier and local DIY shop can offer services and advice which make them an alternative to consider.

Today's home-improver has such a choice of retail outlets it's hardly surprising that he or she is in turmoil when it comes to shopping for the best buys. It's easy to see why many people are tempted by the easy option: the heavily advertised superstores.

But it is worth having a look at the pros and cons. True, you may find just what you need — you can get everything from building materials to paint and wallpapers under one roof — but are you getting the best quality, choice and economy that's perhaps available at the smaller or more specialist suppliers?

Don't be fooled into thinking that builders', plumbers' and decorators' merchants are the domain of the tradesmen. Most offer a substantial range for the amateur handyman — and don't forget the lowly DIY shop, which might have a stock of no-longer-available goods.

Tip

With materials such as filler, for example, it's worth enquiring about the lesser-known products instead of buying whatever is offered in handy tubs or tubes under popular banners: the professional decorator has no time for these, often gimmicky all-purpose products, so why should you not benefit from his preference?

Under one roof

The DIY superstores — notably B&Q, Payless DIY, Texas, Do It All and Homebase — are vast warehouses with ample space to take an enormous range of goods and products (over 14,000 claims B&Q; about 15,000 boasts Homebase). They are arranged like giant supermarkets, with checkouts, trolleys and row-upon-row of stacked shelves.

They are immensely popular — and rightly so, for they enable the masses to drive in (many have ample car parking facilities), drop in and walk out with anything from a tap washer to a complete bathroom suite. They cater for all your homemaking jobs in a central location, meaning you will never need to shop around for bargains — many of their ranges are offered at discounted prices, because there's no middleman, and it's here that they can score above the specialist suppliers.

The ranges of certain — but by no means all — items may be limited to a choice of only one manufacturer's products, even though they may be a leader in the field, although Homebase pride themselves on their extensive range of particular items, designed to offer the customer a wide choice.

It is useful to be able to make comparisons, so if you are after a reliable power tool, for example, you will find a much bigger selection — from makers such as Bosch, Wolf, Steinel and Makita, for example — and find the exact tool you need at a specialist tool supplier. Nevertheless, you can be confident that the quality of materials and equipment sold by the superstores is going to be excellent.

If expert advice is what you are after, you are unlikely to find this readily on tap at a superstore. The staff are well trained about the ranges they sell, and willing to help as best they can, but they are unlikely to be fully conversant with the relative merits of one precision tool against a rival make. Some stores such as Texas Superstores and Homebase, operate information booths, where there's always someone on hand to help with queries. Payless, who also used to run advice booths, are phasing these features out of their stores. Staff training at Homebase involves education on DIY plus suppliers' training courses.

Many items sold by superstores — whether they are small or large — are pre-packed, often shrink-wrapped and not readily available for close scrutiny. Naturally enough, no one would want to buy something that had been unpacked — so if you want to inspect the goods before you part with your money, buy from a smaller outlet, who will be more willing and able to oblige.

One of the greatest advantages of shopping at a superstore is their long opening hours — typically until 8pm, sometimes until 9pm — which generally include bank holidays and Sundays as well.

Help from the professionals

If you are daunted by the prospect of making ignorant requests in a builders', plumbers' or decorators' merchants, surrounded by knowledgeable, chortling tradesmen, you needn't be. These outlets are obviously primarily in business to tend to the needs of the professionals — and many feature only token retail outlets, segregated from the Trade Counter and sparse in display — but here you are likely to receive experienced assistance if you have a tricky prob-

lem, and in all probability they will be able to suggest and supply an alternative product if need be.

Seeing the wood

Buying timber can be quite an art, if you are to end up with good quality materials that won't let down your prowess with a chisel and saw. For large amounts of sawn or planed timber you would be wise to patronise a local timber yard, where you can be sure the wood is stored and seasoned correctly — important to prevent warping, splitting and other damage.

Yards can stack much longer lengths than you will find in DIY stores and superstores, although both these outlets usually stock a representative selection of the most common standard lengths and sections — 1.8m, 2.4m x 25, 38, 50mm sq, for example. Where you need an odd section of timber, most yards have the facility to machine it for you, and some smaller DIY shops may also oblige. In the superstores, their wood is commonly shrink-wrapped in convenient bundles (typically containing four, six eight or more lengths), but Do It all and Homebase, among others, offer a cutting service for boards and timber.

A superstore may have larger stocks of materials but a local DIY shop might give better service

On the electrical circuit

You can buy replacement light bulbs, plugs, fuses and short lengths of flex form many high street stores — Woolworth, British Home Stores, Boots, to name but a few — or electrical goods shops, and many have separate lighting departments offering a range of accessories and fittings.

However, if you are involved in a complete rewire or an extension to an existing set-up, the specialist electrical supplier with trade and retail outlets is the best choice, as here you will be able to buy the bulk quantities of cable, flex, sockets, switches and junction boxes such a task involves.

Some superstores offer electrical fittings and accessories, usually pre-packaged (but often loose in help-

yourself bins) and you should be able to find all you need here, but probably without the technical back-up of a specialist should you have a particular enquiry.

Vehicles for heavy goods

When it comes to bulk-buying of building materials — bricks, blocks, sand, cement and aggregates — it's hard to beat the traditional builders' merchant for a good range of types. However, the big superstores with plenty of storage space are able to stock good ranges of blocks and bricks.

Timber yards are more likely to stock pressure-treated timber (impregnated with preservative), which is a must for large projects where treating by brush with pots of fluid would be too time consuming and not as effective.

Woodworking

Without the correct tools and materials, DIY woodworking can turn into just so much frustration. This year has seen some new variations on time-honoured themes, with improvements on the screwdriver and the clamp. Manufacturers have also introduced three examples of multi-purpose tools which can considerably lighten your toolbox by replacing more than one conventional tool. In addition, you no longer have to choose from a range of boards and plywoods as Medite Medium Density Fibreboard offers considerable advantages over conventional materials.

GRAB A CLAMP

The traditional G-clamp has over the years proved an invaluable aid for gripping work, with a wide range of applications. But when it comes to coping with more awkward items such as small tubes and irregular shapes, there are limitations. Among the dangers here is that the work may be twisted or can slip inside the jaws.

There is now a completely new design call the Crab Clamp which overcomes these problems. This all-steel clamp has a jaw capacity of up to 115mm (4½in) — at least 12mm (½in) more than most popular designs of G-clamp. Since the screw thread is at 90° to the clamp, there is automatically greater clearance around the jaws. With a deeper throat than the G-clamp, the working access to the piece being held is also far greater. It really brings the G-clamp up to date.

Each jaw on the Crab Clamp has four faces. One is plain, and has a hole that takes a 32mm (1¼in) diameter nylon pressure pad, thus removing the

need to insert pieces of padding to protect the work; and the other two have 'V' grooves, one across the face of the jaw and the other down its length. This combination gives you 24 different clamping positions — including the facility to grip two pieces of tube at 90° to each other.

The manufacturers claim that the Crab Clamp can withstand a maximum gripping pressure of 400lb and the screw thread is guaranteed for life. One further advantage of this excellent design is that two or more of these clamps used together will provide a stand for the work if you need to lift it off the workbench — something G-clamps cannot do.

CRAB CLAMP
Manufacturer: JEM Marketing
RRP: £17.95 per pair

EASY SCREW-IN

Starting a screw into its hole when you can't get a hand in to hold it can be a frustrating job, but the Levermore Screw Launcher claims to solve this — at least for slotted-head screws. The Screw Launcher is available in eight sizes, with differing blade diameters and lengths.

Screwdrivers which hold the screw are not new, but the way in which the Levermore works is. The launcher works by having a two-part blade, each half being slightly wedge-shaped. The two halves are moved by pushing on a plastic collar which is located on the screwdriver shaft.

In use, you fit the end of the blade into the driving slot of the screw, then move the collar up the screw launcher shaft. This forces the two blades to slide over each other, and the wedge

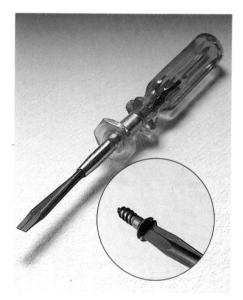

shape ensures that they in effect expand to grip the screw. With the screw held pretty firmly, you can get it started in even the most confined spaces, then switch to a normal screwdriver once the screw is safely located.

The Levermore is also useful for removing a screw which has stripped its thread and is turning freely in its hole. By gripping the screw head, you can pull out the screw without difficulty, and without the usual danger of damaging the surrounding surface if you tried to lever the screw out. The screw launcher works for slotted screws only, not Phillips or Pozidriv ones and is a professional tool available through specialist builders' merchants.

LEVERMORE SCREW LAUNCHER
Manufacturer: Levermore and Co Ltd
RRP: from £4.95

ACCURATE CORNERING

Anyone who has used the traditional mitre box or block will be well aware of the limitations of such items. Particularly annoying is the way in which the slots gradually wear down and result in inaccurate cutting. Not only does the Mitre Maker overcome this problem, but it is also suitably versatile to offer a range of cutting angles.

Barring unforeseen hazards, the Mitre Maker almost guarantees accurate angled cuts in any section of wood that has two adjacent right-angled faces, using a panel saw with 7-11 teeth per inch. It is ideal for such jobs as picture framing and shaping skirting boards, mouldings and architraves. And you can also shape plastic, polystyrene and aluminium, with the right saw.

The Mitre Maker comprises a base unit, into which four bolts fitted with plastic tubes are inserted to act as a guide for the saw. The adjustable fence can be set in position to hold the work at the required angle for the cut. When using the Mitre Maker, you can either hook it over the edge of a workbench or hold it down with G-clamps.

The good news for all left-handed woodworkers is that this device has a symmetrical design, enabling it to be used comfortably by those cutting with their left hand.

Full instructions on how to use the Mitre Maker are included in the pack and spare parts, when required, are available direct from the manufacturer.
MITRE MAKER
Manufacturer: Copydex PLC
RRP: £11.44

BETTER BOLT

Ensuring secure fixings in chipboard has always been a problem, because of the composition of this type of board. Now Rawlplug has introduced its answer — the Harpoon Bolt. The name comes from the design of the bolt, which incorporates a barbed plug that opens out to grip the chipboard as the bolt is tightened into it.

The tools needed include a drill and

countersink bit and a hexagon key to tighten the bolt in place. Alternatively, Rawlplug supplies a special Harpoon Bolt Fixing Kit, which contains the necessary tools plus a drill gauge to ensure the accurate position of fixing holes in the three most common thicknesses of chipboard.

The Harpoon Bolts are supplied with plastic caps, which fit over the top of each bolt to conceal it and give a neat finish. These are available in either white or brown and are simply pushed into place.

Fixing these bolts into chipboard — or other wood, for that matter — is a simple operation. All you need to do is drill the required hole, countersink it, slide the bolt into place and tighten it with the hexagon key. The barbs in the plug will then expand and dig into the wood, giving you a very firm grip. The plastic cap is then fitted on to the top of the bolt head.

According to the manufacturers, you can remove this type of bolt and use it again, as needed.
RAWLPLUG HARPOON BOLT
Manufacturer: Rawlplug Co Ltd
RRP: from £1.98

ALL FOUR ONE

Multi-blade screwdrivers have often caused problems because blades have gone missing and the locking device has worked loose after continual use. The latest idea from Dura-Drive is a multi-purpose screwdriver with a choice of four different heads. The difference with this model, however, is the way in which the blades are stored.

The reverse tapered handle, which sits snugly in the hand, contains four separate blades which can be pivoted easily into the working position. These blades are made from high quality

steel and comprise small and large standard heads and small and large cross-point heads. They are held in position by a steel locking ring, which does appear to be firm enough not to wear loose, even after some considerable hard use.

The added advantage of this screwdriver is that should a screw prove stubborn to shift, one of the other blades can be opened out and used to provide extra leverage.

When not in use, the blades fold back neatly into the handle. This means only one small screwdriver to store away and no separate blades to lose.

DURA-DRIVE SCREWDRIVER
Manufacturer: Dura-Drive Co Ltd
RRP: £6.99

NEW PACKS

If you have ever spent hours hunting for a particular size or type of screw to finish a job, you will appreciate that a supply of different sized screws is always welcome. But the next problem is usually how to store them so you can locate them easily.

The problem is solved by GKN with the launch of its Propack range. Each product in the new range comes in a one-piece transparent package that hangs neatly on to a nail or hook in a section of pegboard. This allows you to find at a glance the type of screw, nut, washer or bolt that you need without scrabbling through a mixed selection in a box or tin.

The packs can be opened and then resealed, so that the remaining contents do not spill all over the floor. If you want a selection of fasteners in one pack, the Rotapack is the answer. All you do is swivel the lid and take out

the size of screw you need.

All the GKN screws in these packs have the latest generation Supafast thread and an improved, recessed head design. They are aimed at providing the DIY enthusiast with a quick and efficient fixing and are specially useful with chipboard.

PROPACK PACKAGING
Manufacturer: GKN Fasteners
RRP: from £0.99

EASY JOINER

For anyone with a storage problem, one practical solution must be the Cabinet Mate produced by Pentabridge. Whether it's a cabinet, cupboard, chest of drawers or shelving you need, this well-designed system enables you to build your own choice of units easily and accurately.

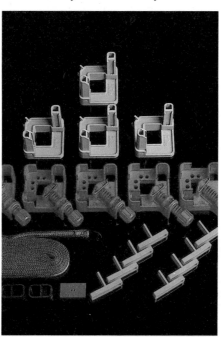

The main advantage of using Cabinet Mate to make storage units against buying ready-made ones is that you can design them to the exact shape and size you require and produce them at a much lower cost. What it does is to help considerably the DIY person who has always doubted his ability to design and assemble his own cupboards (see **Project** page 16).

The Cabinet Mate kit comes with four door clamps, five universal clamps, a webbing strap, drill marker, hinge position guide, various support blocks and door and overlap spacers. The system is designed to help you build storage units using 15mm (⅝in) thick plastic-faced chipboard, although other materials such as blockboard, plywood, medium density fibreboard or just plain wood can be used.

Using the items of equipment supplied with the kit, which includes full instructions for a range of projects, basic construction requires the minimum of skill. The materials and fittings, such as screws, hinges and handles, will be readily available from your local DIY stockist.

All you then need to do is measure up and cut to size the various sections of your unit and assemble it using the relevant fixing guides from the Cabinet Mate kit.

CABINET MATE
Manufacturer: Pentabridge
RRP: £25.00

MULTI-SIZED DRILL BIT

Sandvik has recently added the adjustable drill bit to its range of high quality tools. With this you can bore holes of varying diameters into wood without having to buy a complete set of drill bits. However, it can only be used with a hand brace and is not suitable for an electric drill.

The drill is available in two sizes — 16-45mm and 22-76mm — and any diameter hole can be bored within these limits. This is done by adjusting the setting scale on the bit to the required diameter and holding the cutter in place by tightening the locking screw with either a spanner or a screwdriver. The bit is supplied with two types of cutters — a short one and a long one.

Top quality forged tool steel has been used throughout and the working

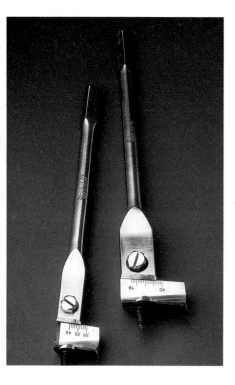

parts of the bit are hardened and stress-relieved for longer life. It is possible to sharpen the cutting edge with a fine flat file as needed.

The adjustable drill bit has been designed with the enthusiast in mind, since it will give a better surface finish and a cleaner cut hole than normal bits. Obviously the other main advantages lie in the fact that two bits will be sufficient to cope with holes from 16mm up to 76mm in diameter and storage problems are greatly reduced.

ADJUSTABLE DRILL BIT
Manufacturer: Sandvik UK Ltd
RRP: £16.97

MULTI-PURPOSE SAW KIT

Multi-purpose saws have always been rather frowned upon by purists. For the DIY enthusiast, however, they are a good value-for-money answer to most wood-cutting tasks. The latest design, from Atkinson-Walker, is the 3-in-1 Saw Kit, which consists of one handle and three different blades — keyhole, hand and tenon.

The tenon blade incorporates a new idea — an adjustable depth gauge. This gauge, which sits in two slots on one side of the 10in tenon blade, helps ensure that you saw to the exact depth when cutting joints and grooves, for example, which you should be able to do with comparative ease.

The hand blade in this kit is suitable for all general work and cuts easily through chipboard and other DIY household materials. When you are faced with awkward cutting situations, the keyhole blade comes into its own. This can saw through floorboards that need lifting, cut holes in doors for letterboxes or catflaps and generally cope with other difficult areas around the house.

All three blades sit firmly in the handle and are secured by a fixed screw and wing nut. Although there should be very little movement between the handle and the blade, you may find after continual use over a period of time that the join does work slightly lose.

As with all such kits, there is no real substitute for individual saws. This particular product, therefore, is aimed at the DIY enthusiast just starting to build up a tool kit rather than the experienced carpenter and is priced accordingly.

3-IN-1 SAW KIT
Manufacturer: Atkinson-Walker (Saws) Ltd
RRP: £6.61

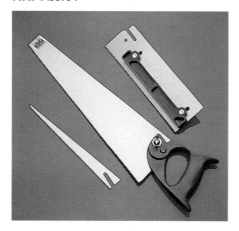

MAN-MADE FIBRE

Medite has recently produced a specially engineered medium density fibreboard (MDF) that combines the best features of hardwood, softwood, particle board and hardboard.

MDF is made from softwood fibres and a small amount of resin, but differs from chipboard in that its composition has a uniform density throughout — chipboard is less dense towards the centre. This means that screws will grip more securely in MDF than chipboard and when working this board you will find it does not splinter, chip or flake. The manufacturers recommend the use of carbide-tipped woodworking tools.

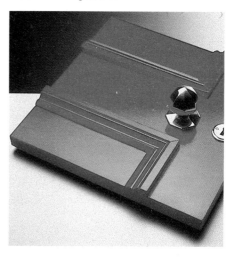

When joining MDF, you can still use traditional woodworking adhesives or standard nails. With screw fixings, sheet metal self tapping screws are ideal.

This board is particularly easy to work and the edges can be moulded or shaped to any design using a router or any other suitable tool.

When applying a finish, you first need to seal the surface with a clear or pigmented sealant. Then put on a coloured base coat, which you can give a grained effect with a brush before completing the work with a clear gloss top coat. Alternatively, any of the normal range of decorative or special effect laminates can be fixed on the MDF.

MEDITE MEDIUM DENSITY FIBREBOARD
Manufacturer: Seaboard International Ltd
RRP: £15.00 for 2.4m × 1.2m × 18mm (8ft × 4ft × ¾in) board

Cabinet Maker

Many people have always thought that designing and assembling a cabinet was beyond them. But the job is now much more straightforward through the use of the Cabinet Mate — a collection of useful assembly tools which are very easy to use once you get the hang of them. Making a bathroom cabinet from melamine-faced chipboard is a good project to start with.

As the size and number of doors determines the overall dimensions of the cabinet, measure the area on the wall where the cabinet will hang, and then buy the doors to fit your measurements — the Cabinet Mate is easiest to use if you choose 15mm (⁹⁄₁₆in) thick doors. The doors used in this project are 300mm (12in) wide and 450mm (18in) high. The cabinet itself is 600mm (24in) wide, 450mm (18in) high and 225mm (9in) deep. The sections, including the shelf can be cut from one 1830mm (6ft) and one 1220mm (4ft) length of 225mm (9in) wide chipboard with little wastage. When measuring, bear in mind that the overall dimension of the unit will be 4mm longer than the width of the door if just one is fitted and 7mm longer if two doors are fitted.

1 Having prepared the doors, clamp them in position. Using the door clamps in the kit, fit these at each corner with overlap spacers between the door and each clamp. Then wrap the webbing strap round the clamps and tighten it to hold them firmly in position. If you are fitting two doors, use door spacers between them to ensure that you get the 3mm gap necessary for opening and closing. In such cases, the door clamps are fitted to the four outside corners.

2 Measure the distance between the top and bottom clamps on both sides of the door and mark these lengths accurately on to the chipboard, scoring the cut lines through

Measuring for the sides

the melamine surface to prevent it from splintering when sawing. Cut the two lengths to form the cabinet sides using a fine-toothed panel saw.

3 Place a universal clamp on each of the door clamps — they fit over the pillars. Now slide the side panels into the universal clamps, and gently hold them in place using the diagonal screws.

Measure the distance between the side panels and cut the top and bottom panels accurately to fit. Loosen the clamp screws slightly, and slide the top and bottom panels into place. Once it is

Clamping the panels

done, tighten the clamp screws once again.

4 Fit the spare universal clamp over the top edge of one corner. Insert the drill marker into this clamp and

Marking the screw holes

using a sharp, pointed instrument, mark accurately the position of the screw holes. Repeat the operation for the other corner clamp on that join. If you are making a very deep cabinet and more than two screws are needed, use the drill marker on its edge to mark the extra holes.

With all the sides marked, drill the holes for the fixing screws — these should be special countersunk cross-head chipboard screws. You can disguise the screws easily using decorative plastic covers which are a snap fit into the screwdriver slot in the screw head. Special stepped drills are available to enable you to bore countersunk, clearance and pilot holes in one operation. Fix this first corner together and then repeat the operation for each of the other corners.

5 It makes sense to fit a shelf into your cabinet as it makes it even more versatile and is quite easily done. First, however, decide on what sort of back you are going to fit to the cabinet (see step 6), since

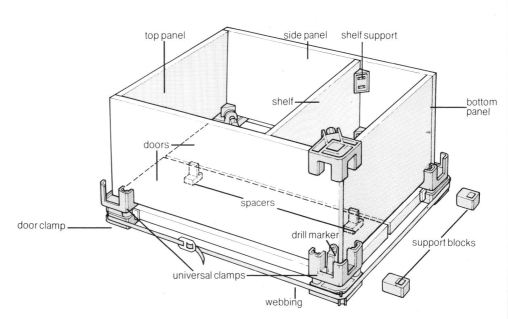

Attaching the shelf brackets

this affects the depth of the shelf. If you are using a hardboard backing, the shelf can be the same width as the rest of the cabinet. If you intend to use 15mm chipboard for it, then the shelf depth must be reduced by 15mm, to compensate for the thickness of the backing.

Mark the approximate position of the shelf on the inside of the cabinet using a pencil and try square. Now remove the universal clamps from one end of the cabinet and replace them with the support blocks. Use the two clamps you have just removed to hold the shelf

Assembling any size of cabinet is made easy with Cabinet Mate's many special features. The cabinet frame is held firmly at all times, making the job as simple as possible

in position on your marks. Check that it is level and adjust as necessary.

The shelf can be fixed in place in one of three ways. First, you can drill holes right through from the outside of the cabinet into the shelf and use chipboard screws, disguising the ends as before. A second method is to use plastic shelf supports which push into holes drilled inside the cabinet. Thirdly, you can use shelf support blocks which are held to both shelf and cabinet by screws. In all cases, use at least two supports per side.

Use whatever methods you have decided on to fix the shelf, then remove the clamps.

6 You can make the back of the cabinet in one of two ways. The easiest method is to cut a piece of melamine-faced hardboard to size and use panel pins to hold it to the rear of the cabinet with the melamine facing the front. You can then finish the cut edges of the board with fine surface filler, and paint when dry. Otherwise, the method is to cut out carefully a suitable section of melamine-faced chipboard to fit exactly inside the opening at the back of the cabinet and then screw this into position.

7 To provide a neat overall finish to the cabinet, fix iron-on edging strip to all visible raw edges of the chipboard, making sure the strip overlaps slightly at all points. You can then trim off the surplus using fine glasspaper wrapped round a wooden block. Work at a 45° angle to give you a neat tapered finish.

8 The ideal hinges to use for each door are concealed cabinet ones often used for kitchen cupboards. These fit into shallow circular holes 26 or 35mm in diameter drilled into the back of each door — go for the 35mm alternative. This type of hinge has several advantages over traditional designs. Because it

Fitting the hinges

has a self-closing, spring-loaded action, you can dispense with the need for a cupboard catch. These hinges are also easily adjustable, which means you can guarantee an accurate fit after the door has been hung.

Mark out where to make the holes with the hinge position guide. You will need a special end mill to drill out the holes. If you use a drill stand, you will find it a lot easier to ensure the holes are drilled squarely. Take care not to drill too deep or you will seriously weaken the doors.

Screw the hinges firmly in position in the back of the door, then hold this in place against the front of the cabinet. Mark out the position for the side fixing screws and drill pilot holes, then screw the arm of each hinge to the side of the cabinet. If the arm incorporates a slot, mark the fixing hole in the centre of this to allow the maximum adjustment of the arm. Mark the positions of the door handles, drill holes to suit the fixing method and secure the handles in place.

The best way to hang your finished cabinet is to use corner hanging brackets, and 35mm (1½in) No. 8 screws.

Masonry & Plastering

Masonry and Plastering products range from the decorative to the supportive. New materials are the story this year, finding their way into many of the products — even the plain old wall tie has been improved.

WALLS WELL TAPED

Small cracks and holes in walls frequently open up again after filling, as the filler dries and shrinks or due to slight flexing in the wall, which ruins your decor.

One new idea comes from Canadian manufacturers Bay Mills, who produce Fibatape, a glass fibre open mesh capable of patching holes up to 80mm across and cracks wider than about 6mm. The tape, very fine, extremely strong yet flexible enough to cope with substantial movement, is self-adhesive on one side for easy application to a smooth, thoroughly clean wall surface.

Fibatape has a dual role as a substitute for traditional paper jointing tape used in drywall and plasterboard ceiling constructions — it's run centrally down the tapered joins between panels from the top without the need to bed it in filler (as with paper tape) then coated with conventional jointing and finishing compounds.

To patch a hole, simply cut three or four strips from the roll and press them

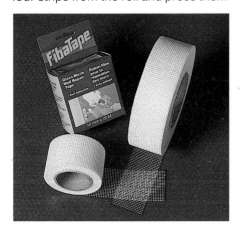

firmly over the defect in criss-cross fashion, keeping the mesh taut to prevent sagging. Immediately, spread on filling compound with a broad-bladed knife. When dry, sand until it's smooth.

You can apply a thin finishing coat of compound, feathering the edges for a smooth unobtrusive finish.

Cracks are dealt with similarly: press the tape along the fissure, then fill and sand as for holes.

Fibatape can also be used outdoors for gutter repairs, roof sealing — and in car body repairs. Available in 20 or 90m long rolls, the tape is stocked by builders' merchants and DIY stores.

FIBATAPE
Manufacturers: London and Lancashire Rubber Co Ltd
RRP: £3 for 20m; £9 for 90m.

Finish off freshly-applied filler with a damp feathering sponge. This eliminates dust due to sanding and makes for a much smoother joint.

ON THE FACE OF IT

Coving, once a standard feature in older houses, adds a finishing touch to a decorating scheme, helping to soften the harsh angularity of a room. Although rare in newer buildings, it's nevertheless a feature that is usually apparent by its absence.

Vencil Resil Home Improvements, in conjunction with Stoneface (who make

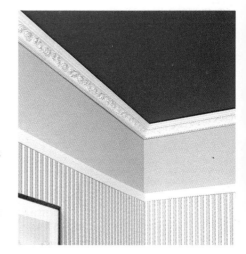

stone cladding), now offer their Plaster-faced Coving. The product comprises reinforced plaster laminated to a lightweight expanded polystyrene core, which can be fixed to a ceiling/wall angle using heavy duty solvent-free coving adhesive.

The marriage is successful, combining plaster's delicate moulding with polystyrene's light weight. The result is eminently realistic — a possible clue to their true make-up could be the joins between the lengths, despite the fact that they are intended to be disguised with plaster or filler.

The coving is straightforward to fit and the simplicity of the two designs on offer — classically linear Regent; intricately floral Garland — means matching lengths need not cause a visual jar.

To install, offer up a suitable length of the coving and draw its outline on the wall and ceiling. Make sure there is no loose or flaky paint or wallpaper within the lines, then apply adhesive to the coving's two angled sides. Press the coving into the ceiling/wall angle (supporting with a few small pins if necessary until the glue has dried).

Butt-join subsequent lengths, mitring them at internal or external corners with the aid of a mitre board and a fine-toothed tenon saw or hacksaw. Smooth cut edges with glasspaper. To finish off the coving, either leave the white finish or paint as required.

PLASTER-FACED COVING
Manufacturer: Vencil Resil Ltd
RRP: £3.00 per length

CONCRETE COLOURS

Concrete may well be tough, durable and hardwearing, and an invaluable material for making hard surfaces, indoors and out, but to look at — frankly, it's dull. Cement pigments for new work have been available for years, but to mask existing concrete's less attractive features it's usual to paint it or clad it. Now, though, you can transform concrete's dreary grey surface with natural stone tints.

Already manufacturers of a range of cement pigments, Readymix Drypack's Wondertone Concrete Stain is a hydrochloric acid-based liquid with dye added, which you simply brush on to the surface. Three colours are available, mimicking popular natural stone colours: Tan, a mellow rust tone; Green, a light pastel tint; and Cotswold, a light yellow.

The stain, which comes in a 2 litre plastic container, is straightforward to apply to any sound concrete surface — whether it's an area of paving slabs, a driveway, path, block wall or pierced block screen. You can even daub the stain on to the walls of a concrete

garage or shed so it blends more easily with its surroundings. Garden ornaments, planters — even drab fence posts — need not be spared a new colour scheme.

Wondertone covers about 10m² (110 sq ft) per litre of liquid, although this is likely to be considerably lessened on very porous surfaces. The liquid dries in about three hours, depending on the ambient temperature and the porosity of the concrete.

WONDERTONE STAIN
Manufacturer: Readymix Drypack Ltd
RRP: Cotswold, £4.79; Tan, £4.95; Green, £6.48

BRICK FACIAL

Bricks are primarily intended as a versatile, structural building material but, laid in numerous simple or complex patterns, they can also be extremely decorative. It's no wonder that — bared and burnished — they are used for features inside the home as an alternative to traditional wall coverings. Naked brick walls make fine feature areas — a chimney breast becomes transformed into a focal point; an entire wall creates an atmosphere rich in texture.

One way to show off a brick wall is to hack off the plaster and clean up the surface. But this method is risky — there's no guarantee that what lurks beneath is good to look at or consistent in quality (or bond), or that you will be able to remove the rendering without chopping off the faces of the bricks. Besides which, the whole process is extremely messy.

A number of companies have hit on the idea of producing slimmed-down brick lookalikes — basically tiles — which you attach to a sound surface. The tiles are typically stuck on using an ordinary ceramic wall tile adhesive and the joints can be pointed with mortar or left as they are for a recessed joint effect.

Many of these brick tiles are moulded from a synthetic material, bearing more resemblance to biscuits than bricks (although some have a charm of their own) — but one exception is Butterley's Brick Faces. These are actually real kiln-produced clay brick slips sliced during manufacture and used to clad walls

both internally and externally.

The slips measure about 215 × 65 × 15mm (8½ × 2½ × ½in) — brick-proportioned, which many poorer relations are not — and come in a range of twelve colours and textures, looking like common brick types — greys, buffs, reds, browns and burnt brick colours with a variety of surface textures that look and feel exactly like any number of different types of bricks — just like the real thing.

Complementing their range of flat faces, Butterley also produce shaped corner tiles — a header and stretcher face in one — which you alternate on each corner of the room to complete the illusion.

Boxes contain 30 tiles — enough to cover about ½m² (5½ sq ft) of wall.

BRICK FACES
Manufacturer: Butterley Building Materials Ltd
RRP: About £16 per box

MASONRY & PLASTERING

COMPOUND INTEREST

Fixing battens, brackets and other objects to walls isn't always a simple matter of drilling a hole and inserting a

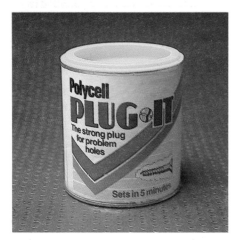

pre-made plug. If the wall is old it may be crumbly or powdery and not even a special soft wall plug will offer any meaningful grip.

Plug-it is a fast-setting powder compound. Mix Plug-it in the proportions of one part water (in a clean bowl) to three-and-a-half parts compound, using a clean knife. Don't mix more than you can use in five minutes, or it will set hard and useless.

Use a pencil or a long nail with a flat head to ram it well in for a good grip. Before Plug-it sets, drive in the screw fully and allow to set for a minimum of five minutes.

When you are fixing an object to the wall, remove the screw before Plug-it sets, leave until it's hard, then fix the object in place, driving the screws through the pre-made threads. Leave the filler to set for five minutes for lightweight objects, one hour for general household items, overnight for heavyweight objects.
PLUG-IT
Manufacturer: Polycell Products Ltd
RRP: £1.25

PANEL GAME

Even the best decorating scheme won't conceal the wall that's rough and pitted due to previous patching — the surface must be sound, dry and flat. Drylining with plasterboard and its derivatives is the foolproof way to prepare walls.

On brick or block walls it's an alternative to wet plaster: it's also a cover-up for old plastered surfaces and for timber-framed walls it's the only option. Where a greater degree of insulation is desirable — on a masonry wall that can't otherwise be insulated — opt for thermal board, with a thick sheet of expanded polystyrene bonded on the back.

Standard thermal boards are either glued to the walls or nailed to a batten framework. But one version, called Epsicon, uses a different method of fixing which should make this job both easier and quicker. It will also absorb minor irregularities in the wall surface to a greater degree than other types of thermal boards. The panels comprise a lamination of three polystyrene sheets, tongued-and-grooved on adjacent long and short edges, enabling the panels — which measure 1.2m (4ft) long and 0.45m (18in) high — to be slotted together. Plasterboard facing is bonded to the front. Unlike conventional boards, Epsicon panels are fixed horizontally.

To install them, a 15mm (⅝in) sq batten is fixed to the floor 15mm from the wall and the first course of panels is slotted on top, working around the room. Plastic connectors secure the panels — they are pushed into every second slot along the top edge of the panels and secured with nailable plugs. The next row of panels are slotted on to the exposed tongues and secured with connectors. The vertical joints are staggered by overlapping the panels by half their width and this gives a smooth finish overall.
EPSICON DRYLINING SYSTEM
Manufacturer: Epsicon Products Ltd
RRP: £3.20 per panel

At the top course, cut the panels about 8mm undersize: saw the connectors from the row below in half, then insert and secure them through the face of the panels. Now slot the other halves into the underside of the top row panels, position them on the wall and secure through the faces.

BRIDGE THAT GAP

Wall ties are vital to the stability of a cavity wall by linking the inner loadbearing leaf to the outer facing

leaf. Inserted in the mortar joints 450mm (½yd) apart vertically, 900mm (1yd) apart horizontally and staggered in each course, ties come in various guises. Twisted wire butterfly ties are used for 50mm (1in) cavities where two different materials — say brick and block — are used for inner and outer leaves, whereas twisted galvanized steel versions are used for cavities 75mm (3in) and more wide.

Now there's Ryton's plastic tie, which offers the benefits of both metal types plus a number of advantages over its predecessors. The tie suits 50mm (1in) and 75mm (3in) cavities, and is made from strong and durable polypropylene, which has the tensile and compressive qualities of a steel tie coupled with the limited flexibility of the wire tie.

The two flat 'bows', ridged on both faces to provide above average pull-out strength, even when the jointing mortar is applied to the top of the tie only, rest on the leaves at each side and a tubular stem links them. The stem features a triple drip ring, which prevents penetrating rainwater from trickling to the inner leaf. Provision is also included for rigid cavity insulation to be attached in the form of a retaining washer.

Although at the time of writing Agrément Board Approval for the tie had not been issued, Ryton expect a favourable assessment.

PLASTIC WALL TIE
Manufacturers: Ryton's Ventilation Equipment Ltd
RRP: £14.00 per 300; £1 per box 100 retaining discs

PATCHING PERFECTION

Plaster repairs give do-it-yourself a bad name, as experts with a trowel will no doubt enthuse, and it's largely true that considerable skill is necessary to make a patch that's flat to the touch and invisible to the eye. But if you baulk at the thought of hiring a professional plasterer to tackle what are really the finishing touches to a project, don't despair because Polycell's Polyskim will help you with patching.

With Polycell's Polyskim you don't have to be a dab hand with the professional's tools — it's a ready-mixed plaster that you apply with a brush, then smooth off with a supplied plastic spreader.

Available in 10kg tubs, mixed to just the right consistency for use, Polyskim can be used to make good alongside sound plaster. Repairing damage caused by failed plasterwork, or

cladding infill brickwork or blockwork (where you have blocked off a fireplace opening, for example) are typical examples of where this material scores, although it's equally well suited to making good where tiles have been removed, or for finishing rough or damaged plasterwork on walls and ceilings prior to decorating.

The substance can be simply spread on to the wall with upward strokes. As the surface becomes covered, you reduce the brush pressure. Once applied, the plaster — which remains workable for several hours — turns matt in appearance, when it can be smoothed over using the spreader. With the extremely long working time you can achieve a satisfactory finish. The thinner the layer, the quicker it dries, and the better your finish ready for decoration.

POLYSKIM
Manufacturer:Polycell Products Ltd
RRP: £3.99 per 3kg; £7.49 per 6kg

Pay particular attention to the join between the new material and the hard plaster edge, spreading on to the existing surface rather than scraping from it, to achieve a ridge-free profile. If the smoothing operation creates a depression in the surface, apply more Polyskim directly with the spreader. By building up thin layers of the material you can achieve a suitable finish for decorating with paint or wallcovering.

BRICKS COME CLEAN

As brickwork gets older, it tends to assume a look about it — but the effects of atmospheric pollution can equally mar an attractive, graceful ageing process with a dirty, smutty coating. There's no way you can remove the staining by scrubbing without damaging the bricks: the porous masonry becomes deeply ingrained and scrubbing with a wire brush would only serve to score and scratch the face. Cementone's Mortar

Clean is an acid-based cleaning solution for cement and brickwork surfaces, which you can use to restore a previous finish or clean small areas of brickwork, although for large areas it would be costly and a chore to apply.

Based on hydrochloric acid, the liquid should be used with caution to avoid splashes on skin or eyes — not easy when you are working on a rough surface. Consequently it's vital that your wear old clothes, PVC or rubber gloves, goggles and a facemask when using the substance — wear a hat and visor if applying it above your head.

The substance can be used neat for heavy deposits on small areas, or diluted with equal parts of water for larger areas of brickwork. Before applying, wet the surface with water splashed on with a brush, or sprayed with a hose and fine nozzle to reduce the absorption of the Mortar Clean.

Mix the solution in a plastic bucket and apply liberally by brush (you can also spray on the substance using a low-pressure sprayer, but beware of using this on a breezy day). Don't allow the liquid to soak into the brickwork, but wash it off thoroughly with clean water applied by a hosepipe fitted with a fine nozzle. Don't allow the hose to play on one area of bricks, or this could soak in, too.

Mortar Clean will dissolve terrazzo, marble and lime silicate bricks, and will attack metal — so keep it well away from old gutters and downpipes. Available in 1 and 5 litre plastic containers, Mortar Clean will cover about 15 to 30m^2 (18 to 36 sq yd) per 5 litres, when it's used neat.

CEMENTONE MORTAR CLEAN
Manufacturer: Cementone Beaver Ltd
RRP: from £2.65

Power Tools

If you've ever used a power tool, you will be hooked. They really do remove the effort and pain of more traditional methods, and add precision to your work. In fact, power tools are obviously extremely popular as manufacturers are increasing their range at a staggering rate, bringing all sorts of jobs within the scope of the average DIY enthusiast. You can now cut foam with a power tool or even indulge in some intricate fretwork. But most useful of all, you can now use a power tool miles from a power source — thanks to the new cordless range.

NO STRINGS ATTACHED

Electric power tools are fast and efficient — but not terribly versatile when restricted by their flex, even though it may be amply long. Battery-

powered versions have been around for some time, but were dogged by flagging power from quickly run-down batteries.

Improvements have meant that longer running and more efficient action are possible.

Makita have developed a range of extensive cordless tools. The drills look like conventional drills, except that the handgrip is bulkier and longer — a niggle all manufacturers of these tools would do well to solve: battery powered tools are not the most comfortable things to hold for a long period — containing the battery (7.2 and 9.6 volts, depending on the power required) — but this doesn't appear to cause problems in use.

The 840DW hammer drill can cope with wood, steel and concrete up to

10mm (⅜in) thick, and delivers 10,000 blows per minute; the 612DL screw drill deluxe features two forward speeds — 250 and 600 rpm — and reverse action for screwdriving; the 6012 torque drill has two powerful forward speeds, 400 and 1100 rpm and a variable torque selector with five strength settings.

Compact and with a cranked chuck, the DA3000DW angle drill can reach into confined spaces. The powerful 6010DWK screwdriver drill will pierce wood and steel up to 10mm (⅜in) thick, whereas the 6010SDW reversible drill is recommended for light use only.

Other tools in the range have impressive specifications, too: the 5600DW circular saw, with a carbide-tipped 160mm (6in) diameter blade, can cut up to 36mm (1⅜in) deep at 45° setting; 55mm (2⅛in) at 90°. It takes a 10.8 volt battery. The 9500DW disc grinder, with a 100mm (4in) wheel diameter makes an excellent, lightweight tool for deburring, smoothing and sharpening.

For cutting glass with precision, consider the 4103DW 80mm-blade cutter, complete with lubricating watertank assembly — it's powerful enough to cut glass and plastic to 17mm (¹¹⁄₁₆in) depth. Another cutter — this time for light wood, ply and thin sheet materials up to 20mm (¾in) thick — the 5081DW runs on 9.6 volts and features a telescopic blade guard for safety in use.

All cordless tools in Makita's range come with a one-hour fast charger.
**CORDLESS POWER TOOLS
Manufacturer: Makita Electric (UK)
RRP: from £62.10**

HOLES IN ONE

A variation on the traditional dowelling jig from Wolfcraft allows you to drill correctly aligned dowel holes for strong, tight-fitting dowel joints 6, 8 or 10mm in diameter. The Universal wood dowelling set consists of a cast metal jig with pre-drilled holes, which enable you to make corner, T and edge-to-edge dowel joints.

The boards to be drilled are cramped into the jig, which is secured to the bench or tabletop. A second device, the dowel clamp, supports the other end of the workpiece. One board

is held under the jig's protruding flange; its mate is clamped above it. The holes are drilled simultaneously through the two sets of guide holes, then the jig is slid along to the next dowel position.

For edge-to-edge joints both boards must be clamped horizontally in the jig and aligned; for corner joints the upper board is clamped vertically so its face edge can be drilled. T joints are more complicated to make, but the kit ensures correct alignment through its clever use of marking notches in the end of the jig. Whatever the joint, the finish is usually much more precise and longer lasting.

UNIVERSAL WOOD DOWELLING SET
Manufacturer: Wolfcraft
RRP: £18.95

ELECTRIC SHAVE

Trimming wood to a smooth, flat finish calls for considerable skill with a hand plane: it's easy to gouge the surface or bevel it unintentionally unless you adopt a smooth arm action. A power planer takes the hard slog out of shaving wood and enables you to trim with greater precision than with the more traditional plane. It's certainly a

real boon to those DIY enthusiasts who could never get on with the manual tool.

Makita's natty blue planer allows single-handed operation — quite out of the ordinary compared to manual planes — and a smooth finish with just one pass of the 80mm (3¼in) wide cutter. The tool is light in weight and is fitted with a powerful 210 watt motor inside a sturdy plastic casing.

Cutting levels are adjustable via a knob on the front of the tool: the planer can shave down to a precision depth of under ½mm, assuring accuracy that would call for some considerable skill

with the more conventional plane.

Black & Decker have a similarly versatile plane, the DN710, which offers the user one-handed operation and adjustable cutting depths, also possible via a knob on the front. Like the Makita model, the Black & Decker tool has a trigger operation on the moulded handgrip.

A version of the plane, the DN720, includes a nifty shavings collection bag, which makes the job of trimming wood so much cleaner and dust-free. The bag is mounted on the right side of the tool. Because of the extra weight of the bag, this model requires two-handed operation, and there's a handle on the front so the grip applied is similar to that of a manual plane.

MAKITA PLANER
Manufacturer: Makita Electric (UK)
RRP: £43.82
BLACK & DECKER PLANE DN710
Manufacturer: Black & Decker Ltd
RRP: £48.99

POCKET SOLDERING IRON

Portasol is a pen-sized soldering iron (only 175mm long × 19mm diameter 7in × ¾in) which is powered by liquid butane gas — the type used for cigarette lighters — and designed for convenient use wherever you happen to need it, freeing you from the hassle of seeking a convenient power supply in which to plug in your electric soldering iron.

The iron produces a maximum tip temperature of 400°C, delivers a power equivalent to a 60 watt electric iron (so it is well capable of matching its bigger counterparts), and runs for one hour continuously on a full

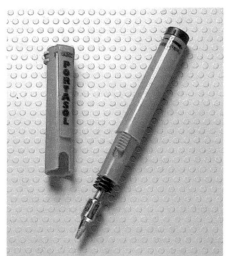

reservoir. The fuel is injected in seconds in the same way as filling a cigarette lighter and a thumb-operated wheel in the protective cap is used to strike the flint and initiate the catalytic conversion, which is responsible for the soldering tip heating up — there's no flame at all. Temperature is adjustable via a regulator at the base of the iron.

Three soldering heads containing the patented catalytic converter are available: 2.4, 3.2 and 4.8mm sizes (⅒in, ⅛in and ⅕in).

We found the heating process difficult to start with the flint but a handy match worked just as effectively.

ORYX PORTASOL GAS SOLDERING IRON
Manufacturer: JEM Marketing
RRP: £17.95

MULTI-PURPOSE TOOL

Peugeot's DIY range includes the versatile Multifac, a tool that defies a generic term, for it is capable of performing numerous tasks — standing, grinding, brushing, polishing and cutting, for example. It is equipped with a selection of interchangeable abrasive wheels, all 150mm (6in) in diameter, and various attachments.

Physically, Multifac resembles a typical jigsaw, with a moulded-on handgrip. There the similarity ends, as there's a side-grip guide handle mounted above the circular wheel head.

Endowed with five speed settings, Multifac is extremely powerful, but includes an automatic overload cut out on its 800 watts motor just in case. Like other tools in Peugeot's DIY range, this can also be used with a flexible hose attachment which connects up to your domestic vacuum cleaner, so all the mess is sucked up as you work and deposited neatly in your cleaner.

MULTIFAC
Manufacturer: Peugeot Power Tools
RRP: £79.95

SAW SOPHISTICATED

Choose Peugeot's new 25S electric circular saw and you need never again resort to cutting chipboard with a hacksaw blade. In fact, you could probably also throw away your club hammer and bolster chisel, for this high speed tool is capable of cutting not only man-made boards and natural timber, but, when fitted with a diamond

blade, it can also cut cement, stone and brick.

Light and manageable, the tool has a single rear handgrip, so it's easy to operate and guide with one hand. It has a 102mm (4in) diameter blade, which rotates at 3000rpm and is able to cut to depths of 25mm (1in).

The deluxe saw, the 25SL, features a multi-purpose tungsten carbide blade, an electronic overload indicator for when the going is even too tough for this powerful tool, and a light at the front to illuminate the cutting line.

Another final bonus: both saws can be used with a flexible extractor hose attachment, so the tool literally cleans up as you cut — no dust to get in your eyes, and no tedious cleaning up when you have finished cutting. However, you must ask for the hose, as it is an optional extra.

PEUGEOT 25S AND 25SL CIRCULAR SAWS
Manufacturer: Peugeot Power Tools
RRP: 25S £39.95; 25SL £52.50

HAVE DRILL WILL TRAVEL

If you are the kind of handyman who is forever losing his drill bits and other accessories, you will appreciate Langdon's Drilltidy. A neat plastic container in violent red, it's designed to hold most makes of electric drill. It comes with a selection of clip-on components into which you can pop drill bits, screwdriver, pencil, screws and any other small items you are likely to need close to hand when drilling.

The drill slots into the central compartment — its side arm must be removed first — and its flex is wound round a holder on the side. The plug sits neatly in the holder — and there is a thoughtful provision for round-pin and foreign plugs, too. A clip on the holder takes the chuck key.

The unit's least attractive feature is the carrying handle which is a flap of thin plastic attached so flimsily that it's bound to drop off under strain of the weight of the drill, ruining your bits in the process. Another attachment is a

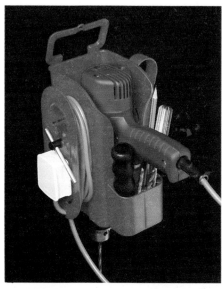

hook, which enables the Drilltidy to be suspended from a ladder rung. Lastly, there's a detachable wall-mounting bracket.

Undoubtedly useful for the absent-minded worker, consider the Drilltidy for its ability to store things rather than as a carrier. It's certainly a useful place to keep all your drill bits.

DRILLTIDY
Manufacturer: Langdon (London) Ltd
RRP: £4.99

SUCKING UP

Hand-sized vacuums have long been seen plugged into the car's cigarette lighter socket, but the new family of miniature cleaners has little in common with their inefficient 'suckability'. Electrically-powered, rechargeable, cordless vacuums are often on a par with their big brothers when it comes to clearing up minor messes.

Black & Decker produce two Dustbusters — models 937 and 938 — which sit happily in their wall-mountable baseplates recharging via a plug charger fitted in a handy socket outlet, so they are always ready for use. Both models come with a range of slot-in accessories — Super

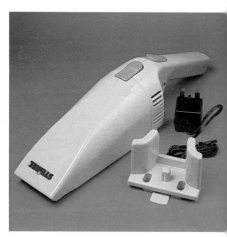

Dustbuster model 938 with crevice tool, filter bag and brush.

Similar in appearance to Dustbuster's elegant cream and brown wedge-shape, Steinel's Vacu-fix 3000 rechargeable hand vacuum cleaner is available in blue or grey with orange buttons, but without accessories. It, too, arrives complete with charger and wall bracket.

Look out also for other hand-held vacuums by Swan, Bosch and Shop-Vac.

DUSTBUSTER 937 AND SUPER DUSTBUSTER 938
Manufacturer: Black & Decker Ltd
RRP: 937 £17.95; 938 £26.95
VACU-FIX 3000
Manufacturer: Steinel
RRP: £17.95

HOT SLICES

Expanded polystyrene is a versatile material that's used widely in home improvements — as ceiling tiles, insulation between rafters and loft floor joists — while its close relation flexible plastic foam pops up as pipe lagging. Rigid foam is also a popular model-making medium.

While the material isn't difficult to cut by hand with a sharp trimming knife, it

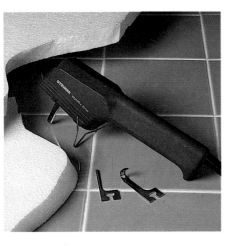

is awkward to shape large panels in this way, especially if you want intricate curves and rounded holes, or to cut through the thick slabs necessary in insulation work. Steinel's Styro Fix 2000 Styrofoam cutter is a mains-powered, electronically-controlled cutting tool, which enables you to make short work of shaping polystyrene and flexible foam.

The tool is a lightweight plastic gadget with a cutting head that takes one of three blades — the standard blade for cutting up to 50mm (2in) deep; the fine blade for curves and fine lines; and the hooked blade for groove-cutting (recessing cables in loft insulation, for instance). The blade is retained in the head by tightening with an Allen key.

To use the cutter, insert the blade then plug into the mains. Wait for about eight minutes for the blade to heat up, then make a test cut on an offcut of polystyrene before commencing with the real cut, which should be clean and strand-free. Once you get used to it, it's a delight to use.
STYRO FIX 2000
Manufacturer: Steinel
RRP: £15.95

FRETFUL

Modelmakers and crafty woodworkers often need to cut quite intricate curves and fancy shapes in thin materials ranging from hardwood, softwood and

man-made boards to plastics and metals. The usual tool they would use is a hand fretsaw.

Thin blades and a shaky hand combine to cause broken blades and frayed tempers. Here's where power and a firm base would ease the job and where Spiralux Handtools have concentrated their efforts with a portable power fretsaw in their Shapercraft range.

The saw, driven by an electromagnetic motor, which causes the blade to vibrate at mains frequency, can cope with most of the previously mentioned materials with the easy insertion of suitable alternative blades. The user is able to work close to the cutting edge in safety

owing to the blade's small vibrations. The workpiece, which rests on the baseplate and saw's motor box, is simply pushed against the blade to cut. The hooked arm, which takes the top of the blade, is broad enough to admit workpieces up to 70cm (2½ft) wide which makes it a very useful tool.
SHAPERCRAFT POWER FRETSAW
Manufacturer: Spiralux Handtools Ltd.
RRP: £19.95

JUST HOT AIR

Efficient the blowtorch may be at stripping paint from woodwork — and excellent for use where there's no electrical supply — but it does have limitations. Indoors, the risk of starting a fire is greater; where you are stripping paint from a door you want to show off for its wood-grained beauty, a gentler source of heat is preferable.

This is where hot air guns such as Steinel's HL500S or Skilten's Hot Air Stripper stake a claim. A far cry from the first generation guns, today's blowers offer a variety of uses apart from their mainstay as paint stripper.

To use in the stripping mode, play the jet of hot air over oil-based paint to soften and bubble the film, then remove with a scraper as you follow close behind the jet.

Most guns come with two air speeds and twin heat settings: for example the Steinel HL1500S produces either 300°C or 525°C, the former suitable for forming plastic and soft metal or in car body filling; the latter for soldering or stripping (melting bitumen adhesive in felt roof repairs).

Optional nozzles are also offered: Skilten and Black & Decker both supply splayed and conical nozzles for directing the heat — for narrow glazing bars or intense heat respectively.

Unlike their forebears, the guns are lightweight — Heat Streak and

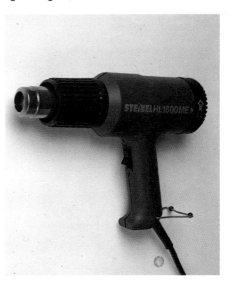

HL15500S (weighing in at 550g) have an inbuilt stand; Black & Decker's gun offers one as an extra, so the tools can be used vertically, with the trigger locked, thus freeing both hands.
HL1500 TWO SPEED HOT AIR GUN
Manufacturer: Steinel
RRP: £27.95
HEAT STREAK
Manufacturer: Skilten Electronics Ltd
RRP: £15.49
B & D HOT AIR STRIPPER
Manufacturer: Black & Decker Ltd
RRP: £15.99

Plumbing

Plumbing is one area of DIY that has never been favoured by the enthusiast — too messy, too risky and fraught with problems. The courage to have a go is usually tempered with fear as you turn on the tap to test your repairs. But visions of flooded basements and ruined carpets can now be a thing of the past. A group of manufacturers have finally come up with some exciting new products which remove the risk and mystery of plumbing and which make plumbing repairs and alterations in the home straightforward, clean and easy to achieve.

TAPS ON DISC

By virtue of their design, traditional taps are prone to leaking with frequent use. The small rubber washers either corrode from contact with water or become compressed by constant use or overtightening the taps. And changing a washer is one of those fiddly jobs that many people prefer to put off until the tap is corroded and the sink or basin stained. Dripping taps can now be a thing of the past.

Replacing the standard tap innards, and especially the lowly washer, there are now modern equivalents using ceramic discs to control the flow of hot and cold water. This innovation in tap design uses these low-friction, hardwearing (even in hard water) and durable discs both to obviate the need ever to change another washer and to improve water control.

Peglars' Regis range of taps and mixers adopts the ceramic system, and demonstrates how the shape of

taps needn't be limited to the conventional styles we are used to. The taps have an easy-action half-turn handle, mounted vertically on the 1/2in and 3/4in pillar taps and horizontally on others in the range.

A number of other manufacturers are also starting to use ceramic discs in their taps, so if you are replacing taps do enquire whether the ones you want are available with ceramic discs.
REGIS CERAMIC DISC TAPS
Manufacturers: Peglars Ltd
RRP: Basin tap £24.90 approx

A SOFT TOUCH

Scale formation caused by hard water is a big enemy of the domestic central heating system. The symptoms — poor flow of water through pipes; abnormally long times to heat up the water; knocking noises within the system — are due to severe furring, but the blame is frequently assigned to different causes.

The scenario is this: waterways are

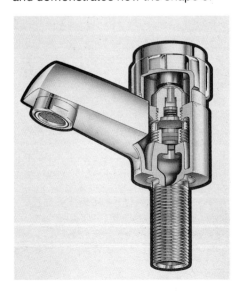

reduced to a mere trickle by scale formation, the heat exchanger is less able to conduct heat, so water in the storage cylinder takes longer to heat up. A puzzled householder resorts to turning up the heating, which only serves to increase energy costs — overheated water straining to circulate through the pipes causes noises within the system as particles of scale break off, produce local hot spots or steam bubbles which, when washed away by cooler water, condense and pop.

All this places a strain on the central heating system and results in inefficient output of heat and increased fuel bills. It's apparent, then, that the softer the water, the less likelihood there is of scale forming. If you live in an area plagued by hard water — your local authority will advise you if you are unsure — a device installed in the

heating system will soften the supply and improve your system's efficiency.

Opella's neat water softener, which is installed in the mains water supply immediately before the central heating system's feed and expansion tank, solves the problem quite neatly. Water flows through a special resin in a filter and thence into the tank as softened water.

Resembling a large vacuum flask — 320mm high × 100mm wide × 88mm deep — the device comprises a cap, seal and bowl with a central core and softening resin. It's easy to install using integral compression fittings (see **Project** page 30) and replacement packs of resin are available.

The entire unit is sold through builders' merchants from whom you can also buy the replacement resin packs. The device must not be installed in drinking water supplies, but is otherwise completely safe in use.

IMI CENTRAL HEATING WATER SOFTENER
Manufacturer: IMI Opella
RRP: £34.50

A TAP ON THE WALL

The convenience of an outside tap means you'll never again resort to carting buckets of water through the house, or have to use the kitchen taps

to attach a hose. Whether you are watering the plants, washing the car or involved in building work, you'll find an outside tap an invaluable aid — and fitted with an automatic hose reel, the tap is transformed into a versatile installation for a multitude of jobs all round the garden.

Opella's recently relaunched Outside Tap Kit provides everything you need to install a garden tap.

Because it uses their Self-cutting Plumbing-in Kit (See **Hole In One**), there's no need to turn off the water supply and drain the pipe to connect the new addition to the mains.

The kit contains: a green plastic bib tap (and hose connector nozzle), which screws onto a brass wall bracket and elbow; a 550mm (22in) length of hand-bendable copper pipe, which passes through the wall for fixing to the stopvalve; and a 1.5m (5ft) length of flexible high-pressure plastic hose for attaching the bendable pipe.

All pipe clips, screws, wallplugs and PTFE sealing tape (for the screw threads) are included, so all you need is a 15mm diameter masonry drill long enough to pierce the wall, a screwdriver to assemble the run and some repair mortar for making good around the pipe where it passes through the drilled hole.

The inclusion of the hose is a great improvement over usual tap kits: commonly you would have to buy a separate length of copper or plastic pipe to span the run between connection point and exit hole, which varies according to particular layouts. The hose, flexible enough to cope with right-angle bends, can be held neatly and rigidly in the pipe clips.

The British-made kit, guaranteed for 10 years, carries National Water Council acceptance — but check with your local authority before installing, as you may, in some cases have to pay an extra charge on your water rates for the added convenience of having a tap outside your house.

OPELLA OUTSIDE TAP KIT
Manufacturer: IMI Opella
RRP: from £16.00

Tip

Hand-bendable copper pipe is easy to use — simply grip it at each side of the proposed bend and bring your hands together slightly — but you should avoid bending it more than once in the same place or you could weaken and rupture the ridged wall. Keep the bend to a large radius.

BLOCKAGE BLASTER

People tend to regard the waste outlets of their sink, bath and other fittings as a way to dispose of all manner of household debris — according to the professionals who are called in to clear them. Although the householder is amply served with proprietary chemical clearing agents, he often has to resort to mechanical aids for the really difficult blockages — typically a straightened-out wire coat hanger.

But now there's a much more sophisticated way to clear a blockage, by blasting it away with Pango's Trouble Shooter. Resembling a large water pistol, the gun uses compressed air to blow pipes clear rather than having to pour in chemicals and leave them to dissolve the problem, or fiddle about with makeshift hooks and plungers.

Made in tough plastic, coloured orange, the gun won't fall foul of rust in this damp environment, and comes with three interchangeable adaptor plugs to suit most sink, basin, bath, bidet and shower waste outlets — you just press the one you want on to the knob on the end of the nozzle.

To use the device you have to pump the plunger on the end of the handgrip, with the gun supported on a firm surface to steady it. Three full strokes are recommended as sufficient to cope with most blockages. The rubber plug adaptor on the end of the gun can then be slotted into the waste hole and the trigger squeezed to force a jet of air into the pipe. Stubborn blockages can be dealt with by repeating the firing, but using greater pressure.

PANGO TROUBLE SHOOTER
Manufacturer: Belco Manufacturing Co Ltd
RRP: £12.50

PLUMBING

DE-BURR IN ONE

To ensure a perfect, watertight seal, copper pipe must be prepared thoroughly before it's connected to compression or capillary fittings: ridges of swarf can prevent an olive from seating properly or metal fragments can be carried down the pipework. Also, grease on a pipe end can mean that the solder won't adhere efficiently and the joint will leak.

Usually, pipe ends are reamed to remove internal burrs caused by the saw cut and filed externally, then both surfaces rubbed with wire wool — it's both time-consuming and messy. Now Opella offer an ingenious device that combines the operations of reaming, filing and polishing in one operation. The De-burr brush can be used on all 15mm and 22mm diameter pipes and is used by inserting the square-cut end of the pipe inside and rotating it.

Opella reckon that the cutters, although as yet untested, will last indefinitely.

DE-BURR BRUSH
Manufacturer: IMI Opella
RRP: £4.50

A HOLE IN ONE

One of the inconveniences of plumbing in appliances such as a washing machine, dishwasher or garden tap is having to turn off the water supply and drain down the pipework so that you can cut the pipe you're teeing into without causing a major flood.

Automatic supply connectors solve the problem simply and quickly without even the need to turn off the water supply. There are various types of connector available and, although the fitting procedure differs, the end result is the same — the device is attached to the pipe and cuts its own hole in the pipe wall.

Opella's Self Cutting Plumbing-in Kit, for use on domestic cold and low-pressure hot water pipes, adopts a gentle method and combines a tee connection with a stopvalve. The unit's base bracket is screwed to the wall behind the pipe you're teeing into, which then rests in the bracket's curved seating. The valve body is then clamped over the top and attached to the base bracket with screws. As the tee connector is screwed home, an offset single steel cutter forms a hole in the pipe. About 75 per cent of the hole area is cut away, so the offcut remains attached: authorities are concerned about types of supply connector that allow the offcut to fall into the pipe, so causing the risk of a blockage further down. Once the new pipework is attached to the tee, the valve can be operated by its built-in tap handle to release the flow.

One problem with automatic connectors is the reluctance of some water authorities to condone them: in some areas interference with the rising main is forbidden, and you should check first before deciding to use such a device.

Nevertheless, Opella's valve has the acceptance of the Water Research Centre.

SELF-CUTTING PLUMBING- IN KIT
Manufacturer: IMI Opella
RRP: £5.50

PUSH-FIT PLUMBING

A type of plumbing connector that needs no tools to assemble is a veritable boon to the ill-equipped handyman, and push-fit fittings are the

answer. Bartol Plastics' Acorn range of tees, straight connectors, elbows, reducing tees and other standard joints complement Uni-Tubes' Plum-in range of kits for installing basins, baths, sinks, garden taps and washing machines.

The fittings comprise a plastic body containing a rubber O-ring seal and a grab ring, which grips the pipe when it's inserted in the socket. The fittings can be dismantled like compression tees for washer changing, should this be necessary, although you don't need to take them to bits for fitting — the prepared pipe end is simply pushed in as far as the internal pipe stop will allow.

You can use ordinary copper pipe in 15mm, 22mm and 28mm diameters with the relevant fittings, or couple up the plastic pipe which is available to suit. Copper and plastic pipes alike can be prepared for fitting by deburring (see **De-Burr In One**) with emery cloth and to assemble the joint you need to lubricate the pipe end with a little silicone lubricant .

The same principle is adopted with Bartol's waste fittings; the larger-scale traps, elbows and straight connectors can be used to join lengths of standard 38mm plastic waste pipe.

Kits containing Bartol's push-fit fittings are sold under the Plum-in banner.

ACORN PUSH-FIT CONNECTORS
Manufactuer: Bartol Plastics Ltd
RRP: from £0.79

PLUM-IN PLASTIC

Conventional copper pipe isn't the easiest material for the home plumber to work with since it requires a comprehensive toolkit to enable you to bend, cut and join it. In addition, there's a high likelihood of leaks from incorrectly-made soldered joints.

Gaining in popularity with DIY enthusiasts (and finding favour with water authorities) is plastic piping which offers a number of advantages over copper pipe. Uni-Tubes Plum-in range, made of tough polybutylene, can be bent to fit round quite tight bends, enabling you to route long uninterrupted lengths around the house without the need for intermediate connectors.

One disadvantage with this pipe is that even though it can be fed under floors without any bother, it requires more support brackets than copper pipe — 300mm (12in) intervals for hot pipes, 500mm (20in) for cold ones.

Plastic pipe is far easier to cut than copper, using a hacksaw, needs only a rub with emery cloth to remove internal and external burrs, and is wholly compatible with standard copper systems. One point to note is that when it's connected to the tees, you have to fit special stainless steel inserts in the cut end to stop the pipe collapsing when you tighten the nuts.

The pipe — which has full National Water Council acceptance — is intended for use with both cold and hot water systems. Because it resists scaling and corrosion, and can withstand temperatures up to 100°C, it's suitable for central heating radiator installations, although it cannot be connected directly to the boiler or other heat-generating source.

Available in coils of 10m, 50m or 100m, Plum-in's pipe comes in standard 15mm, 22mm and 28mm diameters.
PLUM-IN FLEXIBLE PLASTIC HOT & COLD WATER PIPE
Manufacturer: Uni-Tubes Ltd
RRP: from £1.99

SQUIRT A SEAL

Annoying leaks from defective gutters, drains and pipes and tile, slate or felt roofs that let in water needn't spell out total replacement at considerable cost. You can prolong the life of deteriorating seals — if not permanently cure the ailment — by applying a mastic.

Stop That Leak from Mangers is a sprayable asphalt mastic available in an aerosol canister, which you simply have to spray onto the leak to seal it. The 480g container is fitted with a large, clog-free nozzle and dispenses the mastic to form a durable and flexible coating on a variety of materials. You can use it on wet surfaces, as the mastic disperses moisture, and the flexible coating is resistant to sagging and cracking.
STOP THAT LEAK
Manufacturer: J Manger & Son Ltd
RRP: £5.20

INSTANT BURST SEAL

A burst water pipe — whether it's due to a winter freeze-up or a floorboard nail bashed in inadvertently — can easily ruin your decor and in serious cases can result in the collapse of a ceiling. Probably your first thought when a leak is discovered is to turn off the water supply to the offending pipe, but this is impractical in most cases and even with the supply cut off, a long pipe run can hold a surprising amount

of water, which will continue to flow from the breach.

Block the hole — even if only temporarily — and you'll gain time to drain the pipe through more convenient outlets. A burst pipe cure commonly recommended relied on wrapping the pipe with copious bandages around a sealing off-cut of garden hose — neither a successful nor easy task.

Various proprietary clips, clamps and putty-like seals have trickled onto the market but one that seems to offer a realistic alternative is Gerald Coy Developments' Quick Seal burst pipe repair kit. The kit comprises a curved metal plate, rubber seal and a pair of Jubilee clips. To stop the leak you simply hold the seal and plate over the hole, fit the clips on top and tighten the screws to staunch the flow. Two kits are available: the smaller one copes with 15mm pipes, while the large one will seal 22mm pipes. The larger size also fits older ¾in lead pipes.

Thoughtfully, the manufacturers have considered the fact that bursts don't necessarily confine themselves to conveniently straight runs: the metal plate is slit on its four sides so that it can bend along its length and width to accommodate a curve.

Bear in mind that this type of repair is only temporary. It may last for a while, but a permanent repair will be necessary to avoid future leaks.
QUICK SEAL BURST PIPE REPAIR KIT
Manufacturer: Gerald Coy Developments Ltd
RRP: £0.89

For Softer Water

Scale in the central heating as a result of hard water passing through pipes and fittings can mean reduced efficiency and consequently higher fuel bills as the system struggles to meet your demands. A water softener installed at an appropriate position in the pipework can improve matters.

Hard water leaves its mark as the formation of scale in the pipes, which literally reduces the diameter of these vital waterways. As a result the system has to struggle to meet heating requirements and ultimately results in failure of the various components. Softened water leaves no trace as it flows, so a device that causes hard water to become soft has obvious benefits to the set-up.

IMI Opella's Central Heating Water Softener is inserted in the pipework immediately before the system's feed and expansion tank (usually found in the loft, but possibly in an upstairs room cupboard). It works as the water flows through a resin-filled compartment, the material softening it en route, and into the feed and expansion tank. Everything beyond the device then benefits from the process: the cistern's ballvalve, the pipe runs, boiler, pump, radiators and heating coil in the cylinder. This unit must not be used with direct systems.

So that the device can be isolated for servicing (the resin in the filter should last for a number of years) from the mains supply, it's necessary to fit a stopvalve on the inflow pipe. All plumbing fittings are supplied.

Before you proceed, consult your local water authority, as in some areas work on the rising main is forbidden. The mains operating pressure required for the unit is a maximum of 10 bar (150 p.s.i.); check this with the authority, too.

1 First isolate the rising main by turning off the main stopvalve just inside the house (usually under the kitchen sink): this prevents any more water from entering the house. As the water can't flow back through the ballvalves in the feed and expansion tank and the cold water cistern, you can drain the pipe by opening the kitchen cold tap.

Place a bucket or some rags under the pipe you are going to cut to catch any surplus water left inside.

2 It may be easier to fit the softener if the screw-on cap is separated from the base. If you do this, put the filter in a safe place.

Now decide on where you are going to install the unit — the best place is close to the expansion tank.

It's best to fit the stopvalve to the water softener first, then

Fitting the new stopvalve

install the assembly as one unit, so that you don't have to make two separate cuts in the pipe. Cut a short, (say 100mm/4in) piece of 15mm copper pipe then attach it to the softener's supplied com-

pression fittings. Compression fittings are easy to install with an adjustable spanner only. Cut the pipe squarely with a cutting wheel or hacksaw (wrap a piece of paper around the pipe and align the edges to act as a guide).

Deburr the cut ends inside and out with the cutting wheel's integral reamer, a file or a proprietary deburring tool (see De-burr brush page 28). Slip a hexagonal backnut and soft copper olive onto one end of the pipe then insert the pipe into the joint body, as far as its internal stop.

Wind some PTFE sealing tape around the threads of the body to improve the watertightness. Tighten the nut with an adjustable spanner. This causes the olive to be compressed around the pipe, forming a watertight seal.

3 Now slip the nut from the inlet side of the water softener cap (it's marked clearly 'in' and 'out') on to the other end of the pipe then slot the pipe into the cap and secure by tightening the nut. Connect the other end of the length of pipe to the outlet side of the stopvalve (the direction of flow is indicated by an arrow stamped on the valve body), again using the compression fittings.

4 Hold the stopvalve/water softener assembly against the mains pipe and mark the latter for cutting. Allow for enough pipe to be inserted in the compression fittings at each side — use a pencil to find out how much this is and transfer it to the outside of the compression body.

Marking pipe for cutting

5 Turn off the water supply at the base of the rising main and drain the pipe through the kitchen cold tap. Cut the pipe at the marked positions using a hacksaw — catch any water that seeps out in a bucket or with cloths — then deburr the cut ends ready for a clear connection.

Cutting mains pipe

6 You may have to release the mains pipe from the pipe clips at each side of the cut-out, to enable you to provide sufficient slack for fitting the stopvalve/softener assembly. Slip a nut and olive on to each cut end of the mains pipe, then slot the outlet side of the softener cap on to the feed and expansion tank side of the run. Don't tighten the nut yet.

Fitting unit to pipe

Gently flex the pipes to slot the cut end into the inlet socket of the stopvalve. Make sure the connections are tight and square before doing up all the nuts. When you are satisfied, use an adjustable spanner to tighten the nuts. Refix the pipe in the pipe clips and add further clips at each side of the stopvalve/softener assembly for extra support.

The cap includes an adjustable metal bracket for attaching the unit to a joist or wall; swivel this to the required angle and fasten with screws as required. You will probably find that the extra support clips on the pipe line are sufficient to support the unit, but if your pipe runs in such an area where no more clips can be fitted, then you must support the unit through the use of the bracket.

7 Before restoring the mains supply first check that all the nuts have been fully tightened and make sure that the cap and the reservoir are properly tightened down; if you removed the cap from the

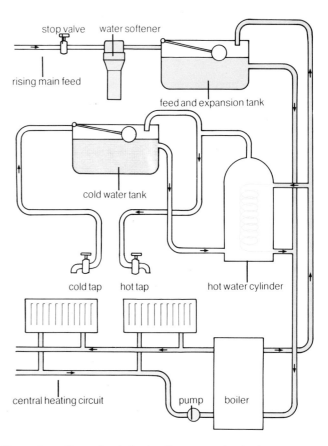

The water softener feeds the heating expansion tank — it does NOT mix with the drinking water supply

Tightening base to cap

reservoir to carry out the work, then reconnect the two now using the special spanner supplied.

Before restoring the mains supply, make sure that the new stop valve is turned to the 'off' position; this is just a preventative measure so that any leaks can be kept to a minimum when the mains stop valve is turned on and your work checked.

8 Turn the main stop valve back on the then, if there are no leaks in your new installation, the new stop valve. In order to make sure water flows through the softener and into the cistern, you will need to drain some water out of the central heating system. Run a few gallons of water into a bucket from the drain cock near the boiler or from the bleed valve on a radiator.

Opening the new valve

Electrics

Developments are moving quickly in the home electrics field. Not only are there more technical tools on the market, but there are now a number of products using the very latest technology. These are mainly house accessories, but they offer considerable benefits to home life. In fact, the Command Centre will virtually keep your house running while you disappear on holiday — an electric home-help and effective burglary preventative rolled into one. And for those who have never been able to wire up a plug, there's the Handy Plug.

LIGHT FANTASTIC

Dimmer switches for domestic lighting have grown in popularity in recent years. As well as the obvious advantages they offer in lighting arrangements in the home, they are also quite simple to install.

Most models on the market incorporate a control knob or roller switch. Some require adjustment each time they are switched on, while others have dual controls and can be left pre-set.

Superswitch has introduced a very stylish and easy-to-operate range of dimmer switches that work simply by touch. By pressing the switch panel the light is turned on. By keeping your finger on the panel, the light level changes. To turn the light off, you simply touch the panel again.

These touch dimmers are available as one- or two-way, single or two-gang switches and there is a choice of two finishes — satin silver and satin gold.

Installation is quite straightforward, since the single dimmer replaces the existing light switch and is connected to the same wiring. For two-way, two-gang dimmers the connections are slightly more complicated. These dimmers are not suitable for use in conjunction with fluorescent lighting.

Useful features are that each dimmer has its own 3 amp fuse and can be used to control up to 400 watts of lighting. An interesting innovation is a time-delay device, which enables the light to dim automatically after a pre-set period of between 2 and 15 minutes. This is particularly useful in such areas as landings and children's bedrooms.

Touch dimmers can also be

operated by remote control and various manufacturers, including both Superswitch and Home Automation, offer that option. By keeping the button on the hand-held remote controller pressed, the intensity of light via the dimmer switch can be altered.

TOUCH CONTROLLED LIGHT DIMMERS
Manufacturers: Superswitch Electric Appliances Ltd
Home Automation Ltd
RRP: from £14.91

CIRCUIT CHECKER

There are occasions when the more technically qualified DIY enthusiast needs to check electrical circuits and supply. In such cases the Steinel Combi-Check electrical tester could prove a useful piece of equipment.

One drawback with this relatively sophisticated unit, however, is that the English translation of the German instructions make its operation difficult to understand fully.

If you manage to master the instructions you will find that the tester

can be used to detect AC or DC voltages in the 6-660 volt range. It can also be used to check on phase to earth, polarity and continuity in the 0-2megohm range.

The small, hand-held 'business' end of the Steinel Combi-Check contains a series of LED displays showing whether the voltage is 6-12, 24, 50, 110, 240, 415 or 660. Another display indicates negative polarity, while the battery contained in the unit's handle provides the power for continuity testing.

There are two test buttons which allow the operator to check on the readings at all times to confirm that the unit is functioning correctly. Where the unit cannot be connected directly to

the power source being checked, a one metre cable probe is supplied.

This unit is only of real use to the technically qualified, rather than those with just a limited knowledge of electrical circuitry.

STEINEL COMBI-CHECK
Manufacturer: Steinel UK Ltd
RRP: £49.95

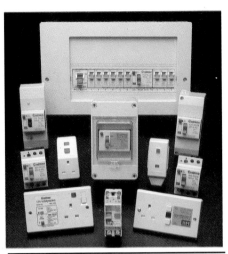

PREVENTING SHOCKS

The majority of homes are now fitted with 13amp socket outlets that are effectively earthed and many appliances are double insulated, which means they need no extra earthing. Despite such safety measures, however, deaths through electrocution still occur in the home.

The most recent safety device introduced for domestic wiring is the earth leakage circuit breaker (ELCB) also known as a residual current circuit breaker (RCCB). Since it works on a different principle to the standard fuse, it will cut off the power instantly in the event of the smallest leak to earth.

This is a major safety improvement and the use of an RCCB is now demanded by the latest edition of the Institute of Electrical Engineers (IEE) Wiring Regulations, particularly in connection with outdoor appliances.

These circuit breakers are made by several manufacturers in a range of types and applications. They can be used in conjunction with complete circuits, (and fitted in the fusebox), combined with power socket outlets or incorporated into individual plugs.

They have the facility to check automatically the circuit of any appliance and will, if a fault exists, trip out so the offending appliance cannot be used. There is a button on these devices to enable you to reset the circuit breakers should they trip out.

The MK Sentrysocket incorporates an RCCB and will replace a double socket outlet. It has a single switch controlled outlet with a reset button.

B & R produces a similar socket outlet, called the Power Breaker S. This is also fitted in place of a double

socket. One useful feature is that the RCCB can be tested by pressing the off button.

Smiths Industries supply an RCCB adapter, which again will fit a normal socket outlet, converting it to an RCCB-controlled one.

RESIDUAL CURRENT CIRCUIT BREAKER
Manufacturers: MK Electric Ltd; B & R Electrical Products Ltd; Smiths Industries Environmental Controls Co Ltd
RRP: from £46.00

LIGHT RELIEF

Fluorescent lighting gives more light more economically than the traditional tungsten filament bulb. The problem has been in designing a fluorescent bulb to fit the standard light fittings.

Philips has now brought out the SL bulb, which will fit straight into the normal bayonet-type socket and thus can replace the ordinary light bulb. The rang of SL bulbs available includes 9, 13, 15 and 18 watt ratings, equivalent to normal 40, 60, 75 and 100 watt bulbs.

Apart from using only a quarter of the power of ordinary light bulbs, the SL has an expected life five times greater, according to the manufacturers.

As with fluorescent lighting, special control gear is needed to start and run the lamp. With the SL, this is incorporated in the base of the bulb, and is replaced with each new bulb.

Although the SL bulb is, as a result, somewhat larger than the standard bulb, it can still be used in a large number of installations.

The SL bulb is ideal where lights are kept on for long periods and you

should be able to justify the additional cost, particularly since Philips claim the bulb will cut lighting costs by half.
PHILIPS SL LIGHT BULB
Manufacturer: Philips Lighting
RRP: £9.00

LOW ENERGY BULB

Normal light bulbs have a limited life, which may be a nuisance when it comes to replacing them, particularly if they are inaccessible.

Bulbs can pose other problems, from the amount of heat emitted, which can cause lampshades to be singed or walls to be stained. And this heat often restricts the strength of bulb you can use.

Thorn EMI has developed a low-energy light bulb called the 2D, which overcomes all these problems. In addition the double 'D' or butterfly-shaped bulb has an expected life of 5000 hours — or five times that of a standard bulb.

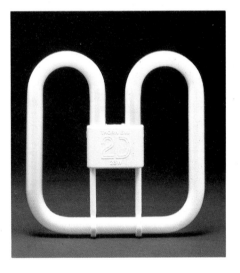

The manufacturers have estimated that you can save up to 75 per cent in lighting costs through using one of the two sizes of bulb — the 16 watt, which is equivalent to the normal 100 watt, and the 28 watt, which gives you as much light as the standard 150 watt bulb.

One great advantage of the 2D bulb is that it remains cool when switched on, thus allowing a much wider range of lampshades and coverings to be used — many have now been specially designed.
THORN EMI 2D LIGHT BULB
Manufacturer: Thorn EMI Ltd
RRP: £6.00

ELECTRICS

TOTAL CONTROL

The Command Centre — again from Superswitch — is a revolutionary new product which offers complete centralised control over up to 16 different appliances or light fittings in the home. The advantages of such a system are many. Specific appliances can be programmed to switch on or off at pre-set times without the need to fit a timing device to each one.

The 'brain' behind all the switching is the Command Centre controller. By plugging this into any convenient 13 amp socket outlet, high-frequency signals can be sent through the normal domestic wiring circuit to any appliances or light fittings plugged into the same circuit. The signal is actually picked up, not by the appliances but by special modules.

These modules are like large 13amp plug adapters, into which individual appliances — such as a washing machine or television — are connected.

The controller sends instructions to each module as required according to its programming. Each module has its own frequency, so that it can detect the relevant instruction from the controller.

You can give the controller up to 24 switching instructions and these can be programmed up to seven days in advance.

In addition to a useful clock and day display, the controller can also check on the status of any or all of the modules and the use of electricity can be monitored at a glance.

COMMAND CENTRE
Manufacturer: Superswitch Electric Appliances Ltd
RRP: £124.64

POWER POINTS

There are some areas in the home where you will need to run a series of electrical appliances or gadgets together. This situation often creates a problem over the number of power sockets available. Typical examples include a television set with a video recorder and possibly a table lamp over the set or a stereo system that incorporates the deck, amplifier and

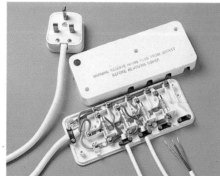

cassette player.

Although such a problem can be solved by the traditional two or three-way adapter, Ever Ready has come up with a more practical and safer solution — the Multi Feed Adapter. This comprises an adaptor box with a capacity of up to four separate connections, each of which is individually fused.

From the adapter box there is a metre length of flex with a 13 amp plug that will fit any standard socket outlet.

To make the job of wiring in to the box that much easier, there is a guide on the back to indicate how much insulation should be stripped off each wire. There is also a red neon indicator to tell when the adapter is switched on.

MULTI FEED ADAPTER
Manufacturer: Every Ready (GB) Ltd
RRP: £8.99

SURGE PROTECTION

Minor fluctuations in the supply of mains electricity to the home can affect the operation of such items as computers, video recorders, burglar alarms and other sensitive electronic equipment. Even a simple action such as switching on a kettle, or the operation of a freezer or central heating system, can easily upset the delicate circuitry of some equipment.

The fluctuation needed to affect

each item varies, but there is always the risk that a change in power will corrupt computer data, alter the quality of the picture on a video recorder or set off a burglar alarm by mistake.

Power International has come up with a solution to this type of problem — 'The Plug'. Designed along similar lines to a standard 13 amp plug, this three-pin model fits into a normal socket outlet, although it is a little taller and there may be situations where you have difficulty plugging it in. It carries a 4 amp fuse for protection.

The Plug contains a solid state voltage clamping device and radio frequency interference (RFI) filter, which the manufacturers claim will give complete protection to the appliance it is used with against spikes, noise and power surges.

The modest cost of The Plug will be repaid particularly in the case of the home computer, where the contents of the memory may be completely wiped out after a power surge.

INTERFERENCE PLUG
Manufacturer: Power International Ltd
RRP: £20.21

RECHARGEABLE TORCHES

There will always be a need for the traditional hand-held torch to see your way into inaccessible places, awkward darkened areas and round the house and in fuse boxes when there is a power failure. The problem with the conventional torch is that the batteries always seem to fail at the most inconvenient time.

Fortunately, a new style of torch is now on the market that can be recharged through the mains electricity supply and will retain this charge at a constant level. Three companies producing these torches are Superswitch, Smiths Industries and Black & Decker.

The Superswitch model is clipped on to a special wall-mounted bracket when not in use. The bracket is wired into the mains supply and keeps the torch fully charged when not being

used. When charged, the light will last for up to an hour and a half and it can be recharged up to 2000 times before it needs replacing. By fitting a special adaptor, you can also charge it from a car cigarette lighter socket.

The Smiths torch can be plugged into a normal 13amp power socket to build up the charge. It incorporates a neon signal lamp which glows continuously when the light is in working order.

The Black & Decker torch slots into a plastic bucket, which can be screwed to the wall. The charger is incorporated into a special 13amp plug. All the time it is in position and the plug is connected, the torch will be charging. When you need to use the torch, you simply unclip it from its holder.

RECHARGEABLE TORCHES
Manufacturers: Superswitch Electric Appliances Ltd;
Smiths Industries Environmental Controls;
Black & Decker Power Tools
RRP: from £8.34

MAKE CONTACT

Talking to people in different parts of the home without leaving the room is a lot easier through the Plug-in Intercom from Superswitch. Simply by plugging the units into standard three-pin 13amp socket outlets in different areas of the house, you can communicate

without the need to undertake a major wiring job.

Up to five units can be installed in any one building and it is possible to talk to just one or all of the units, depending on who you need to speak to and where they are. The Plug-in Intercom converts your speech into FM radio signals, which are transmitted along the standard electrical wiring. This message is then 'translated' by the receiving unit, which can be plugged in anything up to 100 metres away.

Two separate channels allow two different conversations to be carried out simultaneously without affecting each other. However, everyone plugged into your particular channel can listen to your conversation.

The great advantage of this intercom system is its portability — units can be located anywhere in the house and moved from room to room simply by being plugged into a different socket. Where portability is not important mounting brackets are supplied for wall fixing.

If you have a invalid or elderly person at home these units could prove a boon, allowing you easy communication without having to pay high installation costs and as a baby alarm it is ideal. It is not a good idea to use the units while other appliances are connected to the same socket since there is a good chance you will get interference.

PLUG-IN INTERCOM
Manufacturer:Superswitch Electric Appliances Ltd
RRP: £109.50

WONDER PLUG

A neat alternative to the normal three-pin plug is the Tobylec Handy Plug. This new 13amp plug does away with the time-consuming job of wiring up a standard plug and you don't even need a screwdriver or wire stripper.

The top of the plug slides off, revealing a red cover plate that lifts up to give access to the earth, neutral and live connection terminals. On the side of the plug there is a built-in wire stripper with which you can easily remove the necessary amount of insulation from each wire.

Having inserted the prepared flex into the plug, you simply clip each wire in place in its correct terminal, then tighten the cord grip by hand.

Having wired up the plug, you then slide the cover plate back into place and secure it by turning the red lock screw through 90° with a coin.

The Handy Plug, which is fully

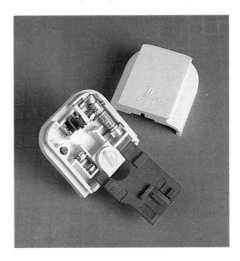

approved to BS1363, comes fitted with a 13amp fuse and can be fitted virtually in seconds. It is a particular boon for those people with large fingers who would normally have difficulty wiring up the standard type of plug.

Tobylec has also come up with an additional device that is designed to be used with the Handy Plug and which will have great appeal for those who have difficulty bending down.

Called the Handly Handle, it slides over the Handy Plug and into the specially designed finger grips, making the plug a lot easier to insert or remove.

HANDY PLUG
Manufacturer: Tobylec Marketing
RRP: £1.25

Decorating

A number of exciting products have emerged in the decorating field this year which will help you achieve neater, cleaner finishes to your decorating projects. And, of course, they will save you time — an important aspect of DIY decoration. If you've tried to hang wallpaper on your own, you will be aware of the problems — glue everywhere, wavy lines where there shouldn't be any, and so much time wasted. Well, at last a manufacturer has come up with a bright idea to ease the pain of hanging wallpaper — the Skarsten Andypaster, the pick of this year's ideas.

NEAT TRIMMER

Even with long-bladed decorator's scissors you will find it difficult to cut a clean line in wallpaper, and a ragged edge will mar your hard work. The new Wallpaper Trimmer from Copydex is designed specially for use with vinyl and washable wallcoverings (although it can be used with a number of other types).

Its job is to trim a neat line where papers butt up to doors, window frames and other obstructions. The tool slides easily and smoothly down or along the wall to give a neat straight edge.

The trimming blade is held in a wedge-shaped plastic body with a portion that protrudes for cutting; each segment of the blade will cut four rolls of wallpaper. Then all you have to do is snap off the blunt edge to leave a sharp new one.

The tool is used flush with the wall and this makes it equally suitable for

right- or left-handed people to hold and use comfortably.

The blade is inserted by unscrewing the two halves of the body and slotting the blade in place before closing up the tool again.

COPYDEX WALLPAPER TRIMMER
Manufactuer: Copydex PLC
RRP: £1.99

PASTING PAL

Wallpapering isn't the most speedy of jobs — pasting, in particular, is fiddly, and keeping the paper unfurled and ensuring the paste is applied thoroughly demands a keen eye. If your time is scarce and you have a lot of rooms to tackle, you will need all the help you can get.

Consider investing in a Skarsten's Andypaster. This neat pasting machine will coat up to 3m (10ft) of wallpaper in five seconds; certainly a way of speeding up the job. It comprises a solid polypropylene tray which holds the paste and across this is a sponge-covered roller that applies the paste evenly to the paper. The roll of wallpaper is held on an adjustable roller above the tray and is fed through two aluminium guide bars that help to hold it evenly over the paste roller.

The pasting machine is positioned on the floor directly below the area of wall to be papered. There is an adjustable guide height which rests on the skirting and allows sufficient adjustment to accommodate high or low skirting boards; this guide should be secured first.

To hang the paper, pull the required length through the machine and position it at the top of the drop, matching the pattern if necessary.

Brush and fit the strip of paper, then tap the bottom of the length into the groove of the guide height fixed on the skirting. Use the carbon steel cutter provided to cut the paper, using the groove as the guide. Then peel the paper from the guide, pull the pasting machine away from the wall and brush the paper back onto the wall. You should have a perfectly trimmed edge.

The Andypaster is ideal for light- and medium-weight papers but for heavyweight papers you will have to cut the paper to length first then pull it through the machine and leave it to soak before hanging.

Although undoubtedly a useful device for straight drops, it's difficult to see how the Andypaster would cope with corners and the usual annoying obstructions such as a pedestal basin or radiators.

SKARSTEN ANDYPASTER
WALLPAPER MACHINE
Manufacturer: Skarsten
Manufacturing Co Ltd.
RRP: £15.99

NEAT AND TRIM

No matter how sleek and streamlined your kitchen worktops look, or how well your new bath blends in with the decor, you can't really consider them wholly part of the scheme until you disguise the gap between them and the walls. In any case, some form of seal is vital to prevent water seeping behind the gap.

Whether you need to seal the gap between the bath and the wall, or seal and finish off your kitchen units, OBO have a range of products that should ensure a neat finish in all cases. Try their Bath Seal — a flexible plastic strip available in White, Ivory, Avocado, Pampas, Wild Sage Green, Alpine Blue, Pale Pink and Damask Red. It forms a completely waterproof seal, which should prevent splashes and condensation seeping down behind the bath. It's also ideal for sinks, shower trays and washbasins.

To fit the Bath Seal, you will need OBO's Bath Seal fixing adhesive — a special waterproof adhesive strip. Place the adhesive along the back of the Bath Seal strip, then press it along the join between the bath and the wall to form a watertight seal.

Hygienic and practical, the Kitchen Worktop seal will bridge that awkward gap between units and wall. There are four finishes to choose from — wood, bronze, white and aluminium

Still in the kitchen, the OBO Kitchen Worktop Trim range offers practical and attractive joining strips for round-edged worktops. There's the straight joint variety for joining runs of adjacent work surfaces; the corner joint for using in right-angled corners and a corner sink joint for joining worktop and sink in a similar position; and an end trim for finishing the edge of work tops. Choose from bronze or aluminium in bright or satin finishes.

OBO BATH SEAL, KITCHEN WORKTOP SEAL, KITCHEN WORKTOP TRIM
Manufacturer: OBO, Douglas Kane Ltd
RRP: from £2.25

GLOWING GROUTING

Porous, stained grouting between ceramic tiles can make your wall look very unsightly — even though the tiles themselves are in fine fettle. Until recently, the only cure for unsightly grouting was to rake it out and apply new grout — a messy job. If the grouting isn't chipped or crumbly you may be able to restore its sparkle using a new product from Polycell.

VersaTile is a water and mould

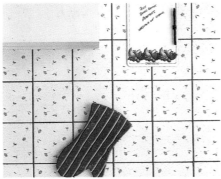

resisting liquid which you can apply to sound material to smarten the grout lines and enhance an area of tiling. In a choice of brown, red, green, beige, and plain white, the liquid is applied directly to the grout with the brush supplied with the pack. There's no need to mask off the tiles: simply daub VersaTile on liberally after cleaning the tiles with sugar soap or detergent.

After leaving the liquid to dry for one hour you then wipe off the excess from the glazed surface using a wet sponge. Once removed a final wipe over the surface with a dry cloth will leave the tiles shining and their grout lines glowing.

VERSATILE
Manufacturer: Polycell Products Ltd
RRP: £4.49

PAINTING BY PRESSURE

Black & Decker's Paintmate is a splendid gadget that means you will never have to dip in your bristles again or risk splattering all and sundry with a freewheeling roller. It's a neat pressurized painting system, which basically combines paint kettle and roller (or brush) in one unit to assure a consistent, continuous painting action.

The gadget comprises a special tub of paint, which fits into a lightweight container that you can carry by its built-in handle or clip on to your belt to leave both hands free. An ordinary soda syphon bulb provides sufficient pressure to suck the paint from the container and force it along the flexible transparent tube that connects it to the applicator head. This may be a foam roller, a flat brush or a paint pad. Paint flow is controlled by a pushbutton on the head.

Until recently Black & Decker's clever device was much hampered by the fact that it was necessary to use only the paint, developed and supplied by Berger, designated for use with the tool. Recently, however, the manufacturers have introduced a Multi-Paint Adaptor Kit, which makes Paintmate so much more versatile.

PAINTMATE
Manufacturer: Black & Decker Ltd
RRP: £17.99

DECORATING

SMOOTH OUT THE ROUGH

Textured paint is ideal for covering up cracked or rough plasterwork but what happens when you get bored with it or if, on taking over a new house, you decide it's not your taste? POB Savident has the answer. Their Textured Paint Remover is a chemical stripper specially formulated to tackle the problem — and sure to be welcomed by those who prefer the subtle approach to decorating.

It's a thick, jelly-like substance that you apply to the textured paint with a brush, working it into all the crevices . Leave it to soften the paint for at least

an hour before removing with a wallpaper scraper.

The substance will remove most vinyl or acrylic-based paints,without any trouble, but for powder-based paints you may need a second application.

The remover is available in 2.5 litre cans and this amount will cover approximately 3m^2 (33sq ft).
POB TEXTURED PAINT REMOVER
Manufacturer: POB Savident Ltd.
RRP:£6.49

SAWS TO TACKLE TILES

Tile cutting is often a hit-or-miss affair, even with a proper cutting blade or pincer-type snapper — if you don't break through the glaze properly it's likely to chip unevenly and a misaligned score line will ruin any tile-cutting job.

From Vitrex comes the handy Tile Saw, which gives you direct control in cutting to a line — even curves aren't a problem, as the tool has a tungsten carbide rod saw blade which is round in section. Set in a square frame with a plastic handgrip, the saw is rather like

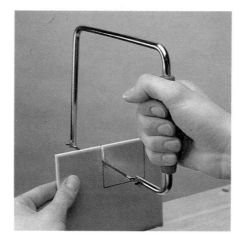

a coping saw in use. The replaceable blade is 150mm (6in) long.

The 'Miracle' blade, also from Vitrex, may not guarantee divine intervention for DIY jobs but it does help to cut a variety of materials, including ceramic tiles (also sheet steel, laminates, slate, stone and glass-fibre). The blade is made of tungsten carbide, is 300mm (12in) long and will fit a standard hacksaw frame.
TILE SAW AND MIRACLE MULTI-PURPOSE BLADE
Manufacturer: Vitrex Tools Division
RRP: Tile Saw, £4.95; Miracle blade, £4.40

COVER-UP

Pipework is obviously a necesssary part of plumbing and central heating systems but it often looks too functional, can mar a decorative scheme by visually breaking up an area of wall and requires special treatment when it comes to painting the room — do you paint it the same

colour as the walls, or match the woodwork?

The dilemma can be easily overcome with a neat idea from Thorsman. Clip & Cover is a pipe fixing system, which incorporates a plain cover strip designed to conceal unobtrusively (see **Project** page 40).

The kit can be used on existing or new heating and plumbing pipework and comprises plastic pipe clamps with moulded seatings for the pipes, which are fixed with screws to the wall. The three screw holes are slot-shaped to allow for adjustment. Ridged plastic ties slot through the pipe seating and are then looped around the pipes to retain them: once fastened they can't be undone.

The cover up is completed with the white PVC rectangular-shaped cover strip, which clips on to the clamp's flanges.

Versions of the system are available to take standard 15mm, 22mm and 28mm diameter pipes. Accessory packs containing extra clamps, ties and cover strips are sold in standard 2.5m lengths. Suitable for either vertical fitting from floor to ceiling height, or horizontal fitting along skirting boards, the strips can be cut to size using a tenon saw or hacksaw, and butt-joined using special joint/junction pieces.

Where pipes disappear midway along a wall, stop-end pieces can be clipped on to form a neat finish. All the screws and wallplugs you need for fixing are included in the packs.
CLIP & COVER
Manufacturer: Thorsman & Co (UK)
RRP: Cover £5.95; Pack £1.85

CLEAN BREAK FOR TILES

Definitely the most difficult part of tiling is cutting the tiles neatly and accurately to size. Plasplugs has added two tile cutters to their range of tiling aids that help to make the job easier.

The Tile Master is a compact two-part tool that contains everything you need for cutting wall tiles. The measuring gauge is an adjustable square that transfers your measurement to the whole tile and ensures that the cut is straight. The cutter has a carbide wheel at one end, which you run down the groove in the

measuring guide to score the tile at the chosen dimension. The other end of the cutter features strong jaws which snap the tile, in a pincer motion, along the scored line. The result is a clean break that does not chip or mark the glazed surface of the tile.

For heavier, thicker ceramic floor tiles, Plasplugs has introduced the new Pro-tiler. It's a sturdy jig which includes a bed for the tile with parallel guide bars above. The cutting head slides along the bars and a lever is used to bring the tungsten-tipped cutting wheel in contact with the tile.

TILE MASTER; PRO-TILER
PRO-TILER
Manufacturer: Plasplugs
RRP: Tile Master, £4.95
PRO-Tiler, £11.95.

LONGER-LASTING GLOSS

The trouble with decorating is that it never stays new for long. This is especially true outdoors, where the rigours of the elements leave their mark. With a conventional paint system of primer, undercoat and gloss, it's likely that you will need to renew the finish every three or four years. Woodwork is particularly prone to deterioration. A longer-lasting finish, therefore, would be a welcome innovation, and Dulux have on offer their new Weathershield Exterior Gloss System, which they say can add at least two years further protection on outside timberwork.

Not just a single product, the system comprises a preservative primer, a flexible undercoat and a high gloss. The three components must be used in conjunction — you can't omit one and hope to use up leftover materials from a previous job.

Four areas where the system's

formulation makes the material longer lived are: elasticity (to cope with natural movement in the wood); permeability (allowing moisture vapour to escape from the wood while resisting the penetration of rainwater); adhesion (better ability to bond to the wood using a penetrating primer); and fungicidal protection.

Weathershield Preservative Primer is clear, of low viscosity to enable it to penetrate deeply into the wood grain, and incorporates a binder to stabilize the surface of new or weathered wood. Its preservative fungicides protect against rot and the material can be applied to damp (but not wet) wood.

The Exterior Undercoat — flexible unlike its ordinary counterparts — has high pigment content which assures good coverage and contains a fungicide to protect against mould.

The Exterior High Gloss has improved flexibility, good colour fastness and stability, plus a fungicide for greater protection. The makers recommend an application on bare wood of one coat of primer, two coats of undercoat and one of gloss.

As you would expect, such a system does not come cheaply (it's being introduced on the professional market and is available only from builder's and decorators' merchants). Can sizes are 5. 2,5 and 1 litres for primer, white undercoat and brilliant white gloss: 2.5 and 1 litre sizes are available for five undercoat colours and ten gloss colours.

DULUX WEATHERSHIELD
EXTERIOR GLOSS SYSTEM
Manufacturer: ICI Paints Division
RRP: from £20.00 approx.

SHARP STRIPPER

Preparation is the tedious part of decorating, but unfortunately it can't be skimped on if you want a finished result to be proud of. It's definitely worth taking advantage of any tool or product that will make the job a little easier — especially a wallpaper tool. Any tool that helps you remove old wallpaper must be worth the price.

Plasplugs' Wallpaper Stripper certainly has the edge over an ordinary stripping knife. It's a sturdy, triangular-shaped tool which is large enough to make the job less tiring while still being comfortable to use. The blade is at one

end of the tool, and at the opposite end is a lubricated roller that keeps the base of the stripper flat. The roller ensures that the blade is always at the correct angle so it doesn't gouge into the plaster.

To use the stripper, first soak the old wallcovering with plenty of hot water containing a little washing-up liquid. Work the stripper along the walls in any direction, collecting the strips of wallpaper as you go along. Particularly stubborn areas may need further soaking. Some wallcoverings are very durable and you may need to score the surface with a knife before soaking, so the water can penetrate the surface and soften the adhesive.

The lubricated roller on the wallpaper stripper also doubles as a seam roller when you are hanging paper. Hang the paper as normal, then run the stripper backwards along the vertical butt joins to ensure the edges are stuck down well.

PLASPLUGS WALLPAPER
STRIPPER
Manufacturer: Plasplugs
RRP: £3.75

Clip & Cover

Exposed pipework is ugly, utilitarian and detracts from your decorating scheme. The usual methods of boxing in pipe runs are fussy, time-consuming — and typically crude. Here's a quick and convenient method of concealing pipes that's slim and stylish.

Although pipework is preferably routed under floors, through walls and in the loft space, solid floors and awkward access means it may have to surface. Whether you want to cover up new pipework, perhaps after having central heating installed, or existing runs that tend to spoil a decorating scheme, Thorsman's Clip & Cover provides the neatest, least obtrusive alternative to boxing in with timber and boarding.

Clip & Cover comprises a twin-pipe clamp (which can be used for single pipes) with flexible ties, which is screwed to the wall behind the pipes and replaces conventional clips on new work, and a durable white, U-shaped PVC clip-on cover strip. You can leave the cover bare or decorate as you wish with paint or wallcovering. Its slim profile take up little space beyond that of the pipes.

There are two pack sizes: No. 56 for pipes up to 15mm diameter; No. 76 for hot water pipes up to 22mm diameter and cold water pipes up to 28mm diameter. Cover strips come in 2.5m lengths and there are joint and junction pieces and stop-ends. All fixings are included.

Little preparation is called for: if you are fitting new pipework, install the clamps as you run in the pipes; if you are concealing existing pipes, start by removing the pipe clips only if they hold the pipes too far away from the wall for the cover to fit. Don't remove the plastic protective sheath that covers the cover strips at this point. Doing this later avoids possible damage.

1 Pull existing pipework away from the clips to expose their fixing screws, re-

Fitting flexible ties

lease and remove the clips — if the clips allow room for the cover to fit on top, just use Clip & Cover's clamps without their ties.

Fit the flexible ties into the slots beneath the curved pipe seating of the clamps, serrated face downwards. It's easiest to bend up the end of the ties before inserting them. Don't close the ties yet — once locked, they cannot be undone.

2 With an existing run, slip the clamps behind the pipes at 450mm intervals; on new work, stretch a string between nails driven temporarily into the wall or skirting at each end of the proposed run as a guide to positioning the clamps accurately.

Hold each clamp in place and mark the wall or skirting through their fixing holes, using a pencil or bradawl. For kit size No. 56, use the central screw slot (this allows sideways adjustment of the clamp); for size No. 76 use the two screw holes diagonally

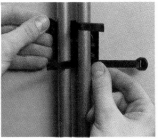

Slipping clips into place

opposite, adjacent to the pipe seatings.

3 Drill holes in the wall to take the plugs provided. Hold the clamps in place — aligning existing pipes with the seatings — and insert and drive home the fixing screws.

With new pipework, don't secure the clamps firmly, but run in the lengths at this stage. Once the plumbing is complete, adjust the clamps to hold the pipes squarely in the seatings — it's worth holding a long straight-edge and spirit level against the edges of several clamps, as irregularity could prevent the cover from fitting properly.

Screwing clamps on to wall

4 Take the ends of the pipe locking ties over the pipes and slot them into the buckles.

Slotting ties into buckles

Pull the ties tightly around the pipes to restrain them — the serrations lock at a given position and can't be released.

Measure up for the lengths of cover strip required, using a retractable steel tape measure for ease and accuracy.

5 Use a try square and pencil to mark the lengths of cover strip for cutting, across the face and down the sides. Place them one by one on a flat surface — a scrap piece of board, for instance — and saw along the waste side of the line with a sharp, fine-bladed hacksaw or tenon saw. To cut evenly, place the cover strip face up and start the saw cut on one top corner with a few backward strokes, then gently lower the blade until the saw is horizontal and cutting to the line: check that it does not wander at the sides.

Smooth the cut ends with fine abrasive paper to remove burrs before fitting to the clamps.

6 Position the lengths of cover strip over the clamps and snap the lip over the outer flange of the clamps. Press home firmly with the heel of your hand. You will find that Clip & Cover is flexible enough to accommodate minor irregularities in the wall surface, but if there are annoying gaps between clamps, apply a bead of flexible non-setting mastic along

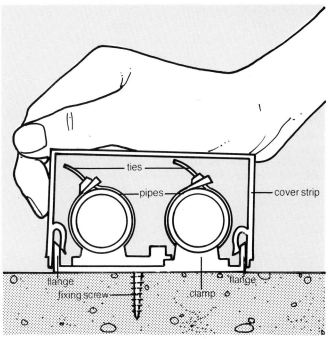

Self-locking ties retain the pipes. The cover strip snaps firmly home over the flanges of the clamp but can be removed if access to the pipes is ever required

Clipping cover into place

the join to fill the space. The time and effort needed to fill the gaps will certainly be repaid by the improved appearance of the finished job.

Where two lengths of cover strip must be butt-joined — necessary if a pipe run traverses the wall vertically from floor to ceiling — fit a jointing piece over the cover to conceal the join. Similarly, a junction where a pipe branches at right-angles to the main pipe run can be tackled by butting up three lengths of cover strip, then clipping a junction piece over the top. For a permanent fixing, attach the joint and junction pieces to the cover strip with a PVC adhesive.

7 The cover strip is attractive left in its natural white colour, but if you want to conceal it further, simply apply wallpaper over it, treating it as for any other obstruction in wallpapering. To enable the paste to adhere well, it's best to rub the shiny cover strip gently with abrasive paper to form a rough key.

If you want to change the colour of the cover strip, again key it with abrasive paper, then apply undercoat and two top coats of gloss paint. Where a pipe run ends in a tap on the wall (in a conservatory, for instance), use a stop-end to finish off neatly, with a cut-out for the tap to slot into.

Fitting stop-end

Damp & Waterproofing

Damp, rot and mould are all persistent problems in the house. Although modern technology has failed to eliminate them completely, there are now a number of easy-to-use and effective products worth trying.

LOFT AIRING

Loft ventilation was never a real problem until loft insulation took off in the late 60s and early 70s. With everyone anxious to stop expensive heat disappearing through the roof, lofts were insulated and often boarded. It was then that the trouble started, because the well-insulated loft also meant bad ventilation, which in some cases lead to an outbreak of rot.

Few houses built prior to 1982 had any system of ventilation installed in the loft, which is why two companies are now providing the answer with soffit ventilators. The soffit is the boarding that runs round the roof just under the eaves.

It would be a simple enough job to make holes in this boarding to allow air to flow through. The problem with this solution is that the holes would also let in birds and insects. So a proper ventilator system is important.

The Homefix pack contains eight rectangular soffit vents and 12 eaves vents. The soffit vents are fitted into holes cut at 1200mm (4ft) intervals in the soffit boards from a template provided. Once cut, the vents can just be slid into position from below. The eaves' vents are fixed between alternate rafters and are slid up to the underside of the roof.

The Swish soffit ventilator is rather more complicated to fit and requires the removal of the soffit boards. Once each is removed, it must be trimmed to allow for the ventilator. This is then clipped to the board and the board fixed back in position. The ventilator has a series of 50 × 5mm (2 × ¼in) slots along its length. These are covered on the inside with a nylon

mesh air diffuser which prevents insects entering the loft through the openings.

Although the Swish system is the more complicated of the two to install, the hire of a mobile tower platform would make the task of fitting considerably easier.

Only the more experienced handyman should tackle this job, since repairs can be expensive if it goes wrong and will leave unsightly gaps in the soffit boards.

HOMEFIX ROOF SPACE VENTILATION KIT
Manufacturer: Willan Building Services
RRP: £18.99 per pack
SWISH SOFFIT VENT
Manufacturer: Swish Products Ltd
RRP: £14.49 per 5m

SEALING OUT DAMP

Marley Damp Seal is a tough two-ply self-adhesive membrane that is impervious to water and vapour. Basically intended for the building trade, its main DIY application would be in the construction or conversion of rooms below ground level, such as a basement or cellar, or when damp-

proofing a solid concrete floor.

To prevent water and damp penetration from the surrounding environment, a very strong and effective waterproof barrier is essential. Traditionally heavy gauge polythene has provided the answer in such circumstance. Marley claims that Damp Seal has four times the resistance to tearing and puncturing and twice the impact strength.

On a concrete floor, a screed can be applied as soon as the Damp Seal is laid down. With walls it is fitted on to primed brick, blockwork or concrete and it is advisable to line the wall afterwards with rigid interior cladding to prevent the Damp Seal being forced off the wall by the pressure of moisture behind.

Care must be taken when using Damp Seal and its application should only be tackled by the more experienced handyman. In any event, you would be well advised to contact the manufacturer first for more detailed advice.

MARLEY DAMPSEAL
Manufacturer: Marley Waterproofing Ltd
RRP: £93.04 per 15m roll

MOULD ELIMINATOR

In areas suffering from condensation, there is often the chance that mould will form. The unsightly black mould, if left for any period of time, is very difficult to remove but Cuprinol No More Mould is a fungicidal spray that claims to overcome these problems.

Available in 500ml containers No

More Mould has a trigger-operated spray and a nozzle that can be closed when not in use. This prevents accidental spraying and makes the product safe to store in the house. Full safety precautions are listed on the side of the container.

No More Mould is a two-action product which first loosens the mould and then, once the mould is removed, is applied again to prevent further mould forming. After the first application, the mould can be removed with a normal cleaning solution. If the stains are really deep, these can be cleaned using a one part water to four solution of household bleach. Remember to check a small hidden area of wall for colour fastness before applying this solution.

No More Mould may also be used for outdoor applications to remove algae, moss, lichen and other parasitic plant growth from greenhouses, roofs and guttering. When working in these situations, you should apply No More Mould only during dry weather.

NO MORE MOULD
Manufacturer: Cuprinol Ltd
RRP: £2.98

You can prevent damp damaging your decorations by covering the affected area with a damp barrier kit. This consists of a laminated paper which is stuck to the wall with a special adhesive.

STOP THE ROT

Wet rot can attack at any time. Usually the first you know about it is when you go to repaint an outside window and find the wood flaking under the brush. You will normally find that if paint is cracked or chipped and water has got in, wet rot soon follows. In some cases, if the wood has been painted before being allowed to dry properly, damage will be caused under a seemingly sound top coat.

However the problem arises, the latest remedy comes from Sterling Roncraft, the producers of the Ronseal range of wood treatments. Called the Ronseal Rot Repair Kit (see **Project** page 46), the three-part treatment is designed to strengthen old wood, fill the affected area and give protection against further rot.

To apply this treatment, the first step is to remove the affected area of timber and leave the surrounding wood to dry. The kit's Wood Hardening Solution is then applied and again the area is left to dry out. Next the Cavity Filler is used. This is a two-pack flexible filler that takes about 20 minutes to dry thoroughly. The area can then be sanded down ready for repainting.

The final treatment from the kit is the injection of small cylindrical pellets into potentially vulnerable areas and in the sound wood around the treated area. The holes drilled to take the pellets are

then sealed with more filler. All the components from this kit are available separately if you don't need the whole system.

RONSEAL ROT CURING SYSTEM
Manufacturer: Sterling Roncraft
RRP: from £2.91

T-BAR PRESSURE

If you've tried to fill the gap between the wall and frame or bath and tile with sealant or mastic and dispensing gun, you will appreciate just how messy the job can be. It takes skill, and it takes some time to acquire the skill.

Well, all of that may be in the past. Hansil have come up with the idea of using aerosol pressure containers for a couple of their products. The idea is that filling cracks and sealing and waterproofing round baths will be an easier, quicker operation with less mess and less waste. Operation is by way of a T-bar finger control, which has an angled nozzle specially designed to cope with those awkward corners.

The two products using the new dispensing method are the Dow Corning Bath and Kitchen Seal and the Hansil Painters Mate. The Kitchen and Bath Seal is a silicone-based sealant which is highly resistant to mildew, fungus, steam, and cooking fats and oils and has a guarantee for 10 years. The 210ml cartridge contains enough sealant to seal an entire bathroom or kitchen, though of course, this depends on the size of the rooms. And it comes in a range of colours to match your bathroom — Wild Sage, Burgundy, Kashmir Beige, Sepia, Avocado, Pampas, Sun King, Blue and Ivory in addition to White and Clear.

Hansil Painters Mate is quite different. It's a flexible filler in brilliant white (although not available in any other colour it can be painted over) and can be used to fill cracks in walls and ceilings, around skirtings, windows and door frames.

Once applied, simply wipe over the surface with a damp cloth — no need

for sanding down. After an hour, you are ready to paint.

In practice, the pressure dispenser works quite well and certainly speeds up the process. But it is hardly easier to use than other dispensers. It takes time to learn the skill, but once learnt, it is certainly less messy. The great advantage is that both products stop coming out of the nozzle when you lift your finger off the control bar — something that doesn't happen with cartridge dispensers.

DOW CORNING BATH AND KITCHEN SEAL; HANSIL PAINTERS MATE
Manufacturer: Hansil Ltd
Builders' Merchants
RRP: £5.46; £3.74

AIR DRYER

Where individual rooms suffer from condensation or a generally damp atmosphere, it is sometimes difficult to check the problem at source. Heating the air may provide a temporary solution, but the trouble is that when the air finally cools down it will contain even more water vapour and the situation will be even worse.

Rentokil has just produced its Mk II Homedryer, a de-humidifier that not only extracts moisture from the surrounding air but also maintains the drier air at a constant humidity level.

Attractively finished in teak with a black front panel, the unit looks like a hi-fi speaker and will be at home in any room. It can be moved about easily, too, since it sits on castors and only

needs a standard power socket outlet.

You can adjust the amount of moisture the Homedryer extracts to suit individual requirements. The maximum extraction rate is about 15 litres in 24 hours.

The unit works on the basis of drawing moist air over a cooling coil, which condenses the water vapour. The cold air is then blown through a hot coil, which warms the dried air before releasing it back into the room.

An automatic control switches the unit on when a pre-set level of humidity is reached, and cuts out when a satisfactory level is achieved. To prevent overflowing, a warning light tells you when the water container is full.

Unfortunately, at £340, the

Homedryer is expensive, but if you have serious condensation problems, this may still prove to be good value.
RENTOKIL Mk II DE-HUMIDIFIER
Manufacturer: Rentokil Ltd
RRP: £340.00

MAGIC CRYSTALS

Secondary glazing, where a second window is fitted inside the existing one, is a common method of helping to reduce heat loss and insulate against noise. No matter how good the seal round the window frames, moisture does find its way in and condensation forms on the inside surfaces.

There are two very good reasons for preventing this condensation from forming. For a start, the window will look dirty and you will not be able to see through it clearly. More importantly, however, if the moisture is left between the panes, mould and rot

can quickly form.

To remove this unwanted moisture, 3M has introduced a pack of anti-condensation crystals. This comprises three trays of crystals narrow enough to fit between the panes of a secondary glazing system. By removing the inside frame, you can lay the trays in the gap. Simply take off the white lids and replace the secondary window. Of course, it is worth checking that the seal round the frames is adequate and making good any deficiencies where you can if it is not, otherwise the crystals may not be able to cope.

It takes about 24 hours for the crystals to absorb any water vapour between the panes. Initially they are blue, but will turn a pinkish white as they absorb moisture. How long they remain active will depend on how good a seal there is round the windows and what level of humidity there is.

When the crystals become inactive, you restore them for further use by taking them out of the trays and heating them in a warm oven for two or three hours. They will then turn blue again.
SILICA CRYSTALS
Manufacturer: 3M United Kingdom PLC
RRP: £22.99

Tip

Damp patches can be caused by mortar bridging the wall cavity. To treat, either remove a couple of bricks from the external wall and clear the cavity, or treat the wall with water repellant.

EASY DAMP PROOFING

Damp walls and floors in basements, cellars and other areas at or below ground level are a constant problem and often the surfaces will be subject to efflorescence. A similar problem in reverse can occur when a concrete lined pool or pond loses water to the surrounding soil.

BP Aquaseal has recently introduced a product that will help you tackle these and other related problems. It's called Heavy Duty Urethane. Used on solid concrete floors, it will give a waterproof, hard-wearing, dust-free surface that is resistant to abrasion and most workshop and household chemicals. Applied to wall and ceilings, it will act as a surface damp-proofer and the advantage here is that you can decorate on top of it.

When put on the walls of a pool or pond the product will provide a suitable non-toxic surface, provided that you leave the treatment for 48 hours before refilling with water.

Yet another practical aspect of this product is that when mixed with sand and cement it provides a hard-wearing waterproof mortar for repairing damage to floors, walls, etc.

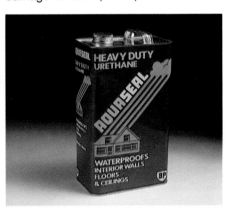

The brown liquid is supplied in cans and care should be taken when using it since is is flammable and abrasive and will therefore cause considerable aggravation if it gets on the skin. Only apply it in well-ventilated areas.

To use it, you brush it on; one litre should cover an area of 5m² (54 sq ft). Since four coats are recommended for full protection, each litre will cover 1.25m² (13½ sq ft) of the job.
HEAVY DUTY URETHANE
Manufacturer: BP Aquaseal
RRP: from £8.56

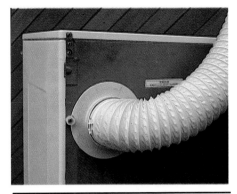

UNIVERSAL CONNECTIONS

Removing the moist air emitted by a tumble drier or similar electrical appliance from a room is vital if the problems of condensation and damp are to be avoided. The difficulty is that many machines are not provided with facilities for attaching flexible trunking which can then be hung out of a convenient window or attached to a permanent vent.

A new flange connector, produced by the London and Lancashire Rubber Company, claims to cure this problem by enabling you to fit 102mm (4in) flexible ducting to almost any tumble drier outlet with relatively little effort.

The flange, which is made from ABS and rubber and comes with a suitable ferrule and clamp, has a wide self-adhesive band that can be cut to size, to match the outlet hole in the appliance. If the outlet is not on a flat surface (some machines have a sunken or raised outlet) you can easily get round the problem by cutting the flange into the correct shape.

Before fixing the flange to the drier, it is important that the area around the hole is degreased to prevent any unwanted air leaks. Also remember that you only have one go at aligning the flange: the rubber sticks instantly on contact.

Don't use the machine for at least 24 hours after fitting the connector to ensure that it sticks fully. The 102mm (4in) ducting needed is readily available, and can be connected in place with the clamp provided in the connector kit.

The flange is rated for use up to a temperature of 82°C, making it suitable for most types of tumble drier outlets.
MAJICON DUCTING CONNECTOR
Manufacturer: London and Lancashire Rubber Company Ltd
RRP: £10.50 approx

DAMP KIT

Cuprinol has introduced the No More Damp range of interior and exterior products to help with the problem of household damp.

The roof products include the No More Damp Flashing Kit for waterproofing joints on roofs, chimneys, home extensions, garages and car ports. Mastic Crack Filler is used for sealing cracks, holes and joints before general waterproofing.

Use No More Damp Roofs-Walls for general waterproofing. A special thick, black bitumen emulsion, Roofs-Walls needs no primer and can be used on a variety of surfaces. No More Damp Roofing Felt Adhesive is a damp-preventative adhesive which will fix roofing felt to concrete, metal and asphalt, as well as to itself.

If you are having problems with gutters, downpipes or joints in roofing sheets, General Roofing Tape could be the answer. Available in rolls 8m (26ft) long and 40mm (1⅝in) wide, the tape is quick and easy to apply.

Waterproofing gutters, downpipes, railings, gates, fencing, corrugated iron, galvanised iron and cold water tanks is best tackled using No More Damp Black Bitumen Paint. This is a special paint giving a decorative glossy finish.

There are two No More Damp products designed specially for walls. No More Damp for Exterior Walls comes in a 5 litre can and is designed to stop rain penetration, while allowing water entering the wall from inside to evaporate. No More Damp Interior Walls and Ceilings is just what's needed for preventing patches of damp from spoiling decorations.
NO MORE DAMP
Manufacturer: Cuprinol
RRP: from £2.48

Rot Cure System

Wet rot is one of the most persistent of all DIY problems. Wherever there is wood and wherever water can get to the wood, it is almost inevitable that rot will set in if the problem is not tackled. But with Ronseal's easy-to-use Rot Cure System, the spread of wet rot can be halted, and the damage minimized.

Wet rot is carried by spores which can penetrate the woodwork through cracks in the paint surface caused by expansion and contraction of the wood. Because the cracks are usually fairly small, the wood has little chance to dry out and the spores flourish in the damp conditions under the deteriorating paintwork.

Since its growth under the paintwork is normally unseen, the rot usually progresses until the timber is left weakened.

The Ronseal Repair kit can be used to tackle almost any affected area of woodwork, but is not suitable for any load-bearing sections of timber. Where rot occurs in more critical areas, such as around door hinges, fascia boards or lintels, you should seek expert advice before attempting any repairs.

1 First check all the exterior woodwork thoroughly for the slightest sign of rot. In-

Testing the wood for rot

spect the paintwork for cracks, which are most likely to occur where sections of wood are joined. Test the surface either by hand or with the blade of a knife. Tell-tale signs of the problem include patches of dark discoloration and a spongy feel to the wood. Particular areas to look at are the bottom rails of windows, the joints between roof fascia boards and the underside of the roof and the lower joints in painted wooden doors. If you can press your thumb through the paintwork and into the surface of the timber, then the area is almost certainly affected by rot and needs treating.

2 Once you have located any defective wood, remove all traces of affected timber with an old screwdriver, knife or wire brush. So as to prevent any possible future contamination of nearby sound timber, immediately burn all the rotten timber which you have just removed.

Having cut the section back to sound, healthy wood, leave the area to dry out thoroughly. If there is any chance of rain or other moisture getting to it before this can be done, protect it with a polythene 'roof' but make sure you maintain a free flow of air to allow the timber to dry completely. If this

Removing rotten wood

is not done, there is every chance of wet rot returning to the same area.

3 Once the affected area has dried out thoroughly, soak it well with Ronseal Wood Hardener Solution. Shake the

Applying hardener solution

can and then apply it with an old paintbrush. Where there are deep holes, pour some of the solution into these and then brush round. To protect and strengthen the wood beneath the rotted area, drill a series of holes and fill these with the solution as well. Leave the treated area for at least six hours to enable the timber to dry out again.

4 Now fill the damaged area of the wood with Ronseal High Performance Wood filler. This is supplied as a two-part kit: the filler which comes sup-

Mixing the filler

plied in a tin and the catalyst which comes in a tub. Since the material sets very quickly when the catalyst is added, you should only mix as much as can be used within say 10 minutes. A lump of filler the size of a golf ball needs about 40mm (1½in) of catalyst.

5 Mix the two together thoroughly and then work the filler right into the hole using a filler knife or old kitchen knife. Make sure the filler is well packed and has reached all the

Applying the filler

crevices, then smooth it down roughly with the knife but leave it just proud of the surrounding wood surface.

6 When the filler is completely hardened, rub it down till it is roughly level with the surrounding area. If the damaged area is more than

Sanding the filler down

25mm (1in) deep, you can save on the amount of filler needed by fixing in a suitable packing piece of wood soaked in Ronseal Clear Wood Preservative. Cover up the remainder of the hole with filler. Although the filler sets hard, it remains flexible enough to cope with the normal expansion and contraction of the timber. You can carve, plane or file it afterwards to match any existing contours in the adjoining wood sections. If you are repairing the bottom of a window sill, do not forget to cut a drip groove in the underside of the filled area.

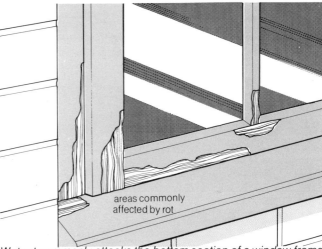

areas commonly affected by rot

Wet rot commonly attacks the bottom section of a window frame – it's a natural spot for water to collect due to the joint between the glass pane and frame

7 Before you rub down your repair ready for decoration, the final part of the rot treatment is to insert the Ronseal Wood Preservative Tablets all round the repaired area. These tablets spread preservative through the wood automatically should it ever become moist again. This action kills off the spores and prevents rot forming.

It is also advisable to carry out this treatment on other potentially vulnerable areas of woodwork not yet affected by rot. The joints in wooden window frames are particularly prone to woodrot, and the wood preservative tablets should extend their life considerably.

To insert the tablets, first drill a series of 10mm ($\frac{7}{16}$in) holes about 25mm (1in) deep into the sound timber around the treated area. Space them at about 50mm (2in) intervals for maximum effect.

Drilling holes for tablets

8 Remove the swarf from each of the holes and then insert a tablet into each hole. Use a screwdriver to push them fully home. The tablet should sit just below the level of the filler. If any of them don't, then remove the tablet

Inserting the tablets

and drill the hole a little deeper, and then insert it once more. Finally, seal each hole with some filler, press the filler in and then allow it to dry.

The area is now ready to be decorated. First sand down the area with a medium grade sand paper, then finish off with fine glasspaper. Brush the area free of dust and then redecorate with primer, undercoat and a top coat of paint.

The finished job should be indistinguishable from the surrounding woodwork and will probably be stronger as well.

Heating & Insulation

Heating costs can be a major strain on the household budget. With this in mind, heating and insulation products are being constantly updated. Installing up-to-date items in your home will soon repay the investment.

SOLID FUEL BOILER

When gas and electricity dominate the domestic heating market, it is reassuring to know that there are alternatives available, particularly if you like the appearance of the traditional solid fuel fire.

In the past, this type of fire may have looked nice but was expensive to run and wasteful in terms of heat given out and lost. Modern designs, which now incorporate a back boiler to supply hot water and feed central heating systems, are a lot more practical.

Dunsley, who produced the first wrap-around boiler, has now given its established Enterprise fire a new — or rather olde worlde — look. Known as the Castle Front fire, this latest style is available in copper, pewter, satin black and persian blue vitreous enamel. The fire comes in two sizes and is fully capable of heating five or six radiators as well as providing adequate domestic hot water.

The latest design in free-standing units, the Condor, has a similar capability. The main adavantage of this

Don't waste fuel when you are using your central heating system. There are a wide range of gadgets — room and radiator thermostats, and timers — which will give you greater control over the entire system.

open fire with wrap-around boiler is that it does not need a chimney. An easy-fit flue adaptor is available to which you can install a 200mm (8in) flue pipe. This means it can be sited in any room.

DUNSLEY SOLID FUEL BACK BOILER
Manufacturer: Dunsley Heating Appliance Co Ltd
RRP: Castle £188.67; Condor £318.87

DRAUGHT FOILER

The value of double glazing in reducing heat loss and the problems caused by condensation has led to the extensive use of a range of systems in the home. Full professional double glazing, however, can cost a small fortune, while the more permanent DIY systems often demand a considerable amount of skill to install.

One simple answer is to fit plastic thermal film. Its main advantages are that it is cheap and easy to fit. But it will have to be renewed each year.

It is certainly not as effective as double glazing and should not be considered as an alternative. But it is a

most useful barrier against draughts if you have loose-fitting windows and window frames.

To fit the film, make sure that the inside of the window and the frame are clean and dry. Also ensure that the air in the room is dry at the time you put up the thermal film — don't have a gas room heater or kettle on at the time.

Stick a line of special double-sided adhesive tape all round the frame, making sure there are no gaps. Then apply the film onto the tape. You can get rid of any creases or wrinkles in the

film by playing a hair dryer over the surface to shrink the film tight. Finally trim round the edges for a neat finish.

This type of insulation goes under the 3M and Baco Homemaster brand. The 3M Thermal Seal insulation comes in two pack sizes. The smaller pack is for windows up to 1500 × 900mm (5 × 3ft), while the large economy pack contains 5.34m (17ft 6in) of film 1.57m (5ft 2in) wide, with sufficient tape to cope with a wide range of window sizes.

Baco supplies its film and tape separately. The film comes in three pack sizes — 1.5 × 1.3m (4ft 11in × 4ft 4in), 4 × 1.5m (13ft × 4ft 11in) and 6 × 2m (19ft 8in × 6ft 7in).

THERMAL SEAL
Manufacturer: 3M United Kingdom PLC
RRP: £4.15
INSTANT WINDOW INSULATION
Manufacturer: Baco Homemaster
RRP: from £3.95

Radiators attached to outside walls have one major disadvantage — much of their heat disappears into the outside world, instead of warming your home. If you fit aluminium foil behind the radiator, it will reflect heat back into the room.

COSY PIPES

With fuel costs constantly rising, any method of preventing heat loss is worth considering to help ensure the heating system runs efficiently. It was often felt that hot water pipes running round a home contributed to heating the property. This has now been proved to be a very expensive and wasteful theory.

All pipes, except those exposed en route to radiators, should be lagged, especially those under the floor and in the loft area. A considerable amount of heat will be lost in such situations and you will be surprised at the increased efficiency once pipes have been lagged.

Ziplock pipe insulation from Frelen, which comes in handy one-metre lengths, is efficient and easy to fit. All you have to do is peel the insulation open, pop it over the pipe and then reseal it. It just snaps back over the pipe, giving complete protection from cold weather and frost as well.

The great advantage of this type of pipe lagging is that no tools or extra materials are needed. And Ziplock comes in three different sizes to suit most domestic pipework.

ZIPLOCK PIPE INSULATION
Manufacturer: Frelen
RRP: from 75p per metre

EASY GLAZE

The use of rigid PVC, acrylic or polycarbonate plastic sheeting as a simple, economic form of double glazing is well known. One major problem with this type of system, however, is that after a period of time the sunlight will turn plastic opaque.

The only way to reduce this effect is to take the secondary glazing down during the summer and store it in a dark place. This involves incorporating a quick and easy method of fixing which does not look too much of an eyesore.

One solution has been provided by 3M Magnotherm. A thin steel strip of self-adhesive backing is stuck on to the window frame. You can paint over the steel strip, to make it virtually invisible.

The magnetic strip is stuck round

the edges of the plastic sheeting — offer the plastic up to the frame and the magnetic and steel strips will stick together. When you want to remove the glazing, you simply pull it gently away from the frame.

Working on a similar principle, but incorporating a thermal break to minimise the condensation, is 3M Magnotherm Plus. The thermal break

is provided in the PVC extrusion magnetic strip that is stuck on to the plastic sheeting. The steel strip that fits on to the window frame is pre-finished in white, thus eliminating the need for painting.

To save you time and effort cutting mitres at the angle joins, special corner pieces are available with strips of magnetic tape for easy fitting.

MAGNETIC WINDOW DOUBLE GLAZING
Manufacturer: 3M United Kingdom PLC
RRP: £6.99

CONTROL IT

The days of basic on-off controls for central heating systems are long gone. With the advent of the microchip, it is now possible to alter the time the heating comes on to within seconds at the touch of a button.

Most of the controls now available are reasonably stylish and the choice is basically about what functions you really need and the price you are willing to pay for them.

Many of the systems now on the market provide battery-powered safety back-up, independent programming for hot water and central heating and

useful features like a single push button to keep the heating on for an extra half-hour without having to reset the controls. Out of the controls on the market we have had a look at two.

Potterton's EP2000 is one of the more stylishly designed heating controls and would look good on the wall of any modern kitchen. This model offers a choice of 10 or 16 programmes, depending on the type of system installed. It also features battery back-up so that it will still work in the event of a power failure.

Small is the name of the game with the latest electronic devices and the Microtimer from Thorn EMI is no exception. It provides a simple automatic time control and is small enough to sit discreetly in most places. Being roughly the size of a single wall tile, it also looks good when used as a digital clock on the kitchen wall.

These are by no means the only new controllers: it is well worth checking other makes such as Randall, Horstman or Landis & Gyr to see whether their products suit you.

POTTERTON'S EP2000
Manufacturer: Potterton International Ltd
RRP: £43.70
MICROTIMER
Manufacturer: Thorn EMI
RRP: £41.98

HEAT TREAT

Thermostatic radiator valves have been generally accepted as efficient methods of controlling the level of heat in individual rooms. In some cases,

localized conditions can affect the correct functioning of the sensor so Danfoss has produced a remote sensor to cope with those situations where heavy furnishings or decor restrict the flow of air round the thermostatic valve.

If curtaining, for instance, restricts the air flow, it will in many cases allow the thermostat to reach a higher temperature than the rest of the room. The result then is that the valve shuts off the radiator before the rest of the room has managed to reach the desired, pre-set temperature. The thermostat, in such conditions, is almost useless.

To cure this problem the RAVL-S Remote Sensor, which is connected

to the valve by a capillary tube, can be sited up to two metres (6ft 6in) from the valve itself.

This means that the sensor can be positioned well away from restricting furnishings and will then register the true room temperature. The neat capillary tube connecting the sensor and the valve is contained within the sensor and you only need to extract enough tube to fix it in the desired position. This has the advantage of providing a neat finished job.

The sensor can be either glued or screwed into place and the tube carefully pinned or stapled to the wall for a neat finish.

RAVL-S REMOTE SENSOR
Manufacturer: Danfoss
RRP: £12.09

KEEP THE HEAT

Around 15 per cent of heat loss in the average home is through draughts and the most common source of these is through windows and doors. Since manufacturers are continually introducing new products or revamping old ones to cope with this problem, it is worth shopping around to check on just what is available.

Homeden's Mr Cosy range now offers Self-stik Pile, which is stuck to the closing faces of door frames to provide adequate draught proofing. This strip, which is relatively easy to fit, is ideal for gaps up to 4mm and, according to the manufacturers, retains its resistance to water for up to seven years.

Draughtlock from Frelen, on the other hand, is designed to cope with gaps of anything from 2mm to 8mm. This is a plastic strip that has two sealing faces, with an adhesive backing for easy fixing. Draughtlock is stuck down the inside angled edges of windows and door frames and seals on the outside edge and the closing face

of the door or window.

Another recent product that copes with the problem of draughts is V-Seal Draught Excluder from 3M. This is a solid but flexible self-adhesive strip which folds on a pre-scored line into a V-shape. It is fitted down the closing edges of a door or window frame and touches along two edges, offering double draughtproofing benefits. According to the manufacturers, this small and easy job reduces air infiltration by more than 70 per cent.

SELFSTICK PILE
Manufacturer: Homeden Ltd
RRP: £2.57
DRAUGHTLOCK
Manufacturer: Frelen Ltd
RRP: £5.74
V-SEAL DRAUGHT EXCLUDER
Manufacturer: 3M United Kingdom PLC
RRP: £2.53

FOOT WARMER

Heating a small modern kitchen can pose particular problems owing to the lack of space available to mount a radiator or stand a traditional heater. With someone constantly moving around in the kitchen, having a traditional heater would be more than inconvenient — it could even be dangerous.

Myson has come up with the ideal

solution in the form of its Kick Space Fan Convector. Neat and shallow in design — just 100mm (4in) in height — this heater has been specially styled to fit in the kick space area between the bottom of the cupboards and the floor. The only part of the heater you can see is the very neat little outlet grille.

The heater plumbs into the existing central heating system and is operated by a remote electrical control switch which can be sited at any convenient point in the kitchen. This control operates an electric fan to regulate the rate of heat output. Should you accidentally switch the heater on before the system has warmed up, the

low-limit thermostat will cut out the fan until the required temperature is reached — neatly thwarting the possibility of having cold air blasted at your feet.

The unit is fairly simple to install, requiring some basic plumbing and wiring skills (see **Project**). The heater itself is mounted on the floor and the 15mm diameter pipe connections can be run below the floor of the cupboard to keep them concealed. Exactly where and how you connect up to your existing central plumbing depends on the location of the pipes and how accessible they are.

No special problems are presented by the electrical supply needed as the unit is rated at just 40 watts. However, because electricity is involved you should not site the heater near water outlets such as the sink.

KICK SPACE HEATER
Manufacturer: Myson Domestic Products Ltd
RRP: £126.50

BLOWING IN THE WIND

There is nothing like an open fire to give that feeling of extra warmth and comfort during the cold winter months — until a downdraught blows the smoke back into the room. With the Colt Chimney Cowl there is a money-back guarantee that this problem can be solved.

The cowl works on the principle that wind blowing in any direction past the aerofoil-shaped sides speeds up the flow of air inside the cowl, thus drawing the smoke efficiently up the chimney. In fact, in its basic form it has been around for years and there are many people who testify to its worth.

But the new model eradicates a potential problem. The original model is made of aluminium, which works well and reliably for those fires using housecoal or wood. But the use of more modern and efficient cokes and smokeless fuels in boiler systems and room heaters meant that the aluminium corroded rather quickly. The answer was to make the cowl in stainless steel — more expensive of

course, but much more resistant to corrosion. In fact, it should last a lifetime.

The great advantage of the Colt cowl is that there are no moving parts to go wrong and it has been specially designed to be fitted easily into existing chimney pots from 150mm to 250mm (6 to 10in) in diameter. This is done simply by lowering the four clamps at the base of the cowl into the top of the chimney and tightening the wing nuts to hold it firmly in place. But you must ensure that the chimney pot and flaunching are sound before you install the cowl.

Apart from the simple method of installation, no maintenance is required and because of the new materials used in its construction your cowl is guaranteed a long and trouble-free life.

COLT CHIMNEY COWL
Manufacturer: Colt
RRP: £44.27

Kitchen Heat

Heating a kitchen has always been a problem, particularly when you have a compact modern design with limited floor and wall space. One of the best and most ingenious solutions is the Myson Kick Space Heater. The heater works on a fan convector principle and is plumbed into your central heating.

The Kick Space Heater occupies space which would otherwise be wasted — the space behind the kickboard of one of your cupboards — and doesn't leave potentially lethal wires trailing through the kitchen. Choose the heater's position very carefully. The warm air needs to be directed towards the centre of the room, and not towards a door. Also bear in mind where existing central heating pipes run — if you plan carefully, you can avoid expense, and tricky runs of pipe.

This project shows how the Kick Space Heater can be installed into an existing kitchen. If you have decided to incorporate the heater into a new kitchen, the job will be much simpler as there will be much less to dismantle, and access will be easier. You should also save time because the wiring and plumbing will be instantly accessible.

1 Start by clearing everything out of the cupboard above the site of the heater. Remove the cupboard door to give you more elbow room. If you still find access difficult, you may find it best to dismantle the entire cupboard, and even the adjoining cupboards as well.

Switch off the boiler, and turn off the main supply to the feed and expansion tank in the loft. Find the lowest draincock in the system, and attach a suitable length of hose. Allow the water to drain safely away.

2 Remove the floor of the cupboard, either by lifting, or by removing the fixing screws. If this is not possible, you will have to cut the cupboard floor to gain access to the space beneath. The piece you cut out will need to leave enough room to allow you to deal with the plumbing to the heater. As the cut out piece should not rest on the heater, it must be supported when it is fitted back into place. Dowel feet screwed to the piece would be ideal, but do not fit them until you are sure that

Marking the kickboard

they will not get in the way of the pipework.

Now remove the kickboard from the front of the cupboard

base — it is usually secured by screws. You will need to cut out a suitably shaped hole to fit the grille of the heater: the instructions specify the size. Use a jigsaw to make the hole.

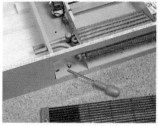

Fitting the heater

Having prepared the cupboard floor and plinth, refit the kickboard and lower the heater into place in the cupboard base. Align the front edge of the heater with the cut-out in the kickboard. Once it is aligned, use a spirit level to check that the heater is level. If necessary, screw wooden battens of the appropriate thickness to the floor. Now use screws to secure the heater either to the floor or to the battens.

3 You now need to make the necessary connections from the heater to the existing central heating systems. Where you tap in the flow and return pipes will depend on the location of the existing pipework. Most circuits with radiators incorporate a two-pipe system, with hot water from the boiler flowing to all the radiators through one pipe, while the cooler water from the radiators returns through another pipe.

Connecting the water pipes

To tap into each of these pipes, you can use one of several T-type fittings currently on the market that are designed for simple DIY installation and will include their own fitting instructions. You should also fit a lockshield flow control valve into the circuit.

Keep the pipe runs to and from the heater as straightforward as possible and avoid sharp bends and elbow fittings. Because of the confined working space it is easiest to use compression-type fittings. Always use compression fittings on the final connections to the heater. If

your heater is at the lowest point on the heating circuit, you must fit a draincock on the bottom section of the pipework so that the whole system can be drained if necessary.

4 Turn off the mains before you start wiring. The electrical wiring to the remote controller and heater must be connected either to a fused spur off the existing power circuit or, easier still, to a normal plug which fits into a convenient power socket. If you choose the latter a 2amp fuse should be used in the plug.

Wiring the controller

Fit the controller to a convenient part of the wall in the same way as any lighting switch. A surface mounting box is provided, or you can fit a recessed one for a neater finish. Connect the wires from the mains to the controller, and run the cable channel, or chase it into the plaster work.

Connecting up wires

Feed the wiring through the relevant wall units to the heater and connect it up to the terminals as specified in the instructions.

If you are in any doubt about the electrical connections, then you must consult a qualified electrician for advice.

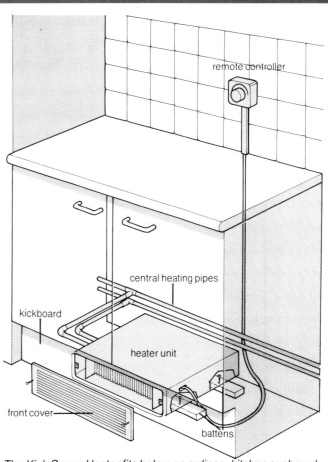

The Kick Space Heater fits below an ordinary kitchen cupboard and is connected to the central heating system

remote controller

central heating pipes

kickboard

heater unit

front cover

battens

5 Once you have completed the installation and checked all your connections, refill the central heating system. Pay special attention to all the new joints in the pipework for possible leaks. Remember to top up the system with corrosion inhibitor.

Switch on the boiler and check the temperature of all the radiators on the same circuit as the new heater. You may find that they remain cold. Try bleeding them to release any air trapped inside. If this does not cure the problem, the chances are that the hot water in the system is taking the easiest route round — through the new heater rather than the radiators. To correct this, screw down the lockshield valve until the radiators reach their normal operating temperature while still keeping the new heater at a reasonable temperature. You may need to make several adjustments.

6 Make a final check on the electrical circuit from the heater to ensure that the controller is working correctly. Remember that because of the low-limit thermostat setting, the fan in the heater will not operate if the water temperature is too low. Finally lag the new pipe runs and then fit the grille to the front of the heater. Replace the cupboard floor and rehang the doors.

Tightening controller cover

Home Improvements

Security has been the real boom in this field with many new and effective products appearing on the market. But don't lose sight of other excellent products such as lookalike wood and expanding fillers.

LOOKALIKE CLADDING

Timber has long been used for its strength, durability and versatility in external house joinery and cladding. Unfortunately, its susceptibility to the effects of rot, and the regular maintenance it demands, can be its downfall. There are many prefabricated plastic lookalikes offering a realistic alternative to timber with a range of benefits.

Celuka from Swish is made from hard-skinned cellular-cored PVC, which is moulded into cladding, fascia and joinery extrusions intended as replacements for traditional timber features, or instead of timber in new constructions.

Cladding, in White, Tame Brown or Sutton Green, comes in Shiplap and Open V profiles (for horizontal only and vertical or horizontal fixing respectively). It is straightforward to install by nailing to a batten framework: the individual strips have moulded tongues and grooves for slotting together, and there's a range of starter channels, drip channels, internal and external corner trims, intermediate trims and cover trims to finish off the installation. Shiplap comes in two cover widths — 100 and 150mm (4in and 6in) — while Open V is only available in the larger size. The material can be worked just like timber — nailed, screwed, sawn — with standard carpentry tools, and will not flake, peel, crack, warp or split.

To fit the cladding, tanalized (pressure treated) battens about 50 × 25mm (2in × 1in) in size are screwed to the wall at 400mm (15½in) intervals, then the starter channels are attached with 25mm galvanized plasterboard nails. The cladding is then slotted on and secured with nails through its upper groove, which is concealed by the next plank.

To complete the infiltration of plastic into our homes, Swish offer PVC windowboards, reveals and sills plus a range of Celuka soffits, bargeboards, fascias, skirtings and architraves.

SWISH CELUKA CLADDING
Manufacturer: Swish Products Ltd
RRP: £10 per 5m length

FILLER FOAM

In the course of home improvements, you are bound to find need for a filler to patch a hole or crack — but which do you choose when each seems suitable only for particular materials and limited locations? New on the market are all-purpose adhesive foam fillers, which have the unique property of expanding to fill virtually any crevice.

The one-part polyurethane foam, sold in aerosol cans under the separate guises of Piccadilly Products' Rollofix X100, Hansil's Fixer Foam and Manger's Mangerfoam, the material

can be used to seal, bond, fill and insulate most building materials such as timber, masonry, concrete, plaster or metal. The foam sets tack-free after about five minutes, can be sawn and shaped, plastered or painted after half an hour and forms an airtight, watertight semi-rigid cell structure that's weather and rot proof on curing.

Hansil's and Piccadilly's canisters come with a pair of plastic gloves and all three with a slim finger-action applicator, which enables you to squirt the foam deep into recesses — say, between a door or window frame and the wall.

Foam can even be applied to damp surfaces (spray a dry surface to improve adhesion and aid curing). Because of the foam's expanding nature, you don't need to use much.

FIXER FOAM
Manufacturer: Hansil Ltd
RRP: £7.48
ROLLOFIX X100
Manufacturer: Piccadilly Products Ltd
RRP: £6.95 for 850ml can
MANGERFOAM
Manufacturer: J Manger & Son Ltd
RRP: £6.99

TIMBER CLADDING

Timber cladding gives a soft, delicate appearance that can either enhance an interesting structure or conceal a drab surface, but if you don't relish the formality of weatherboarding, consider the more random effect of wood tiles, or shingles as they are correctly known.

Shingles are not new: they are often used in countries with less testing climes that our own, although shingle roofs are known in certain areas, albeit usually for small extensions or outbuildings.

Cedar, prized for its excellent weathering and homely good looks, is the choice of Colt in the making of their Cedarlap red cedar shingles. They are intended as an alternative to the usual cladding materials and come pre-packed in sufficient quantities to cover just over 3 sq m (about 35 sq ft), in varying widths between 100 and 355mm (4in and 14in). Using the corrosion-resistant nails supplied, the shingles can be attached to vertical surfaces.

Although not intended for roofing — the makers recommend cladding the garden shed, outbuildings, garage, conservatory, porch.

The shingles can be cut to width to fit the space required, using a sharp trimming knife. They are applied from the bottom up, arranged in overlapping fashion. They are nailed directly to timber surfaces but require horizontal support battens spaced 180mm (7in) apart on masonry walls.

Nails are driven into the centre of the tiles of the first course, then through the centre of the subsequent tiles and through the top edge of the

Use shingles to create a feature of the gable end of your house, or create a random effect using pieces of varying widths.

preceding ones. The vertical joins between shingles must be staggered on alternate courses.

Once attached, the shingles require no further treatment — not even preservative applications — and will not only transform the appearance of the surface to which they are fixed but also offer a degree of weatherproofing and thermal insulation.

CEDARLAP SHINGLES
Manufacturer: Colt International Ltd
RRP: £37.09 per pack

THIEF DETECTOR

With the incidence of burglary and theft on the increase particularly in inner city areas, it is well worth considering having some kind of burglar alarm. Superswitch has come up with a neat device that should detect most unwanted visitors.

The Intruder Alarm is a compact, unobtrusive unit that can be placed almost anywhere — hung on the wall or stood on a table — near to a burglar's likely entry point. It uses an infra-red heat sensor which responds to changes of temperature and detects a body at up to 12 metres (40ft) away.

About 30 seconds after detecting a body, a very loud horn is sounded. This will continue for two minutes. Further movement picked up by the

sensor will set the alarm off again.

There is a tight security system on the alarm itself, which means that the horn can be silenced only by keying in a four-figure security number on a 10-digit keyboard. Should the intruder somehow escape the eagle eye of the sensor and attempt to key in a number or move the alarm, the horn then sounds immediately.

An additional advantage with this alarm is that it is battery operated and power cannot therefore be switched off. A periodic bleeping — quite distinct from the blast from the horn — warns that it is time to change the batteries.

The sensor has a wide arc of operation and should therefore be positioned so that it can cover as many likely entry points as possible.

One important warning though: this device is not suitable for homes which have household pets wandering around during hours of darkness. Even the cat will set off this alarm.

INTRUDER ALARM
Manufacturer: Superswitch Electric Appliances Ltd
RRP: £97.88 approx

ALARMING NEW PRODUCT

Often the presence of an alarm will make a thief reconsider and go in

search of easier pickings. Certes Security, with their Sprint Security System, offer the chance for householders to plan and fit a tailor-made installation which suits their size and type of house.

The basic system contains everything necessary to kit out the average-sized home and there's the option to extend the set-up if required with extra devices. The kit has, at its heart, a mains-operated control panel. It supports closed and open circuit loops for the detection devices, a time-controlled entry/exit circuit and audible warning device, automatic cut-off/reset after ten minutes and automatic battery charger.

The detection devices comprise five door and window contacts, which activate the alarm if a door or window is opened. They are available as easy-to-fit surface-mounted devices or neater flush-mounted versions.

A passive infra-red detector, rare in DIY alarm systems, is a boon for protecting a large portion of the house, such as the living room. The detectors monitor the level of infra-red radiation in the area, and will trigger the alarm if anyone enters the field — the human body emits infra-red radiation.

A personal attack switch, which you can site by your bed or by the front door, remains operative even if the control panel is switched off. The alarm, a self-actuating 108 decibel siren encased in a tamperproof polypropylene box, contains a self-recharging battery. If the siren box is ripped from the wall, or its wire cut, the alarm will still sound.

Completing the kit there is 50m (2ft) of four-core cable (plus clips) for connecting the devices to the panel.
SPRINT SECURITY KIT
Manufacturer: Certes Security Ltd
RRP: £150.00

BROUGHT TO THE BAR

Mugging used to be confined to the street but there's been a rise in the number of personal assaults on householders — particularly the elderly or infirm — when they unwarily open the door to strangers. A good viewer is the best precaution but some extra security is almost vital — most door chains offer little security against a hefty kick and are fiddly to use, can be easily cut, and tend to damage the paintwork with constant use.

From Sandhill comes the slide-

action Bolt Bar Door Guard. Die-cast in polished brass, the precision-engineered device comprises two security measures in one. When closed, it is slid along to act as a tough door bolt; when opened — the door bracket slides along the bar's channels — it allows up to 90mm (3½in) door opening. To open the door fully when you know it's safe, close it and release the bar from the bracket by swinging it back. The bolt bar can't easily be cut and is straightforward to fit with screws provided.

As further benefit, Sandhill bring customers a £25,000 Personal Assault Insurance Certificate provided by Commercial Union Assurance, which applies for 12 months from date of despatch of your order.
BULLION BOLT BAR
DOOR GUARD
Manufacturer: Sandhill Ltd
RRP: £9.95 (£17.95 for front/back door pack)

IF THE KEY FITS

Many burglars enter a house by the window — even if they leave by the

door clutching their spoils. So it's obvious that a good set of window locks is at least a deterrent and provides some piece of mind.

But if your house contains an odd selection of metal and wooden sliding sashes, side-hung casements, sliding patio doors and top-hung vents, you will soon discover that your keyring resembles a warder's, with individual keys for each device.

The Genii Home Security range of window locks from Liberta Hardware has the simple solution — it's possible to match all your locks to a single key. The locks are fairly standard devices:

press locks for wooden windows; sash cams for sliding sashes, for example (although the individual key security device for standard star-drive concealed rack bolts is a neat idea).

A choice of white or brass finish is offered, with aluminium finish for the multi-purpose and press window locks. Key numbers are stamped on the key and marked on the lock packs.
GENII WINDOW LOCKS
Manufacturer: Liberta Hardware Ltd
RRP: from £1.00 to £3.98

A STEP UP

Stairs are basically functional, but there's no reason why they should look unattractive. Sadly modern houses are usually fitted with plain rails or panels; older homes which once boasted elaborate staircases often have had them removed in the name of 'modernisation' — and this strips the property of its character.

You can now restore something of the original charm, or install character where none exists, using the Burbridge refurbishment method. The range of standard parts comprises newel posts (bases and centres), newel caps (mushroom, acorn and ball profiles), spindles in Regency and Georgian designs and fillets.

Parts are easy to assemble. Newel bases can be used to replace existing ones — a hole drilled in the top of each accepts the spigot end of the newel centre; caps slot into holes cut in the top of the newel centres. If an existing newel base is suitable, saw off the old newel and fit a kit centre piece.

Hand and base rails must be cut at

each end to match the pitch of the flight: an adjustable square is used to set this angle. The base rail is screwed direct to the stair string. The hand rail is attached between newels using metal brackets: these have a threaded shank which slots into a hole in the newel and is secured at the opposite side with a nut recessed into a wider hole. A wood screw cover conceals the fixing. Spindles are cut to the pitch of the flight, slotted into the rail's channel — spaced using pre-cut fillets, which also provide a flush finish.

Stair kits are available in light coloured Hemlock, or dark rich Brazilian Mahogany.

BURBRIDGE STAIR RAIL KITS
Manufacturer: H. Burbridge
RRP: from about £280.00 (Hemlock)

RED ALERT

Fortunately there is no fire without smoke and with this in mind

Superswitch has produced its Red Alert Smoke Alarm to provide early warning of a possible fire and so increase the chances of putting it out before too much damage is caused.

This smoke alarm is battery-operated and incorporates an ionisation-type detector. It can be installed in any area where a fire is likely to start — the ideal position for such an alarm is between potential fire points and sleeping areas, such as at the top of the stairs and in bedrooms.

Separate wires are supplied with each Red Alert unit so that if you decide to fit more than one, then all the detectors can be linked. The advantage of this system is that when one alarm is set off, all the others will sound as well.

Each alarm has a loud horn, which will sound continuously at the detection of the slightest amount of smoke.

To ensure that the alarm is

functioning correctly, each unit has a light that flashes approximately once a minute. The batteries that power the Red Alert should last about a year. When the power is running low, the horn will give out a warning pulse to show that the batteries need replacing.

While the importance of such devices to provide an essential safety feature in the home is all too obvious, care should be taken as to the siting of these units as too many false alarms will be very annoying. Avoid such 'dead' areas as the corners of rooms and where steam is often present, such as in a bathroom or kitchen. You should also keep them well clear of forced air ducts or open fires.

RED ALERT SMOKE ALARM
Manufacturer: Superswitch Electric Appliances Ltd
RRP: £17.88 approx

TAILOR-MADE WINDOWS

Finding a replacement window should be straightforward — there's an enormous selection of off-the-shelf frames available. But if your window doesn't comply in size to British Standards, you would have to resort to cutting down a larger frame or have a professional make one up for you.

John Carr Joinery have hit on the answer with their adjustable hardwood window frame. Sold in separate

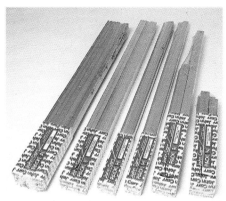

components for home assembly, it's designed to fit any size of opening up to a maximum of 3.05m wide × 1.53m (10ft × 5ft) high. Component packs are in a range of standard sizes and you simply choose the one that corresponds closest to the size of your opening, cut it to fit and assemble it.

Assembly of the frame (see **Project** page 58) uses plastic blocks rather like

KD (knock down) fittings, so no recutting of joints is necessary. Sill, head and jambs, cut to length and assembled, complete the outer frame, which is used to mark out and cut the mullions and transoms, which in turn enable you to size side and top-hung sashes.

ADJUSTABLE HARDWOOD WINDOWS
Manufacturer: John Carr Joinery
RRP: priced individually

SHINE A LIGHT

It's annoying arriving home late at night and having to fumble by the front

door for your key, only to have to go through the same procedure to locate the keyhole. An outside light would solve the problem, but if you leave the house before dark, you don't want to advertise the fact to all and sundry by leaving the light on.

Similarly, burglars who prowl at night aren't lovers of the bright lights, and would likely shy away if suddenly cast in the spotlight, so an ingenious idea from Semiconductor should appeal. The Security Courtesy Light operates automatically when it detects infra-red radiation exuded by the suspecting (or unsuspecting) person.

Measuring 9 × 4½ × 3¾in the 40 Watt light — ample for outdoors — can be connected to other electrical equipment (up to 400 watts), such as a burglar alarm to complete the surprise for an intruder. The light can be adjusted to remain on from 2½ to 5½ minutes after it ceases to detect infra-red radiation.

SECURITY COURTESY LIGHT
Manufacturer: Semiconductor Supplies International
RRP: £89.00

Replacement Window

Fitting a replacement window is straightforward, so long as the opening conforms to standard sizes; if it's something of an oddity, substantial alterations could be necessary — that is, until the arrival of the adjustable window frame.

Despite the vast range of ready-made windows available, replacement of an old one could involve you in bricking up or enlarging the existing opening to accommodate the frame if you can't find a match.

The unique assembly system — using plastic blocks — means that no complicated joints need to be cut, apart from simple halving joints on sash frames.

1 Measure the exact size of the existing window frame, so that you can choose or make up a matching replacement. Take your measurements from the outside: the interior face of the frame will probably be covered by plaster and window board.

Measure the height and width at each end and in the centre and use the smallest dimension, minus 6mm (¼in) from both directions for fitting tolerance.

2 Draw an outline of the frame to scale on squared paper. Compare this with the standard sizes illustrated in the maker's instructions (which you should obtain first). If your window is only about 25mm larger than a standard size, buy the kit and make up the gap with packing as necessary. If the window size is between standard dimensions, in width and height, buy the larger kit and cut down the components to fit.

3 Adhere to certain guidelines regarding structural stability of the frame: basically,

if the window is 1.8m (6ft) wide or more, one vertical mullion should be fitted for strength; if the window is 2.7m (9ft) or more wide, two mullions will be needed. Positions of the mullions depend on the sizes of the opening sashes you want to fit.

Plan out the configurations of windows on your scale plan, working from the illustrations in the leaflet: these include frames with one or two side or top hung casements, top hung fanlights, and fixed panes. Always try to retain the character of the house when designing the window. Look at your existing windows, or those in your street for a guide.

4 For a non-standard window, mark the exact width required on the sill using a pencil against a try square. Cut off the excess from one end with a tenon saw. Place the sill

Cutting the jamb

over the head piece and mark its width and saw.

Mark off a jamb (side piece) to the exact height required,

less 100mm (4in). Square around it with a try square then cut to length. Use the jamb as a template for marking and cutting the opposite jamb.

For standard and non-standard frames, use one of the jambs to mark one or more mullions (centre posts) to length, then cut them to size.

5 Locate and screw a plastic block to each end of the two jambs, using two 32mm (1¼in) No. 7 Pozidriv screws; repeat for the mullion or mullions. Ensure that the blocks are fixed in exactly the correct position and squarely, or the frame will not fit properly.

First construct the opening

Attaching plastic block

sashes. Make a template from a square of plywood with a piece of 50 × 25mm (2 × 1in) softwood screwed across one corner, then use it in the assembly of each corner joint: apply glue then slot the protruding stub of the sash rail into the notch in the end of the sash stile. Insert the star dowels supplied and clamp the assembly to a flat surface with a G-clamp. Repeat for the other corners. Pin two pieces

Making the opening sashes

of 4mm (⅛in) plywood on each side of the sash to give the correct clearance around the frame when positioning the mullions and transoms (cross pieces).

6 Assemble the head, sill, jambs and mullions by push-fitting their plastic blocks into the 12mm (½in) grooves routed in the head and sill. Make sure the groove in the mullion faces the side you want the sash to be fitted.

Lay the frame on the floor with its projecting sill uppermost and check that all joints are firmly located. Measure the diagonals of the frame to check for squareness: if it is square, the measurements are identical; if there's a difference, adjust the components slightly by tapping.

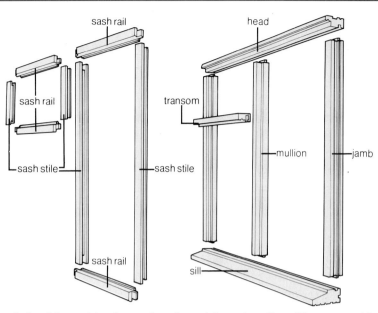

The John Carr window kit consists of a number of special wood sections. These are cut to size and assembled using special plastic blocks

7 Position the opening sashes within the outer frame and tap the mullion gently at top, bottom and centre until the plywood spacers are tight against it. Scribe against the mullion on the head and sill, remove the sash and measure between the inside of the jamb and the mullion. Mark out and cut one T-piece to this length and use

Measuring for T-pieces

a template for cutting two more T-pieces and one transom. Screw a plastic block to each end of the transom.

Remove the head piece from the frame and slot the blocks on the transom into the grooves in the mullion and jamb. Make sure the transom's groove faces the head of the outer frame. Replace the head and slot the three T-pieces into the grooves in the head, sill and transom.

8 Replace the sash and tap the transom up to its ply spacers. Mark the position of the transom on the jamb and mullion. Measure from the top of the T-piece in the sill to the underside of the transom, cut one T-piece to this size and use to cut a second one, then fit them. Remove the sash again. Mark out, cut and fit any other T-pieces to fill remaining grooves in the frame.

9 Pull apart the frame members, leaving the T-pieces in place, then drill through the V-shaped groove in the head and sill using a 4mm (¼in) wood bit to take the 75mm (3in) fixing screws, which pass through the centre hole in the plastic blocks: the hole centres should be 15mm (½in) in from each end of the head and sill. Likewise drill screw holes for the mullions.

Although the timber is

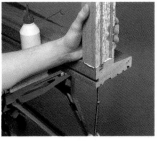

Assembling the frame

factory-treated with preservative, treat all cut ends before assembly. To assemble, apply PVA woodworking adhesive to all meeting faces, slot together the frame and secure with 75mm (3in) No. 10 woodscrews. Glue and pin the T-pieces into their grooves using 30mm (1¼in) nails 225mm (9in) apart; sink the heads. Check that the frame is square then lay it flat until the glue has dried.

10 To make non-standard sized sashes, measure the exact height and width from the outer frame, then deduct 8mm (⁵⁄₁₆in) from the height and width for clearance. Measure off the sash rails and stiles to the new size and recut the joints using a tenon saw. Assemble the sashes with glue and star dowels.

Mark for and cut the 4mm (³⁄₁₆in) deep hinge recesses in the stile or top rail of the sash, depending on the type of sash you are fitting, using a bevel-edged chisel — hinges should be 125mm (5in) from each end of the frame. Screw the shorter leaf of the hinge to the sash and the longer one to the frame using 25mm (1in) No. 7 screws.

Install the windows using screws driven into wall plugs.

Glues & Adhesives

If you want to buy a glue, you will never have any trouble finding one – all sorts of shops seem to sell them. But do you know which glue you want? Or which is the most suitable for your purposes? With so many glues on the market, it's difficult to make a choice. But these tables should help as they list a variety of glues currently available and give their specific applications within the usual DIY repair and maintenance categories.

WOODWORK

Even though most glues are listed as being suitable for use with wood, if you are into serious woodworking, you will get the best results using a proper woodworking adhesive.

PVA adhesives are only suitable where the joints are not going to be exposed to damp.

Water-resistant PVA adhesives tolerate damp conditions, as well as the odd soaking, without the bond becoming weak.

Urea formaldehyde adhesives are very strong and completely water resistant, making them suitable for wet applications.

Resorcinol adhesives are really heavy duty glues used where the work is likely to be constantly exposed to the elements.

No matter which type of woodworking glue you are using, the joint must be clamped until the glue has set. PVA adhesives can be safely handled after an hour or two, but the other types take considerably longer to cure.

Application	Product
PVA adhesives	Cannon PVA Woodworking, Dunlop Extra Strong Wood, Evo-Stik Resin W PVA Wood, Febstik Woodworking, Hermetite Wood, Humbrol Carpenters Wood Fast Grab, Nicobond Timberweld 20, Unibond Woodworker
Water-resistant	PVA Cannon Water Resistant PVA, Evo-Stik Waterproof Wood, Humbrol Extra Bond, Unibond Waterproof Woodworker
Urea formaldehyde	Humbrol Cascamite
Resorcinol	Humbrol Cacophen

SPECIAL PURPOSE

For a specific application, there is often a special glue — these are some of the commoner ones.

Application	Product
Fabrics	Copydex Impact
Ceiling tiles	Evo-Stik Ceiling Tile
Wallboards	Evo-Stik 528, Unibond Unilast Rubber, Unibond Wallboard
Vinyl/vinyl repair	Hermetite Vinyl Repair, Loctite Vinyl Mender, 3M Scotchgrip
Glass	Loctite Glass Bond
Polystyrene	Unibond Polystyrene Tile & Coving

FLOORING

Most manufacturers now supply a range of special-purpose adhesives made specifically for sticking down all kinds of flooring material. While a few adhesives are 'general purpose' flooring glues which will stick most materials, some make them to suit specific types of flooring, so check carefully before buying.

Application	Product
General Purpose	Dunlop Flooring, Evo-Stik Flooring, Marley Universal Flooring, Nicobond Flooring
Cork	Cannon Cork Floor & Wall, Unibond Cork Tile
Vinyl	Febtile Vinyl Flooring, Marley Floorfix
Unbacked Cork	Marley Cork Tile
Foam Backed Vinyl	Nicobond Flooring Acrylic
Thermoplastic & Wood Mosaic	Marley Homelay
Thermosplastic & Vinyl Asbestos	Nicobond Flooring Asphalt
PVC & Sheet Vinyl	Unibond Flooring

EPOXY RESIN

Although epoxy resin glues can be used on almost any material, they are very expensive, and are best kept for small jobs.

The advantages of epoxy resin are that it is heat and water-resistant, and that it can withstand oil and grease too. Furthermore, it gives a very strong bond between materials, although it works best if you are sticking like to like.

Epoxy adhesives are available in two types: quick-setting, and normal. The normal types often give a stronger bond than the 'quick' type but take much longer to cure. These glues are 'two-part' or 'two-pack' adhesives. The kit you buy has two tubes – one contains adhesive, the other hardener. You usually have to work out how much of each to mix together, but some manufacturers make this easy for you by supplying them in a special two-piece dispenser.

Once the two components are mixed, the glue starts to cure. How long it takes to fully harden depends on the type — one of the quick-setting varieties can be handled after 15 minutes.

Products
Araldite, Araldite Rapid, Hermetite Epoxy, Hermetite Fast Set Epoxy, Humbrol Superfast Power Pack, Loctite Tough Bond, UHU Stronghold

WALLPAPER

With so many different types of wallpaper around, it is important to pick an adhesive which is up to the job.

Normal wallpaper adhesive is suitable for a wide variety of papers, from lightweight to textured. It is not suitable for vinyls or washable wallpaper — for this, you must get an adhesive that has a special fungicidal additive to prevent mould.

For heavier wallcoverings, use a heavy-duty paste. Ready-mixed tubs are recommended for fabric wallcoverings.

Application	Product
Ordinary wallpaper	Cannon All Purpose, Cannon Cold Water, Polycell All Purpose, Polycell Heavy Duty, Polycell Plus, Polycell Regular, Solvite All Purpose, Unibond Wallcovering, Unibond Wallpaper
Washable	Cannon Heavy Duty, Polycell All Purpose, Polycell Heavy Duty, Polycell Plus, Solvite All Purpose, Solvite Ready Mix
Vinyl	Polycell Heavy Duty, Polycell Ready Mix, Solvite All Purpose, Solvite Ready Mix, Unibond Wallcovering
Hessian	Cannon Cold Water, Cannon Heavy Duty, Polycell All Purpose, Polycell Heavy Duty, Polycell Ready Mix, Solvite All Purpose, Solvite Ready Mix, Unibond Wallcovering
Anaglypta/chip	Cannon All Purpose, Polycell All Purpose, Polycell Regular, Solvite All Purpose, Unibond Wallcovering, Unibond Wallpaper
Novamura	Polycell Polymura
Polystyrene	Canon Heavy Duty, Polycell All Purpose, Polycell Heavy Duty, Solvite All Purpose, Solvite Ready Mix

CONTACT ADHESIVES

For those general DIY jobs, such as fixing melamine to a cabinet, or even for repairing damaged upholstery.

As the name implies, these glues bond on touch, or when a force is applied.

You can get these glues in three types: non-adjustable (the true contact adhesive); adjustable; and solvent-free.

The non-adjustable type is thinly applied to both materials to be fixed, and then left until touch dry. When the two are brought together, the glue bonds instantly.

Adjustable bond glues have the bonding power of impact adhesives but allow for some adjustment of the two materials before they cure.

Solvent-free glue is non-inflammable and fume-free.

Application	Product
Non-adjustable bond	Evo-Stik Impact, Febstik Contact, Hermetite Contact, UHU Fleximend Contact
Adjustable bond	Dunlop Thixofix, Evo-Stik Time Bond, Humbrol Superstik Contact
Solvent-free	Dunlop Powerfix, Evo-Stik Non Flam, Unibond Non Flam Contact

CERAMIC TILE ADHESIVES

These are normally cement-based and come in two types: ready-mixed paste or powder you mix with water.

Application	Product
General application for indoors in non-wet areas.	Dunlop PVA Ceramic, Evo-Stik Wall Tile, Febtile White Tiling, Nicobond Floor & Wall, Unibond Cerafix
Thixotropic adhesives, used on walls to prevent sagging.	Febtile Non Slip Tiling, Unibond Waterproof Ceramic Wall, Ceramic Wall Tile
Water-resistant adhesives, used on splashbacks, etc.	Cannon Dual Purpose Tile, Dunlop Waterproof Ceramic, Evo-Stik Watertite, Febtile Waterproof Mortar, Nicobond Work Top, Unibond Ceramic Wall Tile Fix & Grout, Unibond Waterproof Cerafix, Unibond Waterproof Ceramic Wall Tile
Waterproof adhesives for use in swimming pools, shower trays, etc.	Cannon Waterproof Tile, Febtile Underwater Curing, Nicobond Waterproof
Flexible adhesives, used on timber wall panels and wood floors.	Evo-Stik Shower & Floor, Nicobond Flexible, Unibond Tile On Wood
Epoxy resin adhesives for use when quick setting.	Dunlop Rapid Set, Febtile Epoxy Quick Set, Nicobond Fast Floor & Wall
Mortar adhesives, where tiles have to be fixed to uneven surfaces or floors.	Dunlop Waterproof Mortar, Evo-Stik Floor Tile, Nicobond Thikbed, Unibond Ceramic Floor Tile Fix & Grout

SUPERGLUES

The range of very powerful quick-setting glues, popularly dubbed 'superglues', are extremely effective for small repair jobs, and will stick almost anything to anything — and that is, in fact, their main disadvantage.

Because they are so quick-acting, if you get any on your fingers, the chances are that they still stick together before you realize what has happened. For obvious reasons you should keep superglues away from children.

Although they come in small tubes and are expensive, you only need a couple of drops for most repairs so provided you use them sensibly, they can be very useful for that odd repair.

Products
Bostik Superglue 4, Hermetite Superglue Plus, Humbrol Wonderbond, Loctite Superglue 3, Loctite Supergluematic, 3M Scotchweld, UHU Supalock

TIP

If you stick your fingers together with superglue, place the affected area under water as hot as you can stand. Then prise your fingers slowly apart with a round-edged flat tool like a spoon handle.

You & Your Home

DIY is not just a story of techniques and new products, it's a part – some would say a vital part – of running a home. *You and your home* widens the horizons of the DIY Yearbook and looks at a range of topics in the home. This half of the book is useful for reference, as well as a source of ideas when planning your home.

There are three help and advice chapters – *Rules and Regulations, Money Matters* and *Getting Specialist Help. Rules and Regulations* helps untangle Planning Regulations, Wiring Regulations, Building Regulations, Gas Safety Regulations and Water Authority Bye-Laws.

Money Matters looks at how to buy a home, from getting a mortgage, to finding a property, to engaging a solicitor or other professionals. For those who already own their home, the section on Home Improvement Loans and Grants contains all the facts about raising money to implement your plans.

Getting Specialist Help contains all you need to know about calling in specialists, ranging from builders to architects. Everyone has some idea of when the limit of their skills or knowledge has been reached, but it's not always clear who to consult.

Saving Energy and *Safety and Security* are two areas of concern for all of today's

householders, and are packed with up-to-date information. The *Saving Energy* chapter will help guide you through the maze of options open to the energy-conscious home owner.

There is no doubt that crime figures are worsening, but there are many ingenious ways to keep out the thief. Read the security section of *Safety and Security* and find the weak spots around your home. Against a backcloth of horrifying accident figures for the home, the safety section will help you make your home a safer place.

The final chapter is the first in a series that examines the origins, designs and construction of Britain's most popular houses. This year looks at the 1930s semi-detached house, the face of suburbia.

The last part of the book is *Useful Information*. Here, you'll find the names and addresses of all the manufacturers and official and professional bodies mentioned

throughout the DIY Yearbook. *Useful Information* is also just that – it's a guide to typical tool prices, cable gauges and types, concrete and mortar mixes, and a whole lot more. This section provides a mine of basic DIY information, with facts and figures at your fingertips.

Metrication charts

To change	Into	Multiply by
Inches	Millimetres	25.40
Inches	Centimetres	2.54
Feet	Metres	0.305
Yards	Metres	0.914
Square inches	Square centimetres	6.45
Square feet	Square metres	0.093
Square yards	Square metres	0.836
Cubic inches	Cubic centimetres	16.40
Cubic feet	Cubic metres	0.028
Cubic yards	Cubic metres	0.765
Pints	Litres	0.569
Gallons	Litres	4.55
Ounces	Grams	28.40
Pounds	Grams	454.00
Pounds	Kilograms	0.454

To change	Into	Multiply by
Millimetres	Inches	0.039
Centimetres	Inches	0.394
Metres	Feet	3.28
Metres	Yards	1.09
Square centimetres	Square inches	0.155
Square metres	Square feet	10.80
Square metres	Square yards	1.20
Cubic centimetres	Cubic inches	0.061
Cubic metres	Cubic feet	35.30
Cubic metres	Cubic yards	1.31
Litres	Pints	1.76
Litres	Gallons	0.22
Grams	Ounces	0.035
Grams	Pounds	0.002
Kilograms	Pounds	2.20

To change degrees Fahrenheit to degrees Celsius, subtract 32, then divide by nine and multiply by five.
To change degrees Celsius to degrees Fahrenheit, divide by five, multiply by nine and then add 32.

Inches	Millimetres
$1/32$	0.79
$1/16$	1.59
$3/32$	2.38
$1/8$	3.18
$5/32$	3.97
$3/16$	4.76
$7/32$	5.55
$1/4$	6.35
$9/32$	7.15
$5/16$	7.94
$11/32$	8.73
$3/8$	9.53
$13/32$	10.31
$7/16$	11.11
$15/32$	11.90
$1/2$	12.70
$17/32$	13.50
$9/16$	14.29
$19/32$	15.09
$5/8$	15.88
$21/32$	16.67
$11/16$	17.46
$23/32$	18.26
$3/4$	19.05
$25/32$	19.84
$13/16$	20.62
$27/32$	21.41
$7/8$	22.22
$29/32$	23.01
$15/16$	23.81
$31/32$	24.60
1	25.40
2	50.80
3	76.20
4	101.60
5	127.00
6	152.40
7	177.80
8	203.20
9	228.60
10	254.00
11	279.40
12	304.80

Rules & Regulations

Safety in design and construction is the key word in DIY work – and for this reason there are simply masses of rules and regulations governing what you can do, how you can do it and what materials you can use. This chapter separates the Regs into 4 distinct categories – Planning Regs, Building Regs, Gas Safety Regs and Water Regs. Each section guides you through the maze by pinpointing the relevant regulations, describing how they operate and how you can safely work within them. Further hints and tips help you cope with officialdom and bureaucracy.

Planning

The Planning Regulations are administered by the Department of the Environment via the Planning Department of your local authority, currently under the terms of the 1971 Town and Country Planning Acts and their various amendments.

Quite simply, their purpose is to provide controls over what you can build, where you can build it and what you subsequently use it for.

The Planning Regulations govern three areas of activity which could conceivably affect a DIY project.

Building work This covers additions and modifications to the external structure of your house, such as installing a dormer window, building a porch, or adding on a carport.

Other work This embraces building work elsewhere on your property; for example, putting up a fence, erecting a greenhouse or building a garage.

Change of use This refers to how you use your home. If you plan to run a business from your home, convert it into flats or turn an outhouse into a separate dwelling, you will require Planning Permission.

However, there are several exemptions classified as 'Permitted Development' for which formal permission is not required (see panel on page 67).

Also (in the same panel) check to see if there are any associated regulations restricting your proposed project's feasibility.

Among the projects certain to require formal Planning Permission are:
● erection of a flagpole or radio mast
● new access from a classified road
● building or conversion of a separate, self-contained dwelling
● conversion of a house into flats
● conversion of a shop or business premises into a domestic dwelling.
● use of a domestic house as a place of business.

How to apply for Planning Permission
You have three choices of how to apply for Planning Permission: you can do it yourself, pay a builder or architect to do it for you, or apply for what is called 'outline permission'.

The first option is generally the most sensible for the majority of DIY projects, since the procedure is quite straightforward. A set 'householder' fee is payable, although there are exemptions including works done for the benefit of a disabled person.

However, if you suspect that your proposals are likely to be contentious, or they are especially complicated, it may be worth paying a professional to make the application since they will 'know the ropes'.

Outline permission means 'permission in theory' and although you pay a smaller fee and don't have to make such a detailed application, you must still apply for formal permission before proceeding with the work. The chief use of outline permission is in convincing prospective house buyers of the value of your land.

Making the application To do this, you must first fill in three or four copies of a standard form obtainable from the Planning Office; these forms are not complicated, and guidance notes are included.

As well as the forms, you will need to draw up two sets of plans: one

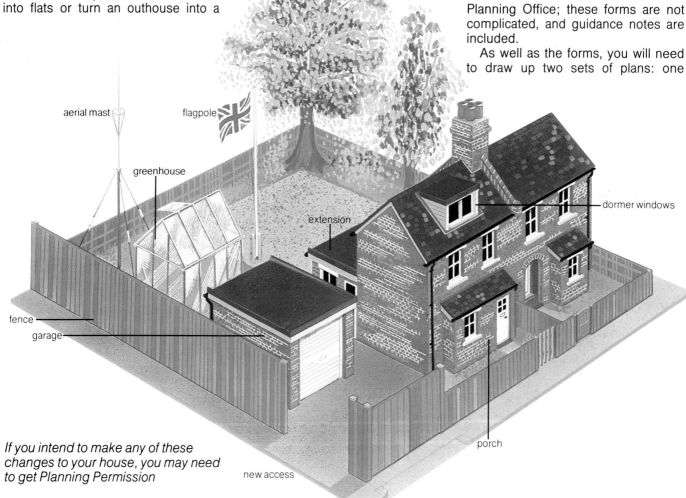

felling trees

aerial mast

flagpole

greenhouse

extension

dormer windows

fence

garage

porch

new access

If you intend to make any of these changes to your house, you may need to get Planning Permission

showing your property in relation to its surroundings, and one detailing the actual construction proposed.

The plans do not have to be drawn to professional standards, but they should be in metric units, and include any information that you think is relevant to your case. In particular, make sure you get all the dimensions and distances correct. And don't hesitate to call the Planning Office if there is anything you are not clear about, before submitting your completed application to the Planning Office, together with the prescribed fee. The Office is then obliged to deal with it within eight weeks.

They will start by considering the

How you present your plans for an extension is crucial in obtaining Planning Permission, but if your plans show a simple design that blends well with the existing building, then your application should be successful

PERMITTED DEVELOPMENT

If your project meets the conditions outlined below, you will not require formal Planning Permission.

Extensions These are exempt providing:
● The volume of the original house is not increased by more than the specified figures. For a terraced house or one in a DOE Conservation Area, the permitted increase is up to 50m³ or one-tenth of the house's volume up to a maximum of 115m³, whichever is the greater. In all other cases it is 70m³ or 15 per cent of the house volume up to 115m³, whichever is the greater.
● No part of the extension is higher than the existing house roof.
● No part projects beyond any wall of the original house facing a public highway (ie beyond what is commonly termed the 'building line').
● No part within 2m of your property's boundary is more than 4m high (roof extension excepted).
● No more than half the garden is built over.
● The extension is not to be a separate dwelling.

Loft conversions These are exempt providing the overall volume of the house is not increased beyond the permitted development limits.

Sheds and Greenhouses These are exempt providing:
● No more than half the garden is covered with outbuildings.
● The structure does not project beyond the building line.
● The roof is no more than 4m high

(pitched roof) or 3m high (flat roof).

The rules also apply to other outbuildings and to swimming pools, providing these buildings are for use by the house occupants.

Conservatories These are treated in the same way as extensions, providing they are attached to the house.

Garages Where these are within 5m of the house the extension rules apply; if they are further than 5m, follow the rules for outbuildings.

Fences and walls If these run along a boundary with a public highway, they are exempt providing their height does not exceed 1m. Elsewhere, a height of up to 2m is allowable.

Drives, paths and hardstandings Conversions and extensions of existing drives and pathways do not normally require Planning Permission, unless building them involves creating new access from a classified road.

Associated Regulations

Any of the restrictions listed below may oblige you to seek Planning Permission — either from the Planning Office or a third party — even if your proposed project would normally be classed as 'Permitted Development'.

Listed Building Consent If your house is Listed, you will need Planning Permission before demolishing or modifying the structure in any way.

Conservation Orders These apply if you live in a National Park, a Conservation Area, or an Area of Outstanding Natural Beauty (as designated by the DOE), and the rules

are administered by the local Planning Office. They operate in much the same way as Listed Building Consent.

Local Planning Restrictions Some localities, in particular housing estates, have conditions attached to the original Approval for Planning Permission. In such cases you may be prevented from carrying out further works even if these fall within the normal permitted development limits; the local Planning Office can advise you.

Tree Preservation Orders If a tree on your property carries one of these, you can't fell it without Permission; again, the Planning Office can advise you.

Deeds of Covenant These are private restrictions on development and will be specified in your house deeds; if you find one is in force, you may have to apply to the County Court for an Order to get it rescinded.

Article 4 Directives

Issued by the local authority to cover a single house, a road or an area, these are the most important associated planning regulations, and frequently a cause of much confusion. Since they override the normal Planning Regulations (including Permitted Development) and can conceivably affect quite minor works such as window replacement or exterior decoration, it's always worth checking with the Planning Office to find out if any are in force *before* you consider the question of formal Permission; often just a phone call will clarify the position.

RULES & REGULATIONS

Your ideas for external decoration may be in marked contrast to your neighbours'. To prevent clashes that reduce both the attraction and value of the properties, Planning Permission is often required

technical feasibility of your project and check with the service Authorities (Electricity, Gas, Water etc) that there are no problems as far as they are concerned. They will then advertise the proposals — either by direct communication, through a local newspaper or by bill posting — to canvass opinion among neighbours and other interested parties.

Do not proceed with the project until you receive a formal notice of approval in writing. If your application is turned down and you believe the reasons for doing so are unfair, you have the right to appeal within six months of receiving the refusal. The exact procedure for making a Planning Appeal is laid down in a free booklet called Planning Appeals: A Guide to Procedure, which is available from the Planning Office.

DEALING WITH BUREAUCRACY

Where Planning Permission is concerned you can do a lot to speed things up by consulting interested parties and endeavouring to sort out potential problems *before* you submit your application. Here, questions of overlooking, obstructed light and spoilt views tend to be the most contentious. And although, in general, neighbours' entitlements in these areas extend no further than 'the provision of adequate natural light', you could find that a diplomatic chat — and perhaps a compromise — does much to help both the Planning Office and yourself.

When it comes to making your application, make sure the plans are legible, to scale, and contain all the necessary details. If you have any questions, save them up and then clarify the points one by one in a single visit or telephone conversation.

Do NOT involve the BCO too early on. One building inspector advises home owners to think things out thoroughly then put their ideas on paper and make an appointment or else send in the drawings in advance of their application and ask the building inspector to contact *them*. Certainly you shouldn't expect a building inspector to visit the site before work has actually commenced.

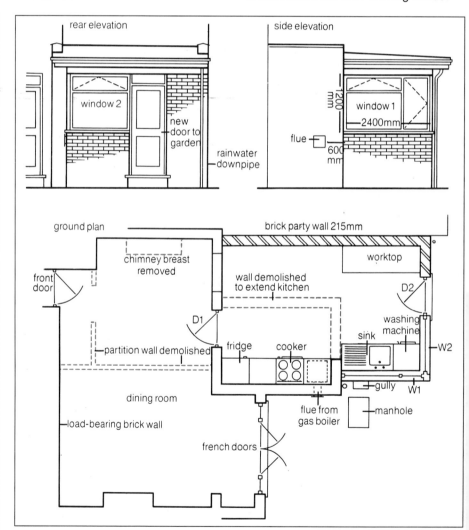

Although you may prefer to get an architect to draw up the plans for planning approval, you can do it yourself. Make sure the proposed changes and measurements are clearly presented

Building

Known popularly as the 'Regs', these are a complicated group of legally binding requirements governing how you build things, what materials you use, and how well you do the job.

In England and Wales, the Building Regs cover virtually all aspects of building work in, outside and around the home, with the notable exceptions of decorating, regular maintenance and electrical wiring.

Scotland and Northern Ireland have their own Building Regulations based on the English system.

Nor do the Building Regs currently apply to Inner London (defined as the old London County Council Area). Building work here is governed by the London Building Acts and the London Building (Constructional) Bye-laws.

In most parts of the country the Building Regulations are administered by Building Control Officers (BCOs) (often called 'Building Inspectors') who work from the Planning Department, Technical Services Department or Building Control Office of your local authority. In Inner London the same job is done by a District Surveyor (DS) attached to the District Surveyor's Office of your local Borough.

The Building Regulations can affect you in three ways. Major jobs such as building extensions require prior approval of drawings (except in London) and must be inspected by the BCO or DS while the work is being done. Smaller projects also require

prior approval (except in London), but inspection by the BCO or DS is at their discretion. Finally, there are everyday jobs for which you can usually get the go-ahead with just a phone call to the BCO. However, even these small jobs must still satisfy the relevant Building Regs, and you can be prosecuted if they don't.

The Regulations themselves are extremely comprehensive, to cope with the majority of different building materials and methods found in the UK. But whereas some of the rules are hard and fast, others are left deliberately flexible and are open to different interpretations. Where this occurs it is well worth having a chat with your BCO.

Coping with the Building Regs calls for a commonsense approach. For the majority of DIY projects you simply need to abide by good building practice, as outlined in any reputable DIY manual, and let the building inspector amend or clarify any points which are not clear. Larger projects — for instance, calculating the size of an RSJ to support an opening in a loadbearing wall — call for complicated calculations outside the scope of most DIY enthusiasts. Bearing in mind that in most cases such jobs also require prior approval from the BCO, it makes sense to call in the expert advice of an architect, surveyor or structural engineer and then let them make the

Both building materials and storage are governed by the Building Regs

WHAT CAN GO WRONG

People often ask; 'Why obey the Building Regulations? What's to stop me 'keeping quiet' and getting on with the job?' Quite a lot, in fact, as the two case histories below so poignantly illustrate.

The first concerns an unfortunate householder who had his loft converted 'on the cheap' by a highly disreputable firm of builders. The work was duly completed without reference to the BCO, but the unsightly dormer window which the builder had installed attracted the unwelcome attention of neighbours, who complained to the council.

Eventually the matter was referred to the District Surveyor, who gained entry to the property, inspected the conversion, and declared it to be in imminent danger of collapse. Steel bracing girders were immediately erected by the council — at the owner's cost.

Furthermore, the builder could not be traced so the owner himself was taken to court. The result was a fine, plus a daily penalty until such time as the conversion was made permanently safe. Needless to say, the project ended up costing many thousands of pounds more than the original quote.

'Horror story' number two involves an enthusiastic builder who

tried to cure a bulging brick wall by demolishing it from the ground upwards. He was spotted in the course of doing so by the District Surveyor, who declared the site a public danger and initiated immediate action. This involved council workmen erecting shoring which closed the street. Once again, the final cost to the householder was astronomical.

As you can see, it simply doesn't pay to short-cut the regulations. If you erect something without Planning Permission, the council can fine you or serve an enforcement notice obliging you to pull it down — and much the same applies to contraventions of the Building Regs.

application on your behalf.

Naturally there are 'grey areas' where you are obliged to apply for prior approval, but can make an informed guess as to what will satisfy the BCO's requirements. A good example would be sizing joists for a loft conversion: on this point the Building Regs contain tables relating joist size to span, so all you need do is consult a copy of the Regs at your local library and prepare plans accordingly.

Some jobs, such as foundation and drain laying, cavity insulation, DPC installation and the fixing of thermal barriers must be witnessed by the Building Inspector at the time they are done, even if they have already been approved in theory.

On other approved jobs the inspector may simply drop in unannounced to check that the work is being done according to plan. Or he may ask to check certain aspects of a job which it was not feasible to assess at an earlier stage.

For relatively minor jobs you probably wouldn't bother to inform the BCO at all, though technically you are still legally obliged to do so. Such jobs must nevertheless be done according to the terms of the Building Regulations, or you risk prosecution. It pays to consult the BCO if you are in any doubt since the Regulations are primarily there for your (and your family's) safety.

Gaining approval

Written Building Regs Approval is required in all parts of the UK except Inner London, where you simply need

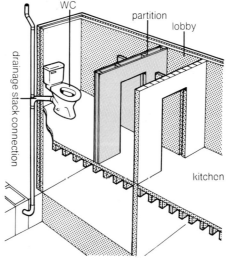

Regulations cover the access to WCs. For instance, there must be two doors between the kitchen and the WC

to give 48 hours' notice of your intention to start work. In Scotland, Building Approval is called a Building Warrant. In all areas a fee is payable with your application, and this is scaled according to the total cost of the works.

The exact procedure for gaining written approval varies from one authority to another but by and large you need to fill in two copies of a standard form, prepare two copies of plans detailing the work, and send these, together with your fee, to the BCO who must respond within five weeks.

As with Planning Applications, the plans don't have to be to blueprint standard, but they should be legible, to scale, and contain any information which you think is relevant.

Once again, actual dimensions and

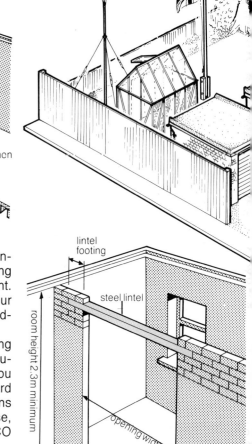

Guidelines to the strength of an RSJ are contained in the Building Regs

WORK REQUIRING BUILDING REGULATIONS APPROVAL

The following categories define the main areas of building work requiring written approval by the BCO (except London).

Suitability of materials The Regs lay down strict guidelines on what materials are suitable for what jobs and often specify a British Standard number to which materials must conform.

Site preparation Standard formulae cover the depth and thickness of foundations and foundation slabs, though these may be amended by the inspector to suit local ground conditions.

Damp proofing Standards of practice and materials are laid down for the protection of walls, solid floors, roofs (pitched and flat) and internal plasterwork. These are quite rigid.

Structural stability All building plans must satisfy minimum standards of stability, assessed against known building practices.

Size of materials Some components, such as roof joists, are sized by reference to tables in the Regs. Others must be gauged with reference to loadbearing calculations made according to accepted practice.

Structural alteration The demolition

or alteration of loadbearing structures such as walls and roof beams is carefully controlled. The building inspector will judge a case according to structural calculations and individual conditions.

Fire precautions The Regs include specifications for self-closing and fire-check doors (particularly in houses converted into flats). Fire-check walls may be needed in some cases, and you may be required to build in adequate provision for escape from a fire.

Thermal and sound insulation All new walls and roofs must satisfy minimum standards of insulation;

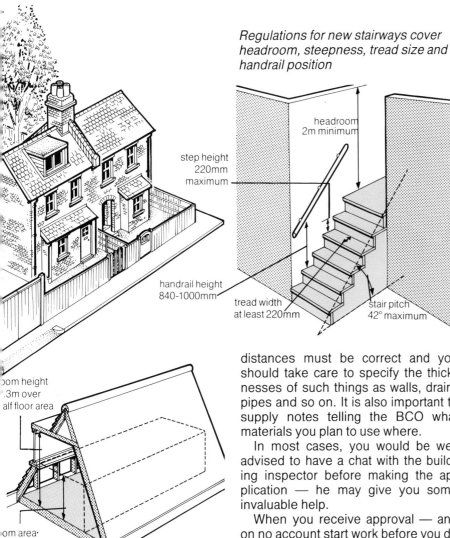

Regulations for new stairways cover headroom, steepness, tread size and handrail position

step height
220mm
maximum

headroom
2m minimum

handrail height
840-1000mm

tread width
at least 220mm

stair pitch
42° maximum

oom height
.3m over
alf floor area

om area
easured at
5m height

Standing room and window area in loft conversions are laid down in the Regs

distances must be correct and you should take care to specify the thicknesses of such things as walls, drainpipes and so on. It is also important to supply notes telling the BCO what materials you plan to use where.

In most cases, you would be well advised to have a chat with the building inspector before making the application — he may give you some invaluable help.

When you receive approval — and on no account start work before you do — the chances are it will be conditional upon the building inspector being present at certain key stages. For these you need to make an appointment — by phone or postcard — at least 24 hours in advance of when you want him to attend.

---

materials are specified and there are strict guidelines on installation.

Stairs and balustrades The Regs include minimum tread and riser heights, maximum slopes, minimum material sizes, handrail heights, and guides on installation within the house structure.

Room classifications For rooms to be classified as 'habitable' the Regs lay down minimum ceiling heights, and rules on the amount of natural light and ventilation that must be provided in relation to floor area.

Fires The Regs specify standards for the construction of hearths, flues and

chimneys with regard to fire protection and the safe disposal of gases.

Installation of heating appliances The Regs are quite specific about any appliances (including cookers) that make smoke or gas.

Drainage Inside the house, the Regs specify pipe sizes, configurations and slopes; there are rules to say where pipes may join a main stack. All other drainage pipes, inspection chambers, gullies and runs are sized according to their carrying capacity.

Loft conversions There are rules to determine ceiling height, natural light and floor strength before a conversion

can be classed as habitable.

Extensions Special rules in the Regs cover the tying-in of an extension to the house structure, with particular regard to damp-proofing.

Plumbing Pipe materials, sizes and jointing methods are specified according to the job they have to do. There are guidelines on the installation of pipe runs so as not to cause airlocks or leaks in the future.

WC Installation The Regs are particularly strict about where a WC may be installed, access between the WC and other habitable rooms, and connection to the main drainage stack.

Wiring

In England, Wales, and N. Ireland, the 'Wiring Regs', as they are usually called, refer to the Wiring Regulations published by the Institute of Electrical Engineers (IEE). First published in 1882, the latest edition is the Fifteenth (published in 1982, with amendments in 1983, 1984 and 1985).

Although the Regs are NOT legally binding, it pays to follow them to the letter. Compliance with the Regs also guarantees that your system will be passed by an Electricity Board inspection, which it must be if the consumer unit is disconnected and then reconnected in the course of a major home improvement.

As with the Building Regs, the Wiring Regs cover all aspects of electrical installation, including materials and correct practices. However, since there is greater standardization and most of the requirements are quite specific, you don't need prior approval before carrying out any work.

Areas covered by the Wiring Regs

Cable sizes These are listed in the Regs and are determined by the current they are expected to carry, since a cable which is overloaded will heat up and may catch fire.

Flex sizes Flexes between appliances and socket outlets are sized in the same way as circuit cables.

Circuit sizes The Wiring Regs allow both ring and radial circuits or com-

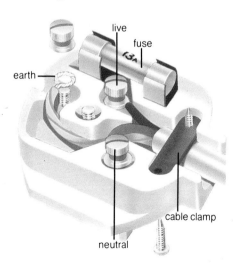

Electrical safety begins with the correct wiring of the plug, securing the cable and fitting the right fuse

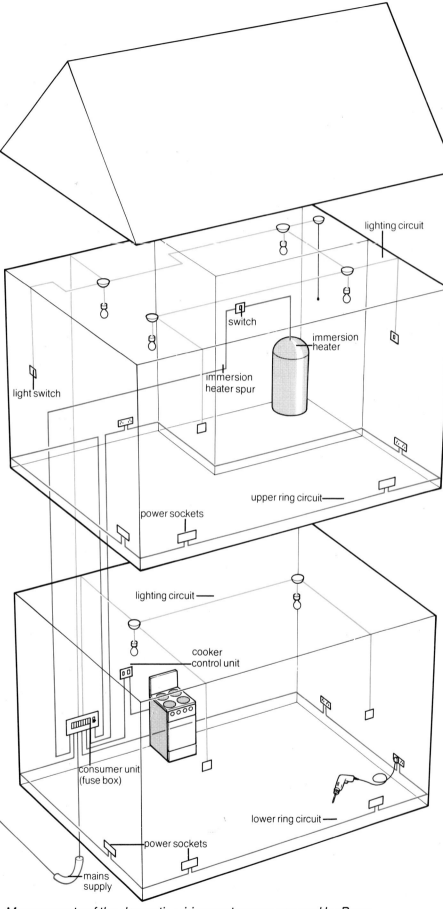

Many aspects of the domestic wiring system are covered by Regs

KEEP IT SAFE!
Basic checks
● Check that plugs are correctly and securely wired and that their flex grips are fitted properly.
● Check appliance flexes and cord outlets for kinks, twisting and fraying.
● Avoid adaptors on a day-to-day basis (especially the three-way sort); install extra socket outlets instead.
● Don't run more than one appliance off a single plug and don't rely on extension leads except on a temporary basis.

Practical checks
Before you can move on to more practical checks, make sure you are familiar with the correct procedure for working on electric circuits. The golden rule is: NEVER WORK ON A CIRCUIT UNLESS YOU ARE SURE THE ELECTRICITY HAS BEEN DISCONNECTED FROM IT.
● Replace cracked, badly worn or obsolete socket outlets, switches and other fittings.
● Check that your circuit cables are the modern PVC-sheathed type —

rewire if you find any other.
● Enclose exposed cable within rooms by encasing it in plastic mini-trunking.
● Make sure the bare earth wires in socket outlets and switches are sleeved with green and yellow PVC sheathing.
● Check for evidence of fraying, excessive heat, or other damage.
● Guard against water coming into contact with electrical fittings.
● Check that heavier radial circuits use cable of the correct rating.
● Check that all plug and circuit fuses are of the appropriate rating.

---

binations of both. However they are restricted in length by the floor area they serve. Lighting circuits can be wired on the loop-in or modern junction box system, and are restricted by the number of light points that can be served by cable of a particular size.

Cable runs The Wiring Regs specify that these must be adequately protected — normally by running them under floorboards, burying them in the wall plaster or cavity, or by encasing them in plastic mini-trunking.

Electrical fittings The Regs specify British Standards for all electrical switches, outlets and fittings.

Installation practice There are many regulations governing this, most of which are concerned with safety. For a start, the Regs specify that outlets and switches should not be positioned where they can easily be touched by

wet hands or running water. In the case of bathrooms and WCs they are more specific: socket outlets are banned; only pull-cord switches are allowed.

Protection against shock and fire These are the most important of the Regulations.

Properly installed electrical systems have several lines of defence against the massive current surges that usually accompany appliance faults. First is the plug fuse, which should be rated according to the appliance it is serving — commonly 3 amps or 13 amps.

Next comes the consumer unit fuse, which may be the rewirable type with a piece of fuse wire, the cartridge type with a fuse like a plug fuse, or a miniature circuit breaker (MCB) — a kind of automatic trip switch. The Regs state that these fuses, too, must be

rated according to the circuit they are serving. The Regs state that a circuit feeding an outdoor supply must be fitted with an earth leakage circuit breaker (ELCB) — a relatively new component that trips the current off whenever current leaks to earth due to an electrical fault.

Your most important protection against serious faults and their consequences is the earthing system. The most common method of earthing is to link the system earth to the domestic rising main; any overloads can be safely discharged to earth via the pipes.

However, now that plastic is increasingly used for water pipes, the Regs provide for a new alternative system known as protective multiple earthing (PME). With this, the circuit earths are connected to the neutral conductor of the supply cable which returns to the local sub-station.

In a PME system, it is vital that all metal pipework and metal fittings around the house are connected — or cross-bonded — to the earthing circuits to ensure good continuity.

If you have a PME system, it should say so on the consumer unit. However, if you are in any doubt have it checked by the Electricity Board.

Who is responsible
Quite simply, the Electricity Board's responsibility ends at the consumer unit. It is illegal for home owners to tamper with the meter 'tails' — the cables linking the consumer unit with the Board's meter — so if you replace your unit or rewire the house then the Electricity Board must be called in to make the final connections.

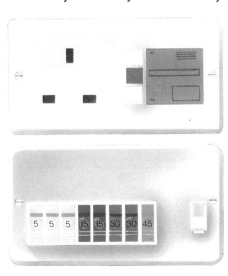

Some consumer units use circuit breakers (above). Outdoor supplies need their own power breaker (top)

Different sizes and types of cable are used according to the current they will have to carry

Gas

The Gas Safety Regulations, which were introduced in 1972, apply to the whole of the UK and are legally binding both on consumers and installers.

Under the Regulations, the street main, service pipe, gas meter, isolating valve and the first 600mm of supply pipework inside the house are all the responsibility of the Gas Board; thereafter, any supply pipes, stop valves and gas appliances become the exclusive responsibility of the householder. But the Gas Board has the power to inspect an installation before connecting it to the mains.

The Regulations also state that only 'competent persons' may work on a gas installation or install new pipework and appliances. This almost certainly excludes the average DIY enthusiast with no trade experience in either plumbing or gas work.

However, the Safety Regs also lay down certain obligations which any householder with a gas supply is legally bound to follow.

Competence It is up to you to ensure that whoever carries out work on your gas system is competent to do so.

Defects You must not use — or let anyone else use — an appliance which you suspect is defective in any way.

Leaks If you smell a leak, you must inform the local Gas Board's emergency service centre immediately, then turn off the supply at the meter isolating valve and do not turn it on until the leak has been investigated.

What else can be done?

Although the Gas Safety panel (above)

GAS SAFETY REGULATIONS — INSTALLATION PRACTICE

The following key points must be adhered to by whoever installs a gas supply or appliance.

Pipes Only certain pipe materials are safe for use with gas. Copper is now the most commonly employed, but plastic and stainless steel are definitely not suitable.

Pipe sizes The standard pressure for most domestic installations is 20 millibars, which means using 15mm pipework.

Pipe joints Only soldered capillary fittings can be used for gas installations. Each new joint must be treated for gas tightness using an approved method.

Pipe runs Gas pipes cannot run in cavity walls, though they may pass through them at 90°. Where pipes pass through walls and solid floors they must be enclosed in a protective sleeve with the intervening space filled with mastic.

Pipe protection Wherever pipes are in contact with material likely to cause corrosion (such as concrete) they should be encased in protective sleeving or be of the type that has a factory-bonded PVC coating.

Pipe laying Gas pipes must be laid in a manner not likely to impair the structure of the building and they should be properly supported.

Ventilation All gas-burning appliances need a supply of fresh air if they are to work effectively. This is usually provided by means of airbricks, or door and window vents. Failure to provide proper ventilation and the blocking up of existing vents both contravene the Safety Regs, since there is a danger of the room filling with carbon monoxide.

Flues The installation and positioning of gas flues is mainly covered by the Building Regulations, which impose restrictions on proximity to windows, doors and other dwellings.

Fire prevention There are several clauses in the Safety Regs dealing with the proximity of gas burning appliances to other combustible materials — for example, shelves above a gas cooker, or curtains near a fire. However, these are mainly a matter of common sense.

Testing All new gas installations must be tested for gas tightness using an approved method. The standard test is to connect a device called a U gauge to the end of the pipe in question; the gauge then measures the gas pressure against atmospheric pressure.

outlines the main considerations attached to the Safety Regs, even if you have some plumbing experience you should still think again before tackling all but the most minor installation jobs.

If your house's electrical installation is earthed by the PME system (see Wiring Regulations), you must have the gas pipework properly cross-bonded by a qualified electrician and install temporary bonds wherever a pipe is to be severed.

In any event, ALWAYS get the system tested by a qualified installer before you reinstate the gas supply.

In a PME installation, continuity must be maintained if the pipe is cut

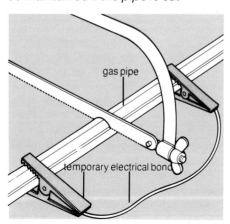

A Gas Board engineer should be called immediately if there is a smell of gas. Before he arrives, turn off the supply at the meter, put out any naked lights and open the windows to minimise any risk of the escaping gas causing an explosion

Water

The Water Regulations are less straightforward. Although the basic guidelines on plumbing work and materials are laid down in the Building Regulations, each local Water Authority has the power to issue bye-laws governing how certain jobs are carried out. These vary widely from region to region, but they are all based on a common plan — The Model Water Bye-Laws — which has specific aims:

● The prevention of contamination of the domestic water supply.
● The reduction of wastage and undue consumption (particularly in the event of a drought).
● The avoidance of knocking and reverberation in domestic pipework.
● The prevention of premature pipe corrosion.
● The maintenance of consistent water pressure through the mains.

Drainage too is covered by the Building Regs and by local Water Authority bye-laws, with the exception of Inner London, where it is the re-

The Water Regulations govern both the use of plumbing components and how and where the pipes are located inside the house

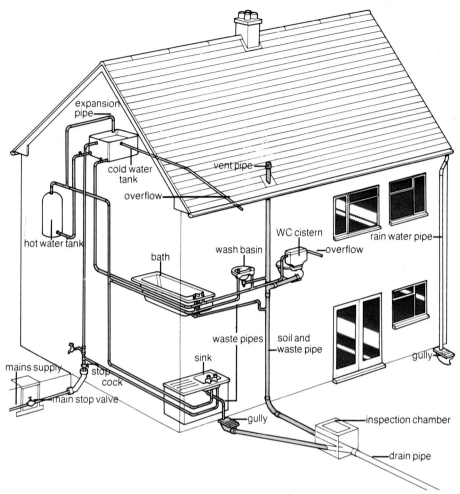

PLUMBING AND THE BYE-LAWS

If you intend to carry out work on any of the parts of a house plumbing system listed below, consult the Bye-laws first.

Stop valves All houses should have a stop valve fitted on the rising main, and this must be easily accessible in the event of an emergency.

Some Authorities insist that stop valves are fitted to each pipe fed from the storage tank, and that there should be additional valves on the cold feed to the hot water system.

Rising main This must be protected from frost, though as far as the main stop valve it is normally the Authority's responsibility. Some Authorities ban any tampering with the rising main whatsoever; others allow you to tap into it to install a garden tap, washing machine or dishwasher — but be sure to check, by giving your local Water Authority a call.

Storage tanks (cisterns) These should have a capacity of at least 200 litres and

be accessible for inspection and maintenance. There are Bye-laws governing the size and positioning of overflow pipes both on storage and WC cisterns.

Pipe materials Copper, stainless steel and plastic pipes are now approved by most Authorities, but this is another thing to check. Plumbing fittings must be British Standard or Water Council approved, and this also includes things like baths, WCs and bidets.

Pipe runs These must be as straightforward as possible and easily drained. U-shaped runs (which can cause airlocks) should be avoided or fitted with a drain cock at their lowest point. Likewise boxed-in pipes have to be reasonably accessible for maintenance, and buried pipes should be joined with either capillary or splayed compression fittings. Pipe runs inside the home must be supported at regular intervals to prevent undue strain and rattling. Pipes buried underground

must be corrosion resistant or else encased in protective sleeving.

Contamination The Bye-laws are particularly concerned with preventing the mains supply from being contaminated with dirty water from a bath, basin or sink — fluctuations in mains pressure could conceivably suck waste water back through outlets such as rising-spray bidets and shower heads.

This means that taps and other fittings (particularly mixer taps) have to be approved by the Authority. Some ban one-hole mixers (where hot and cold water is mixed within the tap itself) on the grounds that the hot water supply could easily be contaminated and find its way back into the mains.

For the same reason, water outlets must be positioned at least 13mm above the top edge of the water container. And shower hand sprays with flexible hoses should on no account be left to dangle in a bath or basin or shower tray.

sponsibility of the Borough Environmental Health Department — not the District Surveyor's Office.

What the Bye-laws affect

The panel on p75 lists areas of plumbing work likely to be affected by the Bye-laws. However, because these laws differ between one regional authority and another, and are often open to considerable interpretation, you would be well advised to get a copy of the Bye-laws for your area before carrying out any plumbing yourself. These are obtainable, free of charge, from the local Water Authority's headquarters. Alternatively, a quick phone call to the Authority's technical department may be all that is necessary.

Certain aspects of water supply and drain maintenance can be tackled only by qualified specialists

WHAT OF THE FUTURE?

The massive boom in DIY which has occurred over the last decade inevitably raises the question of how best to control building work so that enthusiastic home owners have the freedom to do what they want while still maintaining good standards of building practice.

One significant move to help DIY enthusiasts is already being made by the Department of the Environment, who are in the process of updating, simplifying and rewriting the Building Regulations.

It is planned to make the new Regulations short, functional and easy to understand with clearly edited and lavishly illustrated sketch diagrams.

Fewer anomalies

Also on the Building Regs scene are proposals to remove the anomalies that currently exist in Inner London between the UK Regs and the London Building Acts, while making the latter's more streamlined approval system applicable to the country as a whole.

The intention is to reduce the time spent by BCOs at their desk and on minor works, so freeing them to devote more of it to genuinely difficult situations.

Tighter planning

On the planning front, the last couple of years have seen increasing use by local authorities of Article 4 Directives (see page 67).

Among the most common examples of Directives countrywide are bans on rear extensions to properties with small gardens, limitations on caravan parking, strict guidelines on exterior paint colours, and restrictions on exterior decorations such as wall cladding.

Although this might seem like yet more evidence of 'Big Brother' in action, it has to be remembered that with so much DIY activity taking place there have to be some controls over the rights of individuals to alter their property to the possible detriment of their neighbours.

Safer electrics

As yet there are still no formal plans to incorporate the IEE Wiring Regulations into the Building Regs, so making them legally binding. However, local authorities — in conjunction with the relevant Electricity Boards — are doing all in their power to ensure that installations are made as safe as possible.

The most important differences between the Fourteenth and Fifteenth Editions of the Wiring Regs concern the fitting of residual current devices (RCDs) — otherwise known as Earth Leakage Circuit Breakers (ELCBs) — to outside power supplies, so providing greater protection against shocks.

Clear Gas Regulations

Recent public concern over the safety of gas installations has prompted the Department of Energy to prepare a booklet entitled 'Gas Regulations for Everybody's Safety' — yet to be published at the time of writing. Its purpose is to make people aware of how gas installations work so that they can avoid potential hazards.

Perhaps the most confusion concerns Local Water Authority bye-laws, which still vary widely between one part of the country and another. Faced with calls for a more homogeneous Regulations policy, the Authorities reply that their bye-laws are formulated specifically in response to local environmental and operating conditions, and that it would be impossible to produce a truly co-ordinated policy.

To sum up, it does look as if the next two years will see the introduction of building legislation that is more comprehensible to the DIY enthusiast.

Money Matters

In spite of the recession, buying one's own property is more popular than ever — the escalating price of houses is just one indication of how much houses and flats are in demand. So buying wisely is vital — as is maintaining your property. Money Matters aims to unravel and clarify some of the most fundamental aspects of house purchase and maintenance so that you can choose the mortgage that suits you, negotiate a loan that you can afford and also have a clearer picture of what your rates are spent on. Your home is probably your biggest investment — it pays to get it right.

Mortgages

More people than ever before – 62 per cent of the British population – are investing in their own bricks and mortar, enjoying both the practical and financial benefits of home ownership. The fairly free availability of loans which characterised 1984 has continued into 1985 – at a price – and the intense competition in the mortgage market is leading to a better, faster service for the home-buyer.

But the widening choice before the consumer and the fluctuating political and financial situations makes decision-making increasingly difficult. This section aims to answer some of the most confusing aspects of buying a house.

It's worth noting that a number of legislative changes are afoot for 1985 and 1986. The Farrand Committee is due to report on conveyancing. Their findings will lead to a change in the law that will enable non-solicitor conveyancers (to be known as *licensed conveyancers*) to carry out the legal aspects of conveyancing. The Government has published a Green Paper recommending an increase in the scope of the activities of building societies, and 'one-stop shopping' may be possible, in which all aspects of house purchase from house hunting to arranging a mortgage are dealt with under one roof. For the time being, though, the system works as follows.

1. Money

If you are lucky enough to get a 100 per cent mortgage, you will still have to pay costs related to the purchase, such as the solicitor's fees. Your most sensible move therefore is to open a high-interest building society account, where your money will earn a reasonable rate of return, and you will also have established your existence with a lender.

At this stage, consider taking advantage of the *Government Homeloan Scheme*. You have to save with a 'recognised' institution such as a bank or building society for at least two years, when you become entitled to a cash bonus of as much as £110, plus a loan of £600 which is interest-free for the first five years. Further details are available from participating lenders, or

from the Department of the Environment.

How much you can borrow will depend on:

Your income You should be able to borrow around two and three-quarter times your salary, plus the salary of any second applicant. Lenders' policies differ on whether or not they will take into consideration regular commission or overtime payments. If you are self-employed you will normally need to produce your last three years' audited accounts.

The value of the property Most building societies and banks will lend only a proportion of the value of your property – usually 80-95 per cent (of their own valuation, not the purchase price). With higher percentage loans, you must take out indemnity insurance, or a *mortgage guarantee policy* – this protects the lender in the case of a fall in the property's value, or the borrower's default in mortgage repayments.

2. Find your mortgage

If you save regularly with a building society, or you have a bank account, make these your first ports of call. If you haven't saved but have a lump sum to put towards your purchase,

Estate agents' boards advertise a bouyant property market with their signs decorating front gardens. How long a house stays on the market depends on the type of house and area

then save time now by approaching a prospective lender who matches your needs with suitable terms. Compare terms and rates very carefully and check whether a lender has any special first-time buyer schemes, or any lending restrictions.

3. Find your property

When you know that you can get a mortgage – and for how much – the next step is to find a suitable property. First, make a shortlist. You should be sure of your basic requirements – for example, do you really need a flat with a garden? Remember, too, that you are searching for a home that one day you too will want to sell. So steer clear of poor conversions or 'up-market' properties in run-down areas.

Next, sign on with estate agents in the areas you are interested in. You can get their names from the telephone book or, better still, by driving around the neighbourhood and jotting down their phone numbers.

Once you have identified the most

helpful agents, or those with the most appropriate properties on their books, try to keep in regular touch and encourage them to telephone you as soon as something suitable comes up for sale.

There are other ways of finding property – through newspapers or high street 'property shops' for example, and agents' property guides.

4. Make an offer
Before you make an offer for a home, there are a number of important questions to ask:
What are the rates and can you afford them? There's no point considering a reasonably priced property that you can afford if it's in an expensive area where the rates will be well beyond your means.
What is the ground rent and are there any service or maintenance charges? If you're buying a converted or purpose built flat you'll have to pay a *fixed ground rent* annually to the freeholder, and sometimes charges to cover costs of maintenance to the common parts, and services such as porterage which will all cost money.
Is the property freehold or leasehold? In general, houses and bungalows are freehold (meaning that you

own the property outright) and flats are leasehold (when you only own the lease).

If you decide you do want to go ahead with purchase of the property, your next step is to make an offer, which can either be for the full asking price, or a figure below it. This is done through the estate agent – either verbally or in writing – adding that your offer is *subject to survey and subject to contract*. This means that your offer is not legally binding and that you can still withdraw if, for example, your survey reveals too many defects for the property to be a viable purchase. You may, at this stage, have to pay a small holding deposit – usually about £100 – as a sign of good faith. Your deposit will be returned if the sale does not proceed.

5. Return to lender
At this point you will be faced with a number of important decisions, so you should consider the following:
What type of mortgage? Your lender will give you a mortgage application form to be completed as soon as possible, to enable a valuation of the property to be carried out. You will also be asked what sort of mortgage you would like.

Contact your solicitor If you already have a solicitor, you should inform him immediately of your intention to purchase, and at the same time give his name and address to your lender. (If you don't have a solicitor, see the panel on page 80. If you are not using a solicitor make other arrangements now.)

6. Valuation and survey
Your lender will carry out a valuation of the property, to ensure that it is adequate security for their loan, and, if you decide to commission a full structural survey, you could save money by asking for this to be done at the same time as the valuation.

7. Written offer
Provided the results of the valuer's report are satisfactory, you will now receive a firm written offer of funds from your lender.

8. Exchange of contracts
Provided your solicitor's local searches have not turned up any problems (such as the building of a motorway through your front garden), you will now be able to exchange contracts.

At this stage you sign a copy of the contract of sale (the vendor signs another) and hand over the agreed deposit – usually 5-10 per cent of the purchase price. You are now both legally bound to go through with the purchase – if you don't, you forfeit the deposit. Lenders will not normally release any money before completion, so if you are obtaining a large mortgage, you may have to arrange for 'bridging finance' from your bank to cover the difference.

Don't forget to arrange for insurance cover for your new home to come into force now.

9. Completion
Four weeks after exchange of contracts the great day arrives when you are summoned to your solicitor's office to receive the keys of your new home, in exchange for the balance of the purchase money.

Finding a mortgage
Today, more than ever before, the terms offered by different lenders are likely to vary significantly. Choosing the right lender is now as important as

Spoilt for choice — high street banks and building societies now compete for the chance to offer mortgages

choosing the right loan, and could save you much more money than you might imagine.

Building societies

Building societies have just two main functions. They act as a home for peoples' savings, and provide loans to home-buyers, with investors out-numbering borrowers by four to one. Perhaps it's not surprising, therefore, that the societies currently account for well over three-quarters of the total mortgage market. Interest rates now vary considerably, as do building societies' individual lending policies, and you should therefore shop around for the best rates and conditions.

If you save regularly with a building society you will no doubt have a better chance of getting a mortgage when finance is in short supply, and inves-tors are given preference to non-savers.

Banks

The banks' performance in the mort-gage market has fluctuated over the last few years, but the larger clearing banks now seem to be showing a major commitment. Most of the banks offer a 'flat rate' for all sizes of loans (unlike the building societies) which means that you could be paying the same rate of interest for a loan of £12,500 and a loan of £150,000. Note that banks generally charge a fee of £100 on a new mortgage.

Insurance companies

Traditionally, insurance companies deal with the public through interme-diaries such as building societies or brokers, offering insurance-linked en-dowment mortgages. An increasing number, however, such as Legal & General and Confederation Life, are now dealing direct with home loan hunters, and are offering increasingly sophisticated financial packages to the first-time buyer.

Brokers

Mortgage and insurance brokers are intermediaries who match borrowers with suitable lenders. They receive allocations of money from a wide range of sources – building societies, banks and insurance companies – and so boast that they can save a buyer time *and* money.

Brokers can be very helpful, espe-cially in times of mortgage famine when they may be able to get you a mortgage when you would have to wait in your building society 'queue' for a couple of months, or if you have got a particularly difficult mortgage problem.

Employers

Large firms – particularly financial in-stitutions – often offer low-interest mortgages to their long-standing staff. Bear in mind that such a loan would only be in force for the duration of your employment.

Builders

The larger builders are now offering particularly attractive financial pack-ages with a host of incentives if you exchange contracts within a certain period of time, etc., but check what the exact terms are.

What type of mortgage

Once you have found a prospective

CONVEYANCING – THE OPTIONS

A *conveyance* is a method of transfer, and the conveyance of a property is the transfer of ownership from the vendor to the purchaser. Whoever handles your conveyancing will prepare the contracts of sale, carry out a property search (involving questions relating to future development work, etc) and handle Land Registration and payment of Stamp Duty on your behalf. He will handle all the complicated paperwork.

Using a solicitor Solicitors still do most conveyancing – they are often not as costly as rivals claim, and you will benefit from a number of very valuable safeguards. A solicitor is bound by strict rules of professional conduct, has to keep your money in a separate bank account, and is covered by Professional Indemnity Insurance which means that, should you have the misfortune to encounter a dishonest solicitor, the Law Society itself would compensate you. If you have not used a solicitor before, shop around for quotes.

Using a non-solicitor conveyancer Make sure any firm you consult belongs to one of the two professional organisations: the National Association of Conveyancers (NAC) or the National Institute of Conveyancing Agents (NICA). The former imposes strict rules of membership, backing its services with professional indemnity insurance and highly qualified staff. Non-solicitor conveyancers follow the process about three-quarters of the way through – to the stage when the transfer deed has to be prepared by a solicitor. Conveyancers usually charge a 'flat fee' for their services.

Doing it yourself If you have the time and patience, 'doing it yourself' can save you a lot of money. Remember, however, that you will still have to pay a solicitor to carry out the legal work for you in the final stages.

In thriving communities where prices are high, first-time buyers may find it difficult to obtain a mortgage

lender, you will still have to decide what type of mortgage you want to take out.

Repayment mortgage

A repayment (or annuity) mortgage requires you to pay back both the capital and interest levied in regular monthly instalments. Interest on the loan qualifies for tax relief (up to £30,000) and your payments are calculated so that at the end of the term – usually 25 years – both capital and interest have been paid off. Your monthly repayments will remain the same unless interest rates change.

Since the 1984 Budget (which abolished tax relief on life assurance premiums paid under endowment policies) repayment mortgages are the cheapest loan available from the banks and building societies.

Endowment mortgage

Endowment mortgages now account for more than half of all new loans taken out. There are two parts to the loan: the *capital loan*, which is arranged with your lender, and the *endowment assurance policy*, taken out with an insurance company. Each month your outlay consists of an interest-only payment to your lender (eligible for tax relief), and a premium to the insurance company. At the end of the term the mortgage will be paid off with the proceeds of the policy, and there is usually a surplus which can be taken as a tax-free lump sum.

Most lenders charge a higher interest rate for endowments – usually ½-1 per cent above their repayment rate. Note, however, that endowment mortgages have built-in life cover at no extra cost.

There are various types of life assurance policy available for use with an endowment mortgage, as follows:

Low-cost endowment The insurance premiums are lower than with a full-endowment type of mortgage (as above). In order to keep them low, the sum assured is roughly half the amount of the mortgage, the idea being that sufficient bonuses will build up to pay off the mortgage and leave you with a tax-free lump sum.

With-profits A with-profits endowment provides a convenient way of saving as well as paying off your mortgage. The policy guarantees to pay off your mortgage at the end of the term, as well as if you die beforehand.
Non-profits endowment A non-profits policy guarantees to pay off your mortgage at the end of the term, but does not provide any bonuses.

Pension mortgage

A pension mortgage enables you to pay off a loan at the end of its term from the proceeds of a personal pension plan, providing you with a tax-free lump sum *and* a regular pension income. Full tax relief is granted on the premiums, so your pension plan will grow more rapidly than other investments without tax advantages.

You can only take out this kind of mortgage if you are self-employed or do not contribute to a company pension scheme and it may entail higher monthly payments.

COMPARATIVE MONTHLY REPAYMENTS

For a man aged 25 taking out a £30,000 mortgage over 25 years.
Assumes an interest rate of 12.25 per cent.
Assumes 30 per cent tax relief on mortgage interest.

Type of Mortgage	Main Features	Cost £/month
Repayment	Capital and interest	Total 239.40
Low-cost Endowment Mortgage	Premium paid to life company	40.00
	Interest to building society	210.00
		Total 250.00
With-Profits Endowment	Premium paid to life company	98.10
	Interest to building society	210.00
		Total 308.10
Non-Profits Endowment	Premium paid to life company	54.70
	Interest to building society	210.00
		Total 264.79

Home improvement loans

No matter how adventurous – or modest – your home improvement plans are, at some stage they will have to be paid for. Although ultimately *you* will foot the bill (unless you are lucky enough to secure a grant from your local authority – see pages 86-88), there is a bewildering range of short-, medium- and long-term finance available with tax relief for most categories of improvement work.

Of course, you can also increase your tax relief through your mortgage, so before looking for a loan, it may be worth considering the alternative of moving house. Moving up the chain may also provide you with the additional room you were seeking the loan for at a lower total cost. In addition, if you over-improve your house, you may not get your money back when you sell it. So it is worth having a look at house prices (see page 83).

Borrowing money makes good sense. Even if you qualify for a home improvement grant, you will receive only a percentage of the total cost, and you will still have to pay for the remaining portion.

Don't regard 'finding the money' as the final stage of your improvement programme. If you plan well ahead, you will not only make the whole task infinitely easier for yourself, but you are also quite likely to impress a potential lender with your initiative and forethought. This section will explain the options available, and help you assess your own needs.

Probably one of the easiest and most straightforward ways of raising money is to approach an existing lender. Many institutions prefer their customers' finances to be controlled from one source, especially if they know you and have some idea of your reliability as a borrower.

Bank

Further advances If you already have a mortgage with a bank then you can request an additional advance, which usually makes sense if you want to borrow a substantial amount – at least £5,000 – for major improvements.

Most of the high street banks will charge an 'arrangement fee' of around £25, although there may be a degree of flexibility here. You may have to pay for an additional survey, but this will depend on the extent of your improvement plans. As the amount you are borrowing will be added to your mortgage, you will be paying the same rate of interest as for your mortgage.

Re-mortgages If you have a large mortgage with a building society it may actually work out cheaper to obtain a re-mortgage through a bank, because many building societies charge higher interest on 'larger' loans, whereas the banks prefer a policy of a flat rate of interest for all loans.

You will have to *redeem* your current mortgage with your existing lender, and take out a new mortgage with the bank – including, of course, the additional amount for home improvement. For the bank's purposes, you are taking out a new mortgage, so you will have to pay all the associated costs – the bank's arrangement fee, and survey and legal costs.

Personal loans and home improvement loans If you want to borrow less than £5,000, consider a short-term loan. You can opt for one of the fairly standard 'Personal Loans', repayable in monthly payments of capital and interest over three to five years, on an unsecured or secured basis. If you choose the latter you can probably arrange for the payments to be made over a longer period, although you may have to pay a slightly higher rate of interest. Some of the banks also offer special 'Home Improvement Loans' which enable you to borrow about £10,000 for up to ten years.

Interest rates for both Personal and Home Improvement Loans are usually *fixed* in advance which makes budgeting easier – you don't have to worry about a possible increase in your repayments. And most banks provide optional insurance cover guaranteeing payment in the event of your unemployment or sickness.

Overdrafts If you only want to borrow a small amount – a few hundred pounds for some new kitchen units – an overdraft is cheapest. Although you can usually negotiate the rate of interest with your bank manager, you will pay a *variable* rate which moves up and down in line with the bank's base rate.

Overdrafts are a flexible way of borrowing money, but are not intended to provide long-term finance. So, if you eventually find it difficult to shake off your overdraft, it may be more sensible – and the bank will probably advise this anyway – to switch to a personal loan. Do bear in mind also that interest on a bank overdraft does *not* qualify for tax relief, even if it is for home improvement purposes.

Building society

Further advances A large proportion of building society loans is specifically for home improvement, amounting to

---

LOANS FOR HOME IMPROVEMENT
NatWest Bank

All loans are available to existing and new customers (at time of going to press). Check current interest rates with your local NatWest branch.

Mortgages including additional advances and re-mortgages	£12,500-£150,000 up to age 65. Interest rates variable. No differentials for larger loans. Arrangement fee: £100 for new loans, £25 for additional advances.
Personal Loans	£200 minimum with no maximum, available generally on an unsecured basis, payable over up to five years. Interest rates fixed at outset. Arrangement fee: 1 per cent on loans up to 5 years, 1.5 per cent on loans of more than 5 years.
Home Improvement Loans	£500-£30,000 available on an unsecured or secured basis, payable over up to ten years. Interest rates fixed at outset. Arrangement fee: 1 per cent on loans up to 5 years, 1.5 per cent on loans of more than 5 years.

HOUSE PRICES 1985

SCOTLAND					
Property	Pre 1919	1919-45	1946-60	Post 1960	New
Terraced	26,196	*	*	25,514	27,907
Semi-det	34,600	30,878	*	30,240	30,489
Detached	37,802	*	*	41,603	44,443
Flat	22,440	23,199	*	22,655	25,154

NORTH WEST					
Property	Pre 1919	1919-45	1946-60	Post 1960	New
Terraced	16,152	18,433	29,209	20,601	21,938
Semi-det	27,468	24,973	25,478	24,287	24,467
Detached	50,343	48,457	46,846	39,776	43,657
Flat	*	*	*	19,115	21,757

NORTH					
Property	Pre 1919	1919-45	1946-60	Post 1960	New
Terraced	18,137	17,383	*	21,759	22,618
Semi-det	28,859	26,560	27,297	25,330	26,020
Detached	*	*	*	38,884	39,803
Flat	15,701	*	*	17,041	*

WEST MIDLANDS					
Property	Pre 1919	1919-45	1946-60	Post 1960	New
Terraced	17,284	17,175	*	20,874	22,367
Semi-det	25,597	24,292	26,979	23,736	24,760
Detached	45,528	45,383	47,013	38,423	43,645
Flat	*	*	*	19,049	20,816

YORKSHIRE AND HUMBERSIDE					
Property	Pre 1919	1919-45	1946-60	Post 1960	New
Terraced	15,219	16,492	*	19,456	22,458
Semi-det	26,680	22,576	22,795	23,306	23,265
Detached	38,411	44,268	42,059	35,830	36,147
Flat	*	*	*	16,785	*

EAST MIDLANDS					
Property	Pre 1919	1919-45	1946-60	Post 1960	New
Terraced	16,389	16,430	*	20,065	22,126
Semi-det	24,977	22,215	24,002	23,717	22,752
Detached	46,805	37,705	43,928	38,092	43,318
Flat	*	*	*	*	*

EAST ANGLIA					
Property	Pre 1919	1919-45	1946-60	Post 1960	New
Terraced	22,583	*	*	25,373	*
Semi-det	28,048	31,598	*	27,781	26,002
Detached	50,621	*	*	41,649	45,525
Flat	*	*	*	*	*

WALES					
Property	Pre 1919	1919-45	1946-60	Post 1960	New
Terraced	18,883	18,859	*	22,385	21,613
Semi-det	23,421	24,869	*	23,648	23,077
Detached	39,216	*	*	38,143	46,069
Flat	*	*	*	*	*

GREATER LONDON					
Property	Pre 1919	1919-45	1946-60	Post 1960	New
Terraced	43,744	43,795	41,317	47,561	44,740
Semi-det	58,823	55,141	51,025	53,286	47,084
Detached	*	98,435	*	*	*
Flat	36,270	33,535	36,159	36,280	36,716

SOUTH EAST					
Property	Pre 1919	1919-45	1946-60	Post 1960	New
Terraced	31,133	31,987	34,741	34,594	34,699
Semi-det	43,628	42,667	42,223	39,083	37,373
Detached	75,336	69,967	78,201	60,868	62,281
Flat	26,508	27,673	29,122	29,446	30,546

SOUTH WEST					
Property	Pre 1919	1919-45	1946-60	Post 1960	New
Terraced	26,522	26,814	*	26,950	27,197
Semi-det	36,464	32,991	32,015	30,946	28,659
Detached	52,228	52,006	*	47,588	50,171
Flat	25,523	*	*	24,879	24,134

Check the prices of houses before applying for a loan — it may be cheaper to buy. In fact, by moving to a different area, you could find an improved house for only a small increase in your mortgage.

more than one tenth of total lending in 1984. Although it should be relatively straightforward to get a further advance on your mortgage it will depend to a certain extent on the society's availability of funds — in times of mortgage 'famine' you'll get put to the end of the queue in favour of the first-time buyer.

You won't have to pay an arrangement fee if the society does decide to grant you a further advance, but you will find that some societies may ask you to pay a differential of one or two per cent over the basic rate for the extra portion borrowed.

Re-mortgages Again, most building societies will be happy to take over your mortgage from an existing lender, topping it up with the extra finance you want for improvement, but it's really only worth considering this option if it's going to be financially viable.

Maturity loans Some building societies also offer special home improvement loans to elderly home owners with minimal income for repair and improvement. Under the Halifax Building Society's *Home Improvement Low Payment Plan*, for example, up to 60 per cent of valuation of the property (on which the mortgage must have been paid off) is advanced on an interest-only basis, until the owner sells the property or dies, when the loan is repaid from the proceeds of sale. Interest is charged at the normal mortgage rate and is, of course, eligible for tax relief. A maturity loan of this kind can provide a useful way for elderly home-owners to 'top up' a local authority grant.

Insurance company

Additional policy If you have an endowment mortgage, this could be a useful source of extra finance. You may be advised to take out a 'non-profit' policy to cover the additional loan – an expensive option, and one that you should only consider if you can't raise the finance elsewhere.

Existing policy If you've a long-standing with-profits endowment or whole life policy, you should be able to borrow up to 90 per cent of the *surrender value* (i.e. its current value). Repayment terms are often negotiable, and it's usually possible to keep the whole of the loan outstanding until

the policy matures, when the loan will be deducted from the proceeds. Interest charges are reasonably cheap – you'd usually pay around ½ per cent above bank base rate.

Employer

Low-interest loan Many large firms and financial institutions offer their long-standing members of staff low-interest loans. This can be an extremely cheap way of borrowing, but check the exact terms and conditions of the loan. What would happen, for example, if you decided to leave the company before you'd repaid the loan?

Finance house

Personal loans and home improvement loans A personal or home improvement loan from a finance house usually works out to be more expen-

sive than equivalent loans from the sources described above. Rates vary considerably, so it is absolutely essential to shop around. If in doubt, choose a reliable name such as HFC, Citibank, First National Securities or Western Trust and Savings. Look out, too, for the finance houses that are subsidiaries of the high street clearing banks – Midland Bank's Forward Trust, and the TSB Group's United Dominions Trust.

Most finance houses offer *unsecured loans* of up to £5,000, with a fixed rate of interest payable over a period of up to five years. A higher rate of interest is payable on a *secured loan* (or *second mortgage*), but you can borrow a larger amount (up to around £20,000) over a longer period of time - usually up to ten years, although other terms are available.

SECURITY ON YOUR LOAN

All lenders will require some form of security from you before granting a large loan (which will, of course, be known as a *secured* loan) to which they have a claim if you default on your loan repayments.

Today most personal and home improvement loans are dealt with by post. It's essential, therefore, to study carefully any literature relating to the scheme, and make sure you know the answers to the following.

● *What are the monthly instalments?* Are you sure you can afford them?
● *Is the interest rate fixed or variable?* It is important to know whether your repayments could go down or, more likely, up.
● *Can I increase or reduce the repayments?* Sometimes you can't without re-arranging the whole loan.
● *Can I pay the loan off before the end of the term?* Watch out for penalty clauses – some lenders will make a charge for early redemption.

● *How will I have to pay?* Most lenders will require payment by standing order, or transfer from your bank current account. Some finance houses, however, will issue 'pass books' and money will either be collected straight from you or you will be required to pay at an office.
● *What do I get in the way of insurance?* Sometimes insurance is compulsory and the premium will be included in your monthly repayment. to the lender.

Home improvement loans are available for extensive exterior redecoration

Qualifying home improvement

Generally speaking, all 'permanent' alterations and improvements which add to existing accommodation and amenities qualify for tax relief: home extensions; loft conversions; insulation — walls, lofts, double glazing; central heating; fitted kitchens (excluding 'moveable' items such as cooker or fridge; fitted bathroom units/shower; patio/porch; garage/carport; garden shed, greenhouse or conservatory; landscaped gardens; drainage work.

Ordinary repairs and decoration work do not qualify, although there are two exceptions. Firstly, if you bought the property in a dilapidated state you can get tax relief on a loan for repairs resulting from the condition. Secondly, if you are getting a loan intended to pay mainly for home improvements, a small proportion can be spent on redecoration and repair work.

The following jobs may qualify, depending on their exact nature:

Converting the loft into an extra room is a popular job that can be financed by a home improvement loan

Obtaining finance to build an extension is usually straightforward

● reconstruction or retiling of a roof;
● underpinning a house;
● rebuilding a façade;
● installing or renewing a damp proof course;
● rewiring.

To find out whether all, or part of your improvement work will qualify for relief, you should contact your local Tax Office with details of your plans.

NAT WEST LOAN ADVICE

"Probably the most important piece of advice we give to anyone considering improving their home is to *think and plan ahead.*

"People tend to postpone the 'asking-for-a-loan' stage because they fear a gruelling session with their bank manager, or because they feel it's not worth wasting his time for the sake of a hundred pounds.

"Here at the bank we can never stress enough to our customers the importance of arranging the right type of finance. We have a variety of loan schemes to enable people to pay for their home improvements *sensibly*, and in some cases there's no need even to come into the bank.

"First of all, though, you should work out exactly how much you think you'll need to borrow. If you want a substantial amount for a major improvement such as an extension or loft conversion – say, more than £5000 – then you may be required to attend an interview, when your case will be considerably strengthened if you can present a detailed breakdown of the costs involved (e.g. a builder's quotation) and the timing of payments. If you are an existing customer with a branch then they will be familiar with your monthly income and regular outgoings, but if you are not an existing account holder then you should prepare this information beforehand.

"Don't regard an interview as a tiresome cross-examination. Remember that your ability to repay a loan will be assessed according to your existing financial commitments, and your record of honouring your debts, so it's important for the bank to establish what you can reasonably afford to pay off each month. The interview is a *two-way process* – the bank will want to know what your personal requirements are; for example, do you want to pay the loan off as quickly as possible, or would you prefer to spread the payments over as long a period as you are able to? Don't be afraid to ask questions during the interview."

Grants

How many times have you heard the tale of 'the chap down the road' who was able to mend his roof or modernise his bathroom, thanks to a sizeable handout from the local council? Until last year, such stories were all too familiar, and the amount allocated by the government to local authorities for grant assistance was increasing each year in leaps and bounds. Those halcyon days seem to have been ended, however, with the government's announcement of a substantial reduction in its 1985/6 allocation. At local level, the effect has been to cut back the amount of assistance available to the private sector, while councils attend to their priority housing needs — repair and construction of council homes, assistance to housing associations and help for the disabled and the elderly.

However, the Government proposes to replace the current system of home-improvement grants with means-tested, interest-free loans, with simplified administration under which people — not their properties will be assessed for eligibility.

Grants will still be available for people judged to be of sufficiently modest income living in substandard housing, but under the proposed system the four types of grant described below are likely to be amalgamated and

allocated according to a new standard of 'fitness for human habitation'.

The present system is here for a while. So if you are intending to make an application for a grant, check your local authority's availability of funds before proceeding.

Improvement grants

These are designed for homes needing *major* improvements and for larger houses suitable for conversion into flats. Your property will need to be in an extremely poor state of repair, and the grant will also cover some associated repair and replacement work.

When the work has been carried out, the council will expect it to meet a long list of standards. It will, for example, need to be likely to have a useful life of at least 30 years, have adequate natural lighting, insulation and drainage, and be free from damp.

Improvement grants are discretionary – it's entirely up to the council as to whether they decide to give you one. Because of this, the council may well require you to carry out extra work you had not planned, like repointing.

Intermediate grants

Your home may qualify for an intermediate grant if it was built or converted before October 1961 and is missing one or more of a list of standard amenities. The grant can also cover repair and replacement work

that needs to be carried out simultaneously, but if the extra work is substantial (e.g. if an extension has to be built to house a new bathroom), it may be worth applying for an improvement grant instead.

Intermediate grants are mandatory, and you have an automatic right to a grant for whichever standard amenities you want to install at any time. The council must pay the grant at the

Outdated and dangerous kitchens qualify for an improvement grant

maximum rate for which you qualify.

Repairs grants

These are for substantial and structural repairs to pre-1919 properties, covering major work such as re-roofing, replacement of floors and foundations. The rateable value of your property must be no more than £225, or £400 in Greater London, with no limits in Housing Action Areas.

Repairs Grants are normally discretionary, although mandatory awards may be made in cases where a 'Repairs Notice' (under section 9 of the Housing Act 1957) has been served.

Special grants

Of less relevance to the private homeowner, special grants are intended for installation of standard amenities and fire escapes in houses *in multiple occupation*, and for associated repairs and replacement.

Special grants are discretionary, and your council will usually decide the extent of the work to be done.

Calculating your grant

First of all, remember that although

The cost of renovation can be met in part by various grants

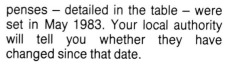

grants are not loans and therefore do *not* have to be repaid, a grant (if you are awarded one) will only cover a certain percentage of the total cost of your improvement work, depending on the area you live in, the extent of the work involved, and your own financial circumstances. The council may assist you with a loan to finance the remaining portion, or you could raise the money in one of the ways described on pages 82-85.

The cost of the work must fall within what is known as an 'eligible expense limit' – this is a maximum figure set for each category of work, and if you spend more than your limit, the extra will *not* qualify for a grant.

The current limits for eligible ex-

Local councils are keen to upgrade their area by giving generous grants

penses – detailed in the table – were set in May 1983. Your local authority will tell you whether they have changed since that date.

The council will award you a *percentage* of the cost of the work that can be considered for the grant, but the maximum you will be awarded in any case is 90 per cent – if the council decides that you could not pay for your portion of the work without undue hardship.

ELIGIBLE EXPENSE LIMITS – ALL GRANTS

	Greater London £	Elsewhere £
Improvement grants		
Priority cases*	13,800	10,200
Non-priority cases	9000	6600
Intermediate grants		
Standard amenities (or additional standard amenities for a disabled occupant)	3005	2275
Repairs element	4200	3000
Repairs grants	6600	4800
Special grants		
Standard amenities	Depends on number of amenites needed	
Fire escape	10,800	8100
Repairs element	4200	3000

*The following constitute 'priority cases':
  (a) Houses in very bad condition – eg, unfit for human habitation, lacking one or more standard amenities or in need of substantial repair;
  (b) Houses in Housing Action Areas;
  (c) Houses needing improvement work for the benefit of a disabled occupant.
Your council will be able to tell you if you live in a Housing Action Area or a General Improvement Area.

APPLYING FOR A GRANT — A STEP-BY-STEP GUIDE

1. Contact your local council (ask for the Grants Section, or the Housing or Environmental Health Department) and establish what types of grant are currently available. If you want a discretionary grant, you may be advised that applications are 'frozen', and asked to re-apply at a later date.
2. A council representative may pay you a visit to discuss your plans in greater detail. In the case of an improvement or repairs grant, they will give you an itemised list of work to be carried out.
3. Have preliminary plans drawn up. You may need to engage an architect for this, although for minor work it may be possible to get a builder to do some simple drawings based on the council's specifications.
4. Go back to the council with your plans and ask for an application form. Make sure your plans are finalised before the next stage.
5. Obtain two or three written quotations from builders and decide, on the basis of the results, which builder you are going to use.
6. Send in your application form, together with the final drawings, an estimate of the total cost of the work, a certificate of future occupation and proof of ownership.
7. The council will let you know its decision. As soon as you have written approval, work can commence, and you will be given a time limit within which to complete it. Your grant will normally be paid in a lump sum, when the work is completed, or in instalments to enable you to pay your builder as you go along. If extra work is found to be necessary during this stage the council may be prepared to increase your grant but make a point of checking beforehand.

MONEY MATTERS

Older houses usually qualify for a grant for re-roofing if battens are weak and felt not fitted originally

Your grant application

Since grants are administered locally, exact procedure may vary and will also depend on the extent of the work to be carried out. Do not under-estimate the importance of your application. Under current rules, if it is refused, you have to wait two years before you can re-apply — so don't jeopardise your chances by giving incomplete or false information, or by failing to comply with your council's instructions. And *don't* start any work until your application has been approved — if you do you could be disqualified completely.

Who can apply? If you are a home-owner, you can apply for a grant if: you own the freehold, or a lease with at least five years to run; or you want to improve your main or only home; or the rateable value of the property is not more than £400 in Greater London, or £225 elsewhere. *Don't* waste the council's time if you're the boss of a property development company, or you want to do up your cottage in the country. Your council may give you provisional approval of your application, if the improvement work is a condition of obtaining a mortgage. So if you are on your way to becoming a home-owner, you will still qualify for the appropriate grant.

"WE HAD A GRANT…"

Steve and Nicola

Council: City of Westminster
Property: One bedroom ground floor leasehold flat, purchased in 1984 for £13,500
Total cost of improvement work: £20,000
Grant awarded: £10,500
Property now valued at: £39,000

Steve and Nicola's friends envy their light, spacious flat in London's West Kensington, but few of them realise they endured 'nine months of hell' while it was being converted from a derelict shell.

"We thought ourselves lucky because the previous owner, the freeholder, had established that an improvement grant was available, and she offered the flat to us at a bargain price.

"Our application was processed very quickly, but we made the mistake of using an architect recommended by the council. The work took nine months to complete instead of the three months we'd been told originally, and he kept issuing 'extension certificates' to the builders – without consulting us.

"In our particular case the council was very efficient and communication with them was excellent."

Martin and Sue

Council: Staffordshire Borough Council
Property: Two bedroom freehold terraced house, purchased in 1983 for £12,300
Total cost of improvement work: £4795
Grant awarded: £3600
Property now valued at: £20-22,000

For Martin and Sue the renovation of their small cottage-style house has been 'a very interesting and satisfying project'.

Martin is a keen DIY enthusiast, and although he originally obtained estimates from a number of builders he has actually done all the major work on the house himself. "I decided it was best not to be too optimistic about what I could do, but the more work I tackled myself, the more I wanted to do.

'The council detailed the improvements we needed to carry out within a week, and have been most considerate and helpful throughout. They released money to me in blocks of £500 – whenever I requested it – and I've contributed about £2000 of my own money.

"We hope to sell in about six months' time and will have made an overall profit of £8000-£10,000."

Some areas in the house are awkward for elderly or disabled people, and grants are available to help buy accessories

Who contributes?

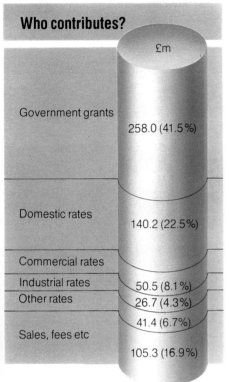

£m

Government grants	258.0 (41.5%)
Domestic rates	140.2 (22.5%)
Commercial rates	
Industrial rates	50.5 (8.1%)
Other rates	26.7 (4.3%)
	41.4 (6.7%)
Sales, fees etc	105.3 (16.9%)

Who spends it?

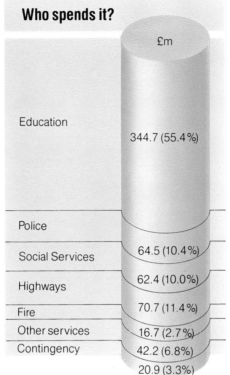

£m

Education	344.7 (55.4%)
Police	
Social Services	64.5 (10.4%)
Highways	62.4 (10.0%)
Fire	70.7 (11.4%)
Other services	16.7 (2.7%)
Contingency	42.2 (6.8%)
	20.9 (3.3%)

What does it buy?

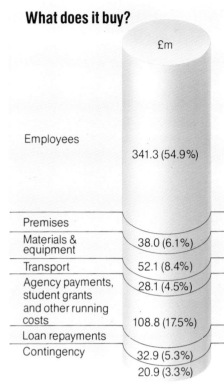

£m

Employees	341.3 (54.9%)
Premises	
Materials & equipment	38.0 (6.1%)
Transport	52.1 (8.4%)
Agency payments, student grants and other running costs	28.1 (4.5%)
	108.8 (17.5%)
Loan repayments	
Contingency	32.9 (5.3%)
	20.9 (3.3%)

Each rating authority has to balance its books and levies rates according to its spending

Rates

Rates are the local taxes paid by the occupier of the property to the local authority to help pay for the services supplied to the community. This rate revenue is boosted by a proportionate grant from central government to individual local authorities. A percentage of every council's rate revenue is then given to the county and metropolitan authorities for the supply of major services such as education, highways, police and fire.

The amount of rates each householder pays depends on the rateable value of the property and the rate in the pound fixed by the local council. If, for example, the rateable value of a property is £200 per year and the local rate is £1.50 in the pound, the rate bill will be £300 per year.

Councils decide on the rate in the pound by calculating the cost of the services they provide, having taken into account the assistance from central government. These rates vary considerably, and reflect the demands on individual local authorities and their level of spending.

The rateable value

The rateable value of a dwelling is primarily based on the likely rent it would attract in the commercial market place. In any valuation the first point considered by valuation officers is the type and style of the property and its location.

Then the age and size of the property are taken into account and the valuer considers such factors as whether the dwelling has extra features like a garage or central heating. Social amenities that would affect the property's rentable value — street lights or pavements — are also taken into account. Conversely, an appropriate reduction is made if a property lacks basic amenities such as electricity, mains water and proper access.

Always check the rateable value of a property before you move in. You may find yourself paying rates on a garage that was never built even though the plans had been submitted.

Rateable value appeal

If you decide to object to the rateable value, first check the rates paid on similar dwellings in the neighbourhood. If your rates are considerably higher, the objection has a better chance of succeeding.

But quirks do occur and it may be

that the slightly different location of your house and its larger garage have contributed to its increased rentable and thus its rateable value. If, after discussing the matter with the local valuation officer, no agreement can be reached, your next step is to appeal to

Less is spent on fire-fighting than many other rate-supported services

Where heavy lorries threaten property, rate reductions may be granted

the valuation court.

At this stage, evidence must be compiled to support the case that the rates on the property are too high in comparison to similar dwellings in the area. A leaflet called 'Rating Appeals to Local Valuation Court in England and Wales', available from valuation offices, will help you to prepare a sound case.

Ratepayers are often content with the rateable value of a property until external changes alter its rentable value. If, for example, a new traffic scheme is instituted that transforms a quiet street into a main thoroughfare, ratepayers may well be entitled to a decrease in rates.

Rate rebates

Domestic ratepayers who have a relatively low income or are unemployed can qualify for a rate rebate. These rebates are available to any owner-occupier or tenant whose rate payments are not already covered by supplementary benefit.

Rate rebates are the repayment of whole or part of the rates due on a property. If you think that your income is sufficiently low to entitle you to a rebate, the first approach should be made to the local rating office. This may also apply if you are a tenant and pay rent that includes a portion of your landlord's rates.

You can find full details and advice on rate rebates at citizens advice bureaux or the local rating office.

Advice and help

Rating law and liability has evolved over nearly 400 years, so it is hardly surprising that few ratepayers fully understand the ins and outs of the present rating system. Generally, however, those who administer the valuation and collection of rates can help with ratepayers' problems.

But time and trouble can be saved if the problem is taken to the correct department. To help decide the best method of approach, this list highlights the four main areas of concern and the departments that normally deal with queries in these areas:

Valuations and assessments – Local valuation officer.

Rate payments – Local council rating office.

Rate rebates – Local council rating office

Rate appeals – Local valuation court.

The address and telephone number of all these offices can be found by calling at the local council offices. Valuation officers are employed by the Inland Revenue and are listed in the telephone directory.

If the authorities are unable to solve the problem a visit to the local citizens advice bureau is recommended. Here general help will be given, together with details of chartered surveyors who specialize in rating problems.

Obviously, expert advice costs money, but in some cases the amount saved in rates will more than cover the fee. Chartered surveyors' fees vary from region to region, but on average are around 4 per cent of a full year's rate liability for negotiation with valuation officers or regional assessors. In smaller cases a minimum fee of £250 may be charged. Finally, if you do not feel that the case is worth spending money on, try approaching your local councillor, where help is free. Any reduction in your rateable value will mean a saving year after year.

Rate reductions will not compensate for freedoms lost to heavy traffic

---

HOME IMPROVEMENT AND THE RATES

There is no legal obligation on ratepayers to tell the valuation officer or rating department of alterations made to property. Under normal circumstances, if planning permission is needed for the alteration, the valuation officer will be informed by the local council.

You will then receive a revised assessment which contains the new valuation. You have 28 days to appeal. A form on which to enter an objection is available from the valuation office, although a standard letter detailing your objections is normally sufficient.

Local authorities now take a straightforward view on property improvements, tending to regard extensions such as garages and extra rooms as rateable items, leaving internal changes such as central heating outside the rating net.

It is always worthwhile making enquiries at either the valuation office or rating department prior to any building work to ensure that it will not greatly increase the rateable value.

Getting Specialist Help

Even the most experienced DIY enthusiast can occasionally find that the job is beyond his or her capabilities. The reason may be that professional help is needed in drawing up detailed plans or that specialised equipment has to be used to complete a particular job. Sometimes, the work is too major and can only be tackled by a firm of builders. In any of these situations, knowing where to go for assistance and how to negotiate the most favourable contract will stand you in good stead and certainly increase your chances of ending up with a job well done and at a satisfactory price.

However skilled a do-it-yourselfer you may be, there will occasionally come a time when you feel a little out of your depth — perhaps you've tried repeatedly to put something right without success, or you've simply hit a problem you can't solve. You need some expert help, and the next step is finding out who to turn to. In this chapter, you will find three main sections full of useful advice, names and addresses that will lead you to the helping hand you require.

The sort of help you need breaks down into: 'advisory' — someone to give you information or tell you what to do; 'creative' — someone actually to carry out a job for you; and 'remedial' — someone to put things right when disaster strikes.

In the first category comes a vast number of trade and manufacturers' associations, many of whom exist to pass on information about their indus-try and its products, and also professional advisers like architects, surveyors and designers who give advice but do not actually carry out physical work for you.

In the second group are the workers — firms and individuals whom you employ to carry out jobs for you, like building an extension or putting in a central heating system.

In the third group are people you need when something goes wrong — you discover dry rot under the floorboards or asbestos in the loft. Often there is some overlap between this section and the 'creative' group, since an electrician might install your lighting and track down an electrical fault, for example.

Only among the first group will you find the help may be free; the others will all cost you money, so it's important to get hold of the right type of help at the beginning.

Architects and surveyors

You are likely to turn to an architect for help if you are building an extension to your home, or planning other large-scale alterations to it. His role includes:
● designing what you want done
● preparing drawings
● obtaining estimates from builders
● submitting applications for planning permission and Building Regulations Approval
● overseeing the work while it is in progress.

You decide whether you want him to do all these things, or just some of them — this probably depends on your budget as much as anything, since jobs like submitting applications and overseeing the builder are things you could probably do yourself.

If someone calls himself an architect, he must be registered with the Architects Registration Council of the United Kingdom. He may also be a member of the Royal Institute of British Architects (RIBA). His fees will be a percentage of the total cost of the work, and will be proportionately higher on a small job than on a large one.

You may find people advertising themselves as architectural consultants, building design consultants or architectural surveyors. They belong to no central organisation, and are not bound by any professional codes of conduct, so their abilities can vary widely. Their fees are generally lower than those of a qualified architect.

A building surveyor can perform similar tasks to those of an architect, but you need to find one who is qualified in design and building work. You can obtain names and addresses of suitable surveyors working in your area from the Royal Institution of Chartered Surveyors or the Incorporated Association of Architects and Surveyors (see under Architects on page 136).

Architects are not allowed to advertise, but some local authorities hold lists of local architects which the public can consult, and registered architects are listed in the Yellow Pages. Architectural consultants and the like are free to advertise their services — usually in local newspapers and freesheets.

Once you have contacted someone who is prepared to take instructions

Large-scale alterations call for the help of an architect. He will prepare the plans and discuss them regularly with builder and owner

If you are worried about structural faults call in a surveyor – he will suggest the best course of treatment

from you, make an appointment at which you can go through the proposals in detail. At this stage, ask to see drawings of similar work he has prepared recently, and enquire whether his plans were approved at the first submission to the local authority — a sign that his proposals are 'in tune' with local requirements.

An architect, surveyor or consultant will be able to give you an idea of the approximate cost of the work at a fairly early stage, but it is only when the plans are put out to tender with various builders that the likely actual cost can be confirmed, so the adviser's fee can only be estimated as a percentage of the total cost once the job has been completed. Remember that members of RIBA or RICS will charge according to their professional scale of fees, but an unregistered consultant can set any fee he likes. If you are using such a consultant, it is a good idea to check what he proposes to charge against the RIBA scale. You can get a copy of this scale by writing to RIBA direct (see under Architects on page 136). If you are unhappy with the fee proposed by your consultant, RIBA will advise you on how to challenge it and how best to negotiate a fee acceptable to the two of you.

Structural engineers

The only situation in which you are likely to need the services of a structural engineer is the unfortunate one of subsidence and settlement of your house. An architect or building surveyor can advise you on what to do if subsidence occurs, but dealing with it is not their speciality.

The tell-tale signs of subsidence are cracks beginning to appear in external (and some internal) walls, often running diagonally across the wall face from the corners of openings such as doors and windows. The problem may be caused in a number of ways from terrain movement to the removal of nearby trees.

Whatever the cause, early investigation by an expert is essential, so that any immediate remedial measures can be taken and long-term restoration can be planned.

When you call in a structural engineer, ask him to submit a detailed report to you in writing of his findings and his recommendations for remedial work needed, and take his advice on

your best choice of local builder to carry out the work. Repairs usually require specialist knowledge, and many firms do not have the necessary expertise. The engineer will help you to obtain quotations, and should be able to advise on whether the figure is reasonable for the job.

If you have buildings insurance against subsidence, you will need to submit a copy of his report to the insurance company in order to make a claim. Check the terms of your insurance carefully: many have detailed exclusion clauses covering damage caused by the demolition of buildings, erosion, alterations such as home extensions, faulty workmanship or defective materials, and there is likely to be an excess figure quoted which you will not be able to recover. If your house is relatively new and covered by a National House Building Council (NHBC) 10-year guarantee, you may be able to recover some of the costs of the correction work. See under Builders on page 136 for the NHBC's address and telephone number.

Settlement or subsidence is a serious structural fault and only a structural engineer is qualified to assess the damage

GETTING SPECIALIST HELP

Finding specialist contractors

If a job is too big for you to tackle yourself, or you feel you don't have the necessary skill or equipment to carry it out — or if the problem is an emergency — you will want to turn it over to a specialist contractor. What you will be looking for is competent workmanship done when you want it and at a reasonable price.

Whatever trade you require, personal recommendation is always the best guide. However, if your own range of contacts doesn't throw up any likely contenders, you are on your own. How you approach the task depends mainly on whether you need someone now to carry out some emergency repairs within hours, or whether you're looking for someone to do a planned alteration or improvement at some time in the future.

In the case of emergencies, your initial response is likely to be to get out the local telephone book and to pick out whatever heading you need — plumber, electrician, drain clearer, roofer, glazier or whatever. Look for firms advertising a 24-hour service — those that don't may not take kindly to being called at 2 am.

Describe briefly but clearly what the problem is, and ask if there is any action you can take before help arrives. Ask there and then what the cost is likely to be, and make a note of the response — it's likely to involve a basic call-out charge, plus labour and materials.

You have little choice at the time but to accept the quotation, but if the sum seems utterly unreasonable when the job has been done you should offer what you consider a fair price for the job (bearing in mind any relevant

factors like the distance travelled, the time of day/night and so on) and make it clear that the tradesman will have to sue you for the difference. If your offer is fair and reasonable, it is unlikely that a court will find against you.

In an emergency it is also worth checking your local newspaper or freesheet for local firms or individuals who could help. Such publications are more up-to-date than any telephone book, and can sometimes offer a wider choice too.

If you want a specialist to carry out a planned job, you can turn to one of the many trade associations listed in the A-Z section; they will usually provide you with a list of their members working in your area. It's worth asking them if they operate a code of practice which

Some specialists give a 24hr service. They may be expensive, but they get the job done when you need it

their members must adhere to, and whether they will handle complaints that might arise during or after the job. The address section on pages 136-138 includes associations for carpenters, decorators, electricians, heating specialists, insulation firms, kitchen installers, locksmiths and plumbers.

Always obtain at least two (and preferably three) quotations for the work you want done, and make sure they are given in writing. Confirm your acceptance of the quotation in writing too, and add details of when work will start (and should finish) and how the money is to be paid.

You can get a fair idea of how satisfactory a contractor is likely to be from his first appearance at your house to estimate for the work. The roofer who turns up without a ladder, the decorator who quotes an all-in price within minutes of arriving, the plumber with a jumble of tools and fittings in a cardboard box in the back of his van, all create an impression of unprofessionalism. Good signs include proper headed notepaper for estimates and quotations, punctuality in keeping appointments, a van with a name and phone number on the side and a list of local satisfied customers.

GAS LEAKS

The one emergency you have no discretion about is a gas leak. If you suspect one, call your local gas service centre IMMEDIATELY — the number is listed in the 'phone book under 'gas'. There is no call-out charge, and you will have to pay for work done only if the cost exceeds £2.50 and the job takes more than 30 minutes to complete. While you are waiting for the fitter to arrive, observe these points:

● Extinguish cigarettes and any naked flames (expecially pilot lights)
● Avoid using any electrical equipment — even a light switch can cause a spark and ignite the gas
● Check that no gas appliance has been left on
● Check whether pilot lights have blown out
● Open doors and windows to disperse the gas as quickly as possible
● Turn off the supply at the meter if appliances on or pilot lights out are not the cause.

Treatment firms

The major areas of remedial work where you might want to call in a specialist firm are the treatment of woodworm, dry rot and damp. It is possible to tackle the job yourself, but many people prefer to leave the job to an expert. Where a guarantee is required — for example, by a bank or building society providing a mortgage, or a local authority approving a grant — you have no choice but to use a professional.

The first job is to find a firm. Most of the larger and more reputable companies belong to the British Wood Preserving Association (woodworm and rot) or the British Chemical Damp-course Association — see page 136 under Damp for their addresses. Both bodies will provide lists of members working in your area and have a code of practice which their members must follow. They will also investigate any complaints that arise. If you prefer to select a firm yourself, contact local builders or surveyors for their advice.

The next step is the survey, which is almost always free. Firms differ widely in their thoroughness, often restricting the survey to obvious areas such as ground floors or the loft. Make sure that they examine the whole property, and ask for a detailed report as well as recommendations for action.

Always get at least two surveys done; this is more likely to uncover all the problem areas, and will also provide a check that unnecessary work is not being included to inflate the price. In particular, diagnosis may mistake wet rot for dry rot, which is much more expensive to eradicate, or suggest woodworm treatment where the attack is no longer active.

When you receive the estimates, make sure you are comparing like with like. Some firms quote an all-in price, others a carefully itemised estimate, and you may find that work like exposing parts to be treated, replastering and so on can cost more than the actual treatment. If this is the case, don't be afraid to raise the matter; it may be possible to do some of this work yourself, or to employ someone yourself to do it more cheaply.

If at the end of the day the estimate seems too high, it's always worth haggling — especially if you can quote estimates from rival firms.

Treating damp is one of many jobs which require specialist equipment

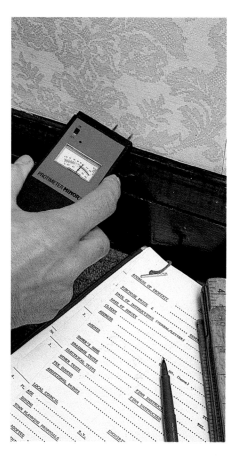

Patches of damp can be checked by a specialist with a dampmeter

When you have accepted an estimate and you know when work is scheduled to start, make sure you are clear what part of the job is your responsibility and what is theirs. You may have to clear lofts, lift carpets and so on before they start.

Once work begins, try to be present — both to check on the thoroughness of the treatment and to keep an eye on the hours worked.

When it is finished, ask how you will know if the treatment has been successful — how long damp will take to dry out, or how to tell if woodworm has returned. Make sure you get a written guarantee, and check that it is transferable if you sell the house.

The trouble with guarantees is that they are not worth anything if the firm goes out of business — unless the firm has insurance to cover its guarantee, which is very uncommon. If you are unable to obtain satisfaction under the terms of your guarantee when something is obviously wrong, you may have to sue in the county court to obtain redress.

Is DIY worth considering?

Many of the jobs for which you could call in an expert can be carried out by a competent handyman. Apart from the time factor, the lack of knowledge and of the right tools probably weigh the balance against doing it yourself, yet getting the right technical information and equipment is nowadays a lot easier than it used to be.

For a start, there is an ever-increasing number of DIY books on the market that are excellent sources of information. Some are very good, others are poor. The most useful titles are those that deal in detail with just one subject area, and which go into some depth of detail.

A good test of how useful a book is going to be is to find a section describing a job you have already tackled and are familiar with, and read it through to see how thorough it is.

DIY magazines and partworks are a useful addition to a small library of books, since they can keep you up-to-date with the very latest in tools and techniques.

You can obtain a great deal of specialist advice from manufacturers' literature, and from the various trade associations, testing establishments and similar organizations listed on pages 136-138. Don't be afraid to

Very little equipment is needed to carry out jobs like cutting and fixing window surrounds and skirting boards

INSULATION AND THE TIMBER-FRAME HOUSE

As a result of adverse publicity in a television programme in 1983, the number of houses being built on the timber-frame principle has dropped substantially — from around 25 per cent at the end of 1982 to half that at the end of 1984. These are national figures; in Scotland, the proportion of timber-frame construction in new houses was over 50 per cent in 1982, and this has dropped to around 35 per cent now.

The programme probably helped in the long run to tighten up on standards in timber-frame construction. Properly built, a timber-frame house will perform just as well as its conventionally-built equivalent, and no major problems need be expected.

However, there have been problems with some timber-frame houses with wall cavities insulated with *urea-formaldehyde foam*. The presence of the foam has been found in a few cases to lead to dampness being transferred to the timber frame, and as a result some building society surveyors have been less than keen to recommend such properties for mortgages, or have valued them below the market price of similar uninsulated properties.

The problem is particularly acute in Scotland. In England and Wales, urea-formaldehyde foam could not be used without local authority permission. In Scotland this rule was not introduced until early 1985, and roughly 5000 houses are reckoned to have been insulated in this way. Their owners are now finding them hard to sell.

The Building Research Establishment's Scottish laboratory (BRE) has been investigating the problem, and recommends that a special survey be carried out on insulated houses to check whether the insulation is causing any damp penetration. The survey involves using moisture meters with long-reach probes to check the moisture content of the timber frame at a large number of points, and its findings should allay householders' fears about the condition of their properties.

No official decision on whether to introduce such a survey has yet been taken by the Royal Institution of Surveyors or the Building Societies Association, so at this stage concerned householders are best advised to contact the BRE for a position report and advice on having the survey carried out. See under Damp on page 136 for the address of the Building Research Establishment.

Some large DIY stores, as well as stocking a wide range of materials, will hire you specialised equipment for as long as you need it

write to manufacturers for information about their products, or to ask for literature in stores (although few stores are at all conscientious about making this available). Establishments such as the Building Research Establishment and the Timber Research and Development Association publish a great many advisory leaflets and other publications on building practices, materials and problems; they are relatively inexpensive, and can be bought from HMSO and Building Centre bookshops or ordered direct from source — see pages 136-138 for addresses.

On the question of specialist tools and equipment, the growing chains of hire specialists (and hire departments within DIY superstores) can now provide almost any item you could possibly require — in fact, a lot of small builders use them for all their requirements, since it solves cash flow problems in buying expensive machinery, and also solves the storage problem.

There are several points to remember about hiring equipment, however. The first is to check the cost; if you need a comparatively expensive item for more than a few days, it will probably pay you to purchase it outright at the start of the job and sell it again at the end.

The second is to check availability; don't expect the firm to have available what you want the day you telephone for it. It's best to reserve items a few days in advance.

The third point is to check the condition of whatever you are hiring, to make sure it is undamaged, safe to use and works properly. If you accept a faulty item, you may be expected to pay for the damage when you return it.

Prices vary widely in the hire business. Firms operating nationwide from shop-type premises tend to charge more than smaller local firms, so it pays to shop around. In particular, compare rates; it is often cheaper to book something for a week, even if

you need it for only four days, than to pay the day rate.

Make sure that delivery and collection can be arranged if you need it, and find out what charge is made for this. Lastly, check the insurance — if the hired goods are damaged or stolen while they are in your possession, you will be expected to claim for them on your household insurance policy.

The savings you make on doing a job yourself represent the labour element of employing a professional — you will still have to pay for materials, and in most cases you will pay more for them than he does (the exception is on a large project, where you may be able to negotiate a discount with your supplier).

The following table gives an idea of the amount you could expect to save doing a range of common DIY jobs yourself; you can get a more accurate figure for a particular job by getting some quotations from professionals and comparing them with your own estimate of costs for materials you would have to buy to do it yourself. Bear in mind that you may have to pay for a number of new tools, but these can be considered an investment as you will always be able to use them again — see Tools, Materials & Prices on pages 139–141.

DIY — THE SAVINGS

Adding a power point	£30
Hanging a new front door	£40
Installing wall lights	£45
Fitting a replacement window	£50
Tiling a wall	£50+
Plumbing in a washing machine	£55
Treating woodworm in a loft	£100+
Laying a drive surface	£120
Painting a room	£125
Plastering a ceiling	£150
Fitting a new bathroom suite	£150+
Papering a room	£175
Removing a load-bearing wall	£250
Fitting kitchen units	£250+
Painting exterior woodwork	£350
Rewiring a house	£800+
Installing central heating	£1000+
Re-roofing a house	£1000+
Building a garden wall	£10/m
Building a home extension	£200/sq m
Replacing slipped roof tiles	£35
Replacing bathroom basin	£40
Replacing old gutters	£190

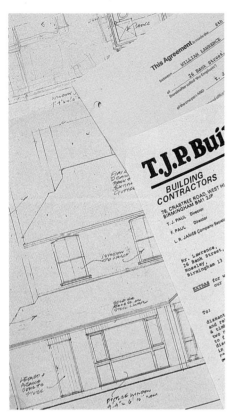

The relationship between builder and householder is more likely to be a happy one if the paperwork – plans, quotation and agreement – is all drawn up and settled before the building work begins

Finding a builder

There are probably more horror stories about builders in DIY folklore than any other trade. Part of the problem is that literally anyone can set themselves up in business as a builder; there is no control over the skill of the people concerned, and no legal requirement (as with architects, for example) to register with a professional body before setting up.

Many such 'firms' are not even companies — just one or more individuals trading under a grandiose business name, a façade concealing Tom the brickie, Dick the plasterer and Harry the odd job man plus one of their wives to answer the phone at one of their homes. Some are very good, many are average and some are downright dangerous: your problem when trying to find someone to do some building work for you lies in obtaining sufficient information to sort out the good from the bad.

So where do you start? Most people seem to choose a builder on personal recommendation from family or friends, and this method does at least have the advantage that you can find out how good the firm was at things like timekeeping and cleaning up as well as being able to inspect their work at first hand.

The problem with this is that good builders are always in demand, and if your best friend's 'gem' of a builder is any good, he's likely to be well booked up for work. The first golden rule, therefore, is to find your builder first and set up your timetable second.

Of course, this method doesn't work so well if you have moved house to a different area. In this case the best method is to walk or drive round the neighbourhood looking for houses where building work is going on. Good builders (and a few bad ones) are keen to advertise, and will usually have a board posted outside the house with their name and address on it. Make a note of it, and call in one evening or weekend at the house to ask the householder for his impressions. Most owners will be pleased to show off the job if it's been well done, and will be able to let you know what the firm is like to work with. You can then contact the firm yourself and discuss your requirements in more detail.

TIMETABLES

If you are employing several different specialists to work on a particular project, it's important to make sure that the right people arrive at the right time — you don't want work held up because a vital cog is missing.

If an architect or builder is coordinating operations, it will be his responsibility to ensure that different trades arrive on schedule. But if you are managing the project yourself, you need to do some careful planning at the very beginning.

Start by talking to the various individuals concerned to find out at what stage they expect to come in and contribute their part to the job. For example, the electrician will want to run in cables and position mounting boxes for accessories before the plasterer tackles the walls, and will then want to return to connect up switches and socket outlets — either before the decorators come in, or possibly after.

Only by checking each trade's requirements in this way can you build up a complete picture and plan accordingly. Ideally, try to get all the contractors together for a meeting to discuss the planning on a large job; on a smaller project involving just two or three specialists you can probably manage just as well talking to them individually.

Now draw up a bar chart divided into days and weeks, and use coloured bars to indicate when each trade needs to be present. Send a copy to each contractor with a written note of the dates on which you expect him to be at work. If any alterations to the plan are needed, make sure you notify everyone in good time, and revise the bar chart accordingly. You can also use it to keep a check on the hours and days worked by each contractor — useful when it comes to account-paying time.

If this method doesn't find you a builder, you can take pot luck with the local Yellow Pages. You will probably have to phone eight to ten firms to get three or four actually to come to the house. Invite them separately — ideally, on separate days; it's awkward having two firms wandering round the house at the same time.

There are two organisations you may like to contact in your search for a builder. The *Federation of Master Builders* (FMB) (see Builders, page 136) is an association of over 20,000 small and medium-sized building firms. All member firms have to have employer's liability and public liability insurance, but member firms are not inspected as a condition of membership unless they belong to the FMB's national register of warranted builders. If they do, they will have had to submit references as to their financial stability and must have been trading for three years immediately prior to joining the register.

If you have work done by a warranted builder you get a two-year guarantee against defects that covers work up to a cost of £30,000. Roof repair work, other than complete renewal, is excluded from the guarantee.

You can get lists of builders belonging to the FMB in your area, plus an indication of the type of work they specialize in, by writing to the Federation at the address given on page 136..

The *Building Employer's Confederation* (formerly the National Federation of Building Trades Employers — NFBTE) (see Builders, page 136) exists to provide business advice services to its members, and does not guarantee any standard of competence in its members. However, you

Major renovations can be tackled if you do not mind using part of your premises as a builder's yard. It is worth hiring a skip if the work involves stripping out existing fittings or clearing rubbish

BUILDER'S CHECKLIST

Quotes Get at least three quotes for all but the smallest job. It obviously helps if you have a clear idea of what you want doing, with sketches and notes on which the builder can give you a firm price for the job (make it clear that this is what you want: an 'estimate' is just that, and is not a guaranteed price). Ask the builder how much of the work will be subcontracted; people who don't actually work for him are often the biggest source of hold-ups in work of this sort. Check that he has adequate insurance to protect his workmen and the public — you and passers-by. Ask for the quotation in writing, and write your acceptance of it back to him.

Contracts An oral contract to do a job for an agreed price is just as legally binding as a written one, but a lot harder to enforce when something goes wrong. For all but the smallest job it will save a lot of time if you have a written contract covering the following points:
● A description of the work to be done plus the finish and standard of workmanship expected.
● The start and completion dates for the job, plus either a damages clause for delays or at least a promise to negotiate over late completion.
● The price, and how the money is to be paid. It is not generally a good idea to hand over any money until work has at least started, and reputable firms will usually submit an account only when work has been completed. On large or complex jobs it is common practice to retain say 5 per cent of the total, to be paid after an agreed time.
● Variations; any changes to the original specification should be agreed by both parties *and* put in writing.
  Your builder may offer to use (or you can obtain) a standard pre-printed contract such as that supplied by the Royal Institute of British Architects or the Royal Institute of Chartered Surveyors (see Finding an architect and also see page 136 for useful addresses).

Inspection It's in your best interests to keep a close eye on the work at every stage. You can then make sure that quality is satisfactory on things that will be hidden later, and raise any queries at a stage when putting things right is still easy. Carry out a final detailed inspection as soon as the work is finished.

GETTING SPECIALIST HELP

can at least find out how long a firm has been in business, how many people it employs and so on. The Confederation has regional offices from whom you can get lists of member firms working in your area.

The *National Home Enlargement Bureau* exists to give advice on the best way of extending your home, and can provide lists of builders specializing in work of this sort (see Builders, page 136).

Scaffolding can be hired to give better access to upper storeys, but it is advisable to get a specialist to erect and dismantle it for you

In certain circumstances a specialist may recommend a builder to you — if you've used an architect, for example, or are buying a 'package deal' such as a loft conversion or kit home extension. In these cases, don't be afraid to ask for references so you can inspect some of the firm's work and talk to previous clients before accepting the recommendation.

Once you have found a builder who seems satisfactory and expresses an interest in working for you, you should make sure from the beginning that nothing is left to chance — especially when he is to start work, when he is to finish and how he is to be paid, in stage payments or a lump sum.

THE ASSOCIATIONS BEHIND THE PROFESSIONALS

The problem area	Who to call in	The association to contact
Building design	Architect	Royal Institute of British Architects
		Incorporated Association of Architects & Surveyors
	Surveyor	Royal Institution of Chartered Surveyors
Building work (general)	Builder	Federation of Master Builders
		Building Employers Confederation
Decorating	Decorator	British Decorators Federation
		Scottish Decorators Association
	Interior designer	British Institute of Interior Design
Electricity	Electrician	Electrical Contractors Association
		National Inspection Council for Electrical Installation Contracting
Heating	Plumber	Institute of Plumbing
		National Association of Plumbing, Heating & Mechanical Services Contractors
	Heating specialist	Confederation for the Registration of Gas Installers
		Heating & Ventilating Contractors Association
		Solar Trade Association
		Ventilation Advisory Bureau
	Chimney sweep	National Association of Chimney Sweeps
Insulation	Specialist installer	Cavity Foam Bureau
		External Wall Insulation Association
		National Association of Loft Insulation Contractors
		National Cavity Insulation Association
Kitchens	Specialist installer	Kitchen Specialists Association
Noise	Consultant	Association of Noise Consultants
Plumbing	Plumber	Institute of Plumbing
		National Association of Plumbing, Heating & Mechanical Services Contractors
Roofs	Roofer	National Federation of Roofing Contractors
		National Society of Master Thatchers
	Builder	Federation of Master Builders
Wood treatment	Damp specialist	Timber Research & Development Association
Walls	Builder	Federation of Master Builders
	Decorator	British Decorators Federation
		Scottish Decorators Association
	Damp specialist	British Chemical Dampcourse Association
Windows/doors	Installer	British Woodworking Federation
		Glass & Glazing Federation

Most areas of specialisation in the building industry have their own professional associations who keep a list of their members and often produce useful booklets which are available to the public

Saving Energy

One of the trends in modern living has been towards central heating and constant hot water. Nobody now expects to live in the way that our great-grandparents used to, with a coal fire in the living room as the main source of room heating and a kettle on the stove to heat water for washing. The price of fuel, particularly oil which is now low owing to a world glut, will continue to rise but there are a lot of ways in which the householder can reduce heating bills whilst actually increasing the level of comfort in the home — effective insulation will pay for itself in a matter of years.

Heating

Whatever the source of your heating, the origin of that supply involves the burning of a natural resource — whether coal, oil, wood or gas. The demand on resources grows each year, as homes become equipped with more and more labour-saving gadgets.

Despite the obvious deterrent of the rising cost of fuel, domestic energy consumption continues to increase. At present, fuel is not in short supply, but there is bound to come a time when this is no longer the case.

Manufacturers of heating appliances lay considerable emphasis on the fuel saving advantages of particular types and models and research is continuing into making the various heating appliances and equipment on the market more efficient and cost effective.

To encourage energy saving on heating, grants are available to help provide loft insulation in those homes where it is insufficient or lacking altogether (see **Insulation** page 108).

Financial help may also be given to improve the efficiency of some parts of the plumbing, such as the hot water cylinder and pipe runs in the loft.

The relevance of this energy saving campaign is twofold. First, if less energy is used, existing natural resources will last longer, allowing more time for viable alternatives to be found. Second, there is a positive advantage to be gained from taking precautions to save energy in the home. Without reducing the level of comfort, it is possible to cut fuel bills by as much as 50 per cent.

Fuel facts

Six basic types of fuel are available for domestic use in providing energy for heating and hot water — electricity, mains gas, oil, coal and smokeless fuel, wood and LPG (liquefied petroleum gas). Each of these has their benefits and disadvantages and these we discuss below along with their average 1985 prices. Bear in mind that local clean air regulations may rule out coal and wood as possible choices.

Annual costs are average running costs for heating and hot water in properties with loft insulation and lagging only. Your own costs may be above average if you are at home all day or need to keep very warm.

This conservatory, heated by the sun's rays, has louvres and blinds to control the temperature

Electricity

Unit price: 5.64p per unit (average).

Annual cost: Ranging from £150 for a two-bedroomed intermediate storey flat to £460 for a three-bedroomed detached house. In the case of the flat, the system comprises two storage heaters, four panel heaters and one bathroom heater, with Economy 7 water heating. With the house, the system includes four storage heaters, five panel heaters and one bathroom heater, with Economy 7 water heating.

Electricity can be used to fuel individual heating units, boilers, central heating systems, storage and panel heaters and to heat domestic water in sufficient quantities to meet the demands of all households.

Gas

Unit price: 37p per therm.

Annual cost: Ranging from £210 for a two-bedroomed intermediate storey flat to £420 for a three-bedroomed detached house. In the case of the flat, the system comprises a central heating boiler and six radiators. With the house, the system includes a central heating boiler and nine radiators.

Gas can be used to fuel individual heating units, back and standard boilers, including full central heating systems, and instantaneous domestic water heaters.

Oil

Unit price: 20p per litre (approx.).

Annual cost: Ranging from £485 for the average semi-detached house to £625 for a three-bedroomed detached house. In the case of the semi-detached house, the system comprises a floor-standing boiler and eight radiators. With the detached house, the system comprises a floor-standing boiler and nine radiators.

Special considerations: Oil is available to any property that can accept deliveries by road tanker.

A large tank, conveniently sited, is needed in which to store oil. Not only should this be reasonably close to the property to reduce the pipe run into the home, but it also has to be accessible from the road or driveway for deliveries. Unless communal facilities have been made available, this fuel is not a practical proposition for flats or some terraced houses. Once suitable storage has been arranged, oil is fed automatically to the boiler while the supplies last.

Oil can be used to fuel a boiler supplying hot water for both domestic and full central heating systems. Its only other use is in firing a combined cooker/boiler unit.

Solid fuel

Unit price of house coal: £108.00 per tonne (approx.).
Unit price of smokeless fuel: £132.00 per tonne (approx.).
Annual cost: Ranging from £225 for a two-bedroomed intermediate storey flat to £460 for a three-bedroomed detached house. In the case of the flat, the system comprises a smokeless fuel room heater with back boiler, six radiators and an electric immersion heater for hot water during the summer. With the house, the system includes a housecoal room heater with back boiler, nine radiators and an electric immersion heater.
Special considerations: A sizeable bunker, shed or suitable cupboard area is needed in which to store solid fuel. Such facilities should be conveniently sited to provide adequate

The traditional way – coal and smokeless fuels are still competitive for home heating systems

access for deliveries, and equally for carrying the fuel to the relevant appliance. For these reasons solid fuel may not prove a practical alternative for flats or terraced houses.

Solid fuel has, in most cases, to be carried to the appliance and fed into it. Hopper-fed units are now available that make this job less frequent and new methods of clearing out are a lot less messy.

An underfeed refuelling technique, as already used in industry, is being developed which greatly reduces — and should eventually eliminate — the need for refuelling by hand. Ash disposal may pose an additional problem, as will the need to supply hot water during the summer months, when running a boiler will not prove cost effective.

Solid fuel can be used to fire individual heating units and back and standard boilers to provide domestic hot water and operate central heating systems. Its use will to an extent be determined by the existence and location of suitable chimneys.

Although vast improvements have been made in controlling the rate at which the fuel burns, this form of fuel cannot be switched off. And when left to burn down, it will take some time to reach a desirable level of heat again.

Wood

Unit price: £30.00 per tonne (approx.).
Annual cost: Ranging from £240 for a two-bedroomed intermediate storey flat to £350 for a three-bedroomed

Wood for burning should be stored under cover so that it can be air-dried over a period of time

detached house. In the case of the flat, the system comprises a central heating cooker with six radiators. With the house, the system includes a central heating cooker and nine radiators.
Special considerations: A shed, store or convenient area outside is needed for storing wood. Such facilities need to be accessible for deliveries and for carrying the fuel indoors. With certain types of property, such as flats and terraced houses, wood may not be a practical option.

Appliances which burn wood need to be refuelled at regular intervals and will also have to be cleared and cleaned periodically. An immediate supply should be made available near the appliance and this will require some space in the relevant room.

Wood can be used to fuel individual heating units, stoves from which central heating systems can be run, and central heating cookers. Its use will to an extent be determined by the existence and location of suitable chimneys.

While it is possible to control the rate at which this fuel burns and therefore the amount of heat given off, it cannot be switched on and off instantly.

ANNUAL COST OF HEATING AND HOT WATER IN AN OLDER TERRACED HOUSE			
Heating system	Cost of system	Without draught proofing	With draught proofing
Electricity	£1338	320-330	240-250
Mains gas	£1500	300-330	240-277
Oil	£2000	470	370
Solid Fuel	£1600	380	320
LPG	£1700	570	460

ANNUAL COST OF HEATING AND WATER HEATING IN A SEMI-DETACHED HOUSE			
Heating system	Cost of system	Without draught proofing	With draught proofing
Electricity	£1300	340-346	320-330
Mains gas	£1400	320-360	310-330
Oil	Not used owing to storage and delivery difficulties		
Solid Fuel	£1600	390	370
LPG	Not used owing to storage and delivery difficulties		

Liquefied petroleum gas (LPG)

Unit price: 18p per litre (approx.).

Annual cost: Ranging from £660 for the average semi-detached house to £840 for a three-bedroomed detached house. In the case of the semi-detached house, the system comprises a wall-mounted boiler and nine radiators.

Special considerations: While small cylinders that are used in conjunction with free-standing room heaters should cause few problems, when LPG is required as a more general source of fuel a special, large supply cylinder will have to be installed. As with oil, access will have to be provided for refuelling from time to time. LPG may not, therefore, prove a practical fuel for flats and terraced houses.

LPG can be supplied throughout the home in the same way as mains gas, through pipes to the required outlets and appliances.

All appliances run off LPG are instantly controlled, in the same way as those fired by mains gas, and respond immediately. Time, programme and thermostat controls will require electricity with which to operate.

Liquefied gas, like fuel oil, is delivered in bulk and stored in a tank ready for immediate use

Heat and heaters

Sources of heat in the home can range from localized heating provided by individual fires to a complete central heating system with radiators or storage heaters strategically placed throughout the house. To some extent, the type of heating chosen will depend on the size and design of the building, the number of people living there, and the day-to-day use of each area.

In most cases, balanced central heating is considerably more efficient and cost-effective than individual fires, assuming that the house has been adequately insulated and well draught-proofed. This is also assuming that suitable controls have been installed to ensure the system runs efficiently, maintains the required temperature and operates only when needed. The following is intended as a guide when considering what form of heating to choose for your home, taking into account convenience and cost.

Central heating

Installation costs are relatively high, depending on the size of the property and the number of radiators or heating outlets used, but the price of running a complete system should more than justify this initial outlay.

The cost-effectiveness of any system is dictated by the type of fuel and appliance used and also the amount of insulation (see **Insulation**) provided in the home. The more efficient the insulation, the cheaper any system will be to run.

Electricity: The systems available include Electricaire ducted warm air, ceiling and underfloor heating, all of which can prove economical if installed during the building or conversion of a property. They would otherwise be too expensive and disruptive to fit into existing properties. But electricity is only truly competitive in price terms when used through the Economy 7 off-peak tariff (see panel page 107).

Alternatively, overall heating may be provided by a combination of storage heaters using off-peak electricity and panel and skirting heaters.

Gas: Around 80 per cent of central heating installations in Britain are fuelled by gas. These systems can be supplied by wall-mounted or free-standing boilers or back boilers that combine with a gas fire. The latest style of gas boiler incorporates a storage cylinder, which avoids the need for long, heat-wasting pipe runs to a separate hot water cylinder.

In single storey homes and flats, it is also possible to install a pre-plumbed cold water storage unit complete with feed and expansion pipe, which sits above the boiler.

A ducted warm air system can also be fired by gas.

Oil: Like gas, oil can be used to fire free-standing boilers supplying central heating systems. The latest range includes combination units as well, which eliminate the need for water storage tanks in the loft or a separate hot water cylinder.

Solid fuel: Boilers fired by solid fuel have become considerably more popular since their operation has been improved. The latest designs include hopper-feeding and a booster fan to make the boiler respond faster.

Room heaters and free-standing fires in modern styles also incorporate

back boilers that are capable of supplying hot water for many radiators.

Wood: In the last few years woodburning stoves have found popularity, not just for their looks but also because some models will provide hot water for central heating systems. A number of central heating cookers can also be run with wood.

A closed stove burns fuel much more efficiently than an open fire

A woodburning stove adds considerable charm to a room and radiates a surprising amount of heat

Supplementary heating

For those who cannot afford the expense of a full central heating system, there are plenty of other types of heater capable of keeping the home warm at a reasonable cost. And even in those homes where central heating has been installed, an infra-red wall or ceiling heater may well be the ideal boost when temperatures are low.

Electricity: This source of energy offers the greatest range of heaters to suit all situations and needs. Panels and skirting heaters and oil-fired radiators, for example, will provide a useful source of background heat and can be controlled by a thermostat or timer to increase their efficiency.

More direct instant heat can be obtained from fan, convector and infra-red heaters, which are ideal for warming up a cold area quickly or boosting existing background heating. There is also a wide range of traditional radiant heaters, which are available with flaming coal and log effects.

ANNUAL COST OF HEATING THE LIVING ROOM ONLY

Heater		Cost of heater	Without double glazing	With double glazing
⚡	Electricity	£150-170	80-90	70-80
🔥	Mains gas	£140	90-130	80-120
	Paraffin	£40	120	100
	Solid fuel (open grate)	£40	160	140
	Solid fuel (room heater)	£200	90	80
	LPG	£70	160	130

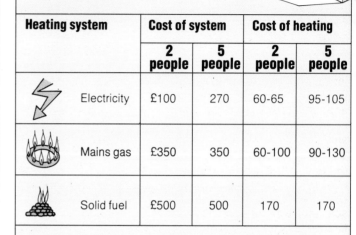

COST OF HEATING WATER ONLY

Heating system		Cost of system		Cost of heating	
		2 people	5 people	2 people	5 people
⚡	Electricity	£100	270	60-65	95-105
🔥	Mains gas	£350	350	60-100	90-130
	Solid fuel	£500	500	170	170

Whether or not you have central heating, it is always handy to have a separate means of heating the living room and of providing hot water. The system you choose will depend on how much store you set by 'flick the switch' convenience and whether you wish to move the heater from one room to another. Storage and delivery difficulties may rule out the possibility of using either oil or LPG

Gas: Here the choice is more limited. Apart from the portable free-standing gas heaters run off small cylinders, individual fires have to be fixed in position. The traditional wall-mounted or floor-standing fires come in a range of styles, some of which incorporate a back boiler to provide hot water. Thermostatically controlled wall heaters are also available which can be fitted to any suitable outside wall.

Oil: The only individual unit for supplementary heating using this type of fuel is the paraffin heater. The design and style have improved much over the years and in certain circumstances this source of heat may be a viable alternative to some of the more obvious supplementary heating equipment.

Solid fuel: The traditional open coal fire still retains its appeal and adds considerable charm to a living room. This fuel has been made a lot more efficient for direct heating with the latest types of free-standing and inset fires and room heaters, some of which also provide hot water through back boilers. You should check on the type of solid fuel used in the model you want as some models will function efficiently on only one type of fuel.

Wood: The options here are similar to other forms of solid fuel and burning wood on an open fire is for many an ideal way of supplementing existing background heating. Wood-burning stoves have made this fuel a lot more cost-effective and, as well as looking attractive, can supply hot water.

Water heating

Heating water was the traditional function of the domestic boiler, although nowadays the options and alternatives are numerous.

The problem with domestic boilers is highlighted by those fired with solid fuel, which cannot be simply switched on or off at a minute's notice. Here, in particular, it would be totally uneconomic — not to mention uncomfortable — to have such a boiler running throughout the warmer months of the year. Whether or not you have a central heating system installed, there is a strong argument for using supplementary methods for heating water.

You could, for example, use an immersion heater, which is fitted into the hot water cylinder and can be used to heat small amounts of water for general washing or larger amounts for those wishing to take a bath.

Instantaneous hot water heaters are ideal in this situation, as they provide just the amount of hot water needed

A modern wall-mounted gas boiler takes up no more room than a wall cupboard and can supply heating and hot water for an average house

and there is no waste of valuable fuel. And shower units incorporating their own water heaters are particularly cost-effective — not just in the summer but all the year round.

Electricity: This fuel offers the widest range of choice for heating domestic water. Apart from the Economy 7 boiler, and the immersion heater and instantaneous heaters already mentioned, wall-mounted kettles and over- and under-sink storage heaters can prove very practical where smaller amounts of hot water are required.

Gas: Hot water is available through a range of gas boilers, combination units and back boilers. Gas-fired instantaneous water heaters are also available and can be fitted over a bath or kitchen sink to save switching on the boiler — or in smaller houses or flats where no boiler is installed.

Oil: The only method of heating domestic water with this fuel is through an oil-fired boiler. Again, an immersion or instantaneous water heater is a useful secondary source of hot water.

Solid fuel: The limitations of this arrangement for providing hot water have already been mentioned. All the time the boiler is running, there will be plenty of hot water.

Wood: While supplies of hot water can be obtain from central heating cookers and wood-burning stoves, the limitations here apply in the same way as for solid fuel.

ECONOMY 7

Economy 7 is a special off-peak tariff which is available from all regional electricity boards. It can make a great difference to the amount you pay for the electricity consumed in providing heating and hot water.

It operates on the basis of using electricity overnight and allows you seven hours of cheap-rate fuel between midnight and 8am every day.

The advantages of using this tariff is that normally heavy consumption appliances such as storage heaters, and immersion heaters can be run for under half the normal unit rate. Although this varies according to where you live, the Economy 7 tariff offers electricity at just over 2p per unit, whereas the normal supply averages out at about 5½p per unit consumed.

BOURNVILLE SOLAR VILLAGE

Bournville Solar Village in Birmingham comprises some 300 houses on seven sites, and two homes for elderly people. The present development is the third phase of a long range solar energy program. In earlier phases, two homes for the elderly were fitted with 'active' solar systems in which roof mounted collectors supplied domestic hot water. The system had to be augmented by conventional auxiliary heating.

The solar energy project has been commissioned by the Bournville Village Trust (BVT), set up by George Cadbury (of the famous chocolate manufacturers) in 1900, with an interest in improving housing conditions and construction methods. Finance for the project comes from BVT, the Commission of European Communities, and the Housing Corporation.

All buildings in phase three are built to 'passive' design principles — the building itself is constructed to maximize the use of the sun's energy. Large south-facing windows take in as much of the sun's heat as possible while double glazing, a high standard of insulation, tightly fitted windows, and thermal blinds for night use, reduce heat loss to a minimum.

From 1985 to 1988, the energy performance of the houses will be monitored by computers, and the various elements of the design properly evaluated. The cold winter of 1985 certainly allowed the first inhabitants of the Solar Village to test the benefits of their new energy-efficient homes.

A special demonstration house combines both active and passive technology, and is designed to test the most up-to-date solar space heating and water heating methods. Two separate systems supply water and space heating, using roof-mounted selectively coated collectors, and a phase change heat store. Space heating is by underfloor piping. The water heating is interesting because it uses the newly-patented Variable Volume, Variable Flow-Rate method, which increases the system's efficiency significantly.

Passive technology (everything that is not concerned with actually heating the water) includes a specially-designed sunspace to the south, while heat losses are reduced by mechanical shutters. The house has concrete floors throughout, covered with quarry tiles to reduce heat loss, and to even out temperature changes in the rooms.

The solar village's efficiency is now being studied.

SAVING ENERGY

Heat from an uninsulated house will be lost to the outside atmosphere in the proportions shown

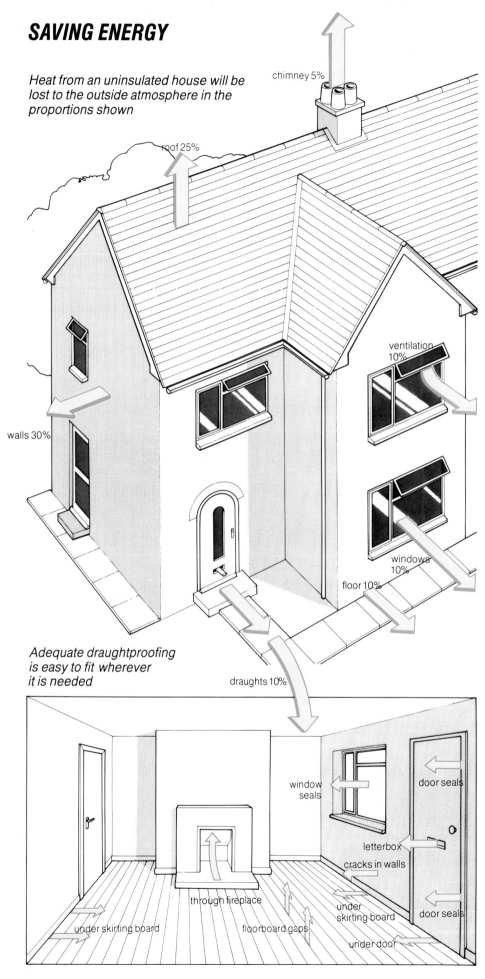

chimney 5%

roof 25%

ventilation 10%

walls 30%

windows 10%

floor 10%

Adequate draughtproofing is easy to fit wherever it is needed

draughts 10%

window seals

door seals

letterbox

cracks in walls

through fireplace

under skirting board

floorboard gaps

under skirting board

door seals

under door

Insulation

Apart from limiting consumption by controlling the supply, the only way to make the most of the energy used is to control the rate at which the heat escapes from the house — the slower the rate of heat loss, the less fuel you will use and the lower your bills will be.

If you consider that certain types of insulation can reduce the heat flow out of the home by up to 80 per cent, then it makes sense to take some precautions, at least to protect the more vulnerable areas. Just where the vulnerable areas are varies from one type of house to another and so the cost-effectiveness of each kind of insulation will also vary. For example, more heat could be lost though the walls of a detached house with four exposed walls than through the three exposed walls of a semi; consequently wall insulation will be more effective in the detached house.

Heat loss

There are two basic principles which explain where the heat goes to in any type of home. The first is that hot air rises. This means that heat will pass up through ceilings and eventually disperse out of the roof. The second is that hot air will always travel from a warmer to a colder environment. This is why, for example, single glazed windows are such a major factor in heat loss — as are open doors and thin, uninsulated walls.

Although it is almost impossible to totally eliminate heat loss, you can insulate those parts of the home through which most heat is lost. The inevitable loss will be reduced to more acceptable and less costly levels.

It is no surprise that the three areas in the home for which grants may be made available — the loft, the plumbing fittings in the loft and the hot water cylinder — are three of the major sources of heat loss. Fortunately insulating these areas is generally inexpensive.

The loft lining is probably the most important insulation job in any home. When you consider that as much as 25 per cent of heat — and possibly more — can be lost through the roof, the need for proper loft insulation becomes obvious.

The easiest escape route for heat is

108

through gaps in the basic structure of the house — round ill-fitting doors or windows for example. And you could be losing as much as 10 per cent of valuable heat this way. Since the various forms of draughtproofing available provide the cheapest method of insulation, sealing off gaps and cracks with draughtproofing materials and with mastic or sealant is the next most effective job to consider.

The walls are the worst offenders when it comes to losing heat. External walls, in particular, can account for around 30 per cent wastage or more. The cost of insulation here is slightly greater, but generally very worthwhile.

In more recent houses, built with double-skin walls, cavity infill insulation is available in a range of materials. When this type of insulation is unsuitable — such as for those houses with solid walls — there are internal and external insulation materials available, which comprise extra wall lining.

As well as escaping through ceilings, heat also finds its way out through floors, particularly through gaps between floorboards and under skirting boards. Up to 10 per cent of heat can disappear this way. The remedies here can be very cheap and include laying down newspaper, fitting wood moulding or using a proprietary sealant. More unusual methods such as underfloor insulation can be expensive. A thick well-fitted carpet is one of the best methods of floor insulation.

The problems of heat loss through windows are not restricted to gaps around the opening of fixed frames and therefore draught-proofing these areas will not provide the complete answer. About 10 per cent of your heating escapes through the glass itself, unless some form of double glazing is fitted. Provided an air gap is created between the inside and outside surfaces, even the crudest of systems can have some effect.

The cost of double glazing can vary enormously, depending on whether DIY or professional systems are fitted. Furthermore, glazing can be as simple as a plastic film similar to food wrapping right up to a complete tailor-made replacement window.

Loft insulation, whether the mat type shown here or loose-fill, will make the whole house feel cosier

It is certainly worth bearing in mind that heavy lined curtains and strong blinds can make a considerable difference to the amount of heat escaping through the window, although this is normally only a practical insulation method when it is dark.

One important aspect which must not be overlooked, especially where fuel-burning appliances are being used, is that a certain amount of ventilation is essential. However well you may insulate a room, you must ensure that air bricks and ventilation grilles are not blocked up or covered over. Where neither of these vents is fitted it is best to leave the top of a door uninsulated — while it may let in a small amount of draught, it will cause little wastage in heat, and no discomfort at that height.

Different insulations

Having highlighted those areas in the home where the most heat is lost you can look in greater detail at what exactly can be done to make your home more comfortable and more efficiently heated.

Here it is not only important to consider the various types of insulation but also how effective each one is in terms of pounds spent. With this in mind, follow the procedures given here.

Hot water cylinder jacket

Special lagging jackets are made to fit the various different sizes of hot water cylinder. These should be at least 80mm (3in) thick and conform to BS (British Standard) 5615:1978. Most designs come as a number of plastic covered foam strips held together by a collar round the top of the cylinder. The plastic or metal straps are fixed to secure the sections tightly in place, with no gaps between them.

A thick lagging jacket around the cylinder can save up to 75% of the heat losses from an unlagged one. Since a jacket of this sort only costs around £10, it will soon pay for itself.

Loft insulation

The minimum recommended thickness of insulation on the loft floor, between the joists, is now 100mm (4in) — if you have less than 30mm (1¼in) of insulation, you will probably be able to get a grant to help with the cost of topping up or installing insulation where none at present exists.

There is a range of different materials available, some of which you can lay yourself, while others will need to be installed by a contractor. The material used and the contractor both need to be checked with your local council if you want to claim a grant — you may be able to install it yourself. The two

basic types are *mat* and *loose-fill* and both are readily available from builders' and plumbers' merchants, hardware and DIY stores.

The mat insulation is sold in rolls of various lengths, widths and thicknesses which are laid in place between the joists and cut to fit. Loose-fill material comes in bags and is poured into place and then levelled off to the correct depth — it is also easy to lay around obstructions. When laying these types of insulation, leave a small gap for ventilation by the eaves. In the case of loose-fill, you will need to block off round the edges with boards.

Some materials need to be blown into place. This requires special equipment and the job will have to be carried out by a recommended specialist.

Although costs vary from £100 or so up to £250, in terms of fuel saving this can be recovered in about two years.

These methods of insulation are suitable for any property with a sloping roof. Flat roofs pose special problems and it may be necessary to call in professional help. Unless the area of roof is fairly large, the cost and bother involved may well not prove worth the trouble. If you are in doubt, ask a specialist for advice.

Installing cavity wall insulation is not a DIY job as it requires highly specialised equipment

Tank insulation

Having insulated the loft, the space under the roof will be much colder and so the chances of the cold water tank, pipework and central heating feed-and-expansion tank freezing up in severe weather are increased. All of these must be insulated at the same time as the loft itself.

The simplest way of protecting a rectangular tank is to buy pre-cut insulation panels to fit round the sides and over the top. These can be taped in place. Alternatively, you can use the same mat material as you used for the loft and secure it with wire, tape or netting. Loose-fill insulation is more of a problem, since you will have to make a box round the tank to hold the material in place. The mat material is the only option if your house has a round tank.

With both types of tank, only insulate the sides and top (use a board to prevent the mat falling in) and do not insulate underneath, since by allowing some warm air up through the floor you will help stop the tank freezing.

Where water pipes have not been covered already by the loft floor insulation, these should be lagged, either using strips of mat material wrapped round like a bandage, or the more convenient moulded pipe sleeves, which can be bought in different sizes, to match the diameter of the pipes.

Tank insulation should be at least 25mm (1in) thick, while the pipe lagging needs to be 32mm (1¼in).

Draughtproofing

It is worth remembering that not only does draughtproofing reduce heat loss but it also increases the comfort in a room by helping to eliminate unwanted draughts. Depending on how much draughtproofing has to be carried out, the cost can be as little as £30, which should easily be recovered within a year or so.

Compression seals, which are made of plastic, metal, rubber, bristle or a combination of these materials, as well as the cheapest self-adhesive foam, are applied in strip form and, as the name suggests, are compressed when the door or window is closed. Wiper seals are also available with nylon brush strip and this type slides over a closing surface. They are best suited for doors and large casement windows.

One area that can be a source of draughts is the join between the frame and the wall. Here any gaps can be filled with a proprietary sealant, which is applied using a special tube or gun.

These methods will normally be suitable for all types of home, but there may be problems with older houses that still have sash windows. Often a combination of compression and wiper seals is necessary.

Many of these procedures for reducing heat loss can be carried out by anyone with cheap materials and ordinary household tools, but jobs like cavity wall insulation must be left to properly equipped specialists.

For further advice and help on the different types of insulation see **Insulation and Draughtproofing** on page 137 for addresses.

Wall insulation

As a longer-term investment, this type of insulation can be worthwhile, depending on the property and wall construction.

There are several types of material used to insulate cavity walls and all offer effective protection against heat loss. You must check with a reputable contractor as to the one best suited for your property, since some materials are not suitable for all types of wall. The basic materials are expanded polystyrene beads, bonded polystyrene beads which adhere once inside the cavity, rock or glass fibre, and urea formaldehyde foam.

The principles of installation are similar in all cases. Holes are drilled at regular intervals through the outer leaf of the wall and the material is then pumped or blown through these holes into the cavity.

Current costs of insulation vary, depending on the type and size of the property. But the process will cost in the region of £500 for the average two-storey semi-detached house. This means a pay-back period of up to 10 years, although this should be taken as an average figure.

As its name suggests this treatment cannot be carried out on a property with solid walls. Instead it will be necessary to insulate either the inner or outer skin of the wall.

Internal insulation involves putting up a false inner wall using suitable boards mounted on battens, inside which insulation material and a vapour barrier must be fitted. Alternatively, special insulation board can be used. Problems can occur when working round electrical fittings, windows and doorways and the costs will vary from about £12 per m^2 if you do the job yourself to £15 or more per m^2 if you use a contractor.

Walls are usually insulated externally by fixing or bonding suitable insulation material to the wall with a protective rendering on top, or by using a rendering that combines an insulating material. External lining or cladding can cost £25 per m^2 — or more than £2000 for a two-storey semi-detached house. It may also be necessary to get planning permission if the exterior appearance is being changed. One major advantage is additional weather protection.

As well as providing insulation, double-glazed doors look attractive

Double glazing

Because there are now so many different systems available for double glazing windows, it is virtually impossible to access accurately the cost-effectiveness of this form of insulation.

Before committing yourself to a particular system you should make a number of decisions — if you want plastic or aluminium frames, for example. You can choose glass or acrylic panes, and fixed, hinged or sliding sections, depending on whether windows need to be opened or not. You will need to look at the various systems to see whether they can be mounted on to the existing frame or have to be fitted to a subframe, as in the case of metal-framed windows, for example.

Always check the state of the existing frames before choosing your system. If these are in a poor state of repair, it may work out cheaper in the long run to buy double-glazed replacement windows, despite the greater initial cost.

Depending on the type and extent of the double glazing you need, it will at present cost anything from £1000 to £2000 or more, with DIY systems working out, on average, at about half the price. In terms of a pay-back period you could be looking at between 10 and 20 years. You should recoup some of your investment when you come to sell your house.

Fully-fitted carpet can be expensive but is an effective insulator as well as being an important part of the furnishing scheme

Floor insulation

Since the measures taken to cut out draughts through the floor could cost anything from a few pence to hundreds of pounds, it is impossible to assess the cost-effectiveness of this type of insulation accurately.

Gaps round skirting boards can be filled with a proprietary sealant or covered with strips of wood moulding nailed in place. Equally, gaps between floorboards can be filled with sealant,

Metal foil behind a radiator will reflect heat back into the room

strips of newspaper or papier maché. floorboards can be lifted and loft-type mat insulation laid on to strips of nylon netting stapled to the sides of the floor joists. This job involves quite a lot of work, including lifting the floorboards.

Additional floorcoverings such as carpets will help enormously, and although they are expensive they can be regarded as money well spent on decorating.

One important point to remember here is that timber floors need some ventilation to prevent the formation of damp and rot. So never be tempted to block up ventilation airbricks in the outside walls in order to rid the house of every little draught as this will soon lead to condensation. Poke through the holes in the air bricks with a stick to make sure they are clear.

HEATING AND INSULATION TIPS

Some forms of insulation will also reduce noise levels. Double glazing is particularly effective here, while polystyrene rolls or panels will absorb a certain amount of sound when fitted on ceilings and walls.

A simple temporary way of double glazing a window is to tape sheets of clear polythene or kitchen food wrap across the frame.

Don't waste your fuel. Fit the necessary controls such as room thermostats and timers to the system, and have heat when and where you want it.

Don't block radiators by placing furniture right in front of them. Make sure that the heat is allowed to circulate round the whole room.

There is no point in having a radiator which heats up an outside wall. If you fit aluminium foil behind the radiator, it will reflect heat back into the room.

If you are using room heaters, make sure the output is enough for that area, but never more than is needed.

Have your boiler serviced annually for maximum efficiency.

Check your thermostats and turn them down a degree or two. While you won't notice the slight fall in temperature, you will notice the saving in fuel.

When you are airing a room, there's no point in throwing away valuable heat. So switch off the heating until you shut the window again.

If you run storage heaters off Economy 7 tariff and have an immersion heater in the hot water cylinder, then have this linked to the Economy 7 metre as well.

As a temporary insulating measure a rug rolled up and laid against the bottom of a door will help to reduce draughts, particularly if the room has not got a fitted carpet and there is a large gap under the door.

If you have thermostatically controlled radiator valves, keep the bedroom radiators set at a lower temperature than the living room radiators.

Check round all your doors and windows for sources of draughts. You should be able to detect these by running your hand round the edges of the frame or holding a lighted candle up to them — be careful not to set fire to curtains or burn coverings. Deposits of dirt round window frames will indicate gaps. One way of checking gaps round internal doors is to stand in a darkened room with the lights on in the area behind the door and check for shafts of light.

Wind will whistle through the front door unless this is draughtproofed. Special excluders are available for the letterbox, or as a cheap alternative use a block of compressed foam cut to size.

As soon as it starts to get dark, close the curtains. Make sure they hang over the windowsill and behind radiators where fitted. Line thin curtains for extra insulation. It's a good idea to hang heavy curtains over external doors too.

Don't leave unused chimneys open. Screen off the opening but make sure you leave a gap and fit an air grill to provide adequate ventilation.

GRANTS

At present, grants are only available for specific types of insulation: in the loft and around pipes and hot water cylinders. To qualify, there must be no insulation 30mm (1¼in) or more thick in any part of the loft and to claim you will have to insulate any tanks and water pipes in the loft and also the hot water cylinder wherever it is sited.

In 1985, the amount of grant available is 66 per cent of the cost, up to £69 — or, in special cases, 90 per cent or £95. For further conditions and the availability of such grants, check with the local environmental health officer.

Safety & Security

Government figures for 1984 show that burglaries in England and Wales increased by 10 per cent and some areas show even twice that growth rate. Figures for death and injury in the home while not increasing at such an alarming rate, are running at an unnecessarily high level. In this chapter, we look at how you can ensure that this is not the story of your home. Many of the recommended measures are just commonsense and involve no extra costs, while others entail considerable expense. A careful appraisal of your home will make it safer and more secure in 1986.

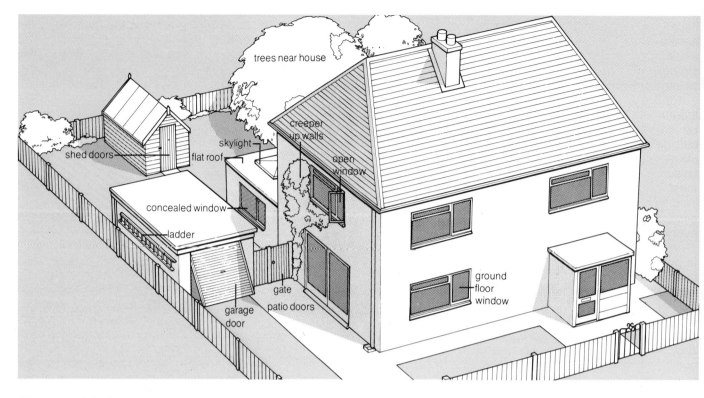

Check carefully for any weak spots in your home's security which would allow easy access

Security

Every home is a potential target for a thief. Many people assume that it is only the rich or those with something particularly valuable who need to bother about security. Nothing could be further from the truth — in most burglaries the thief's pickings are very small.

In fact most thieves are opportunists who go for the easy target — houses where the windows are left open, or where the doors are flimsy. That's why people who haven't taken any special precautions are the most at risk. But looking on the bright side, you may not need to do very much or spend a great deal of money to deter the casual thief. Nine times out of ten, if they can't see an easy way in they won't bother.

The first practical step you can take is to look round the building to make sure that your house isn't the thief's first choice. Then you can go about making things even harder for the criminal. But first, think about who you are trying to keep out.

Recent surveys show that two thirds of all break-ins are committed by people between the ages of 14 and 21, few of whom have any professional skill. This is why you are unlikely to

have to spend a fortune to deter such burglars. Most casual thieves don't carry skeleton keys and other special tools, so even quite ordinary locks and simple precautions will deter them. They won't want to arouse suspicion, and so won't spend very much time to work on the outside of the house.

Of course, there is another sort of thief — the well equipped professional. But these are few and far between, and will certainly know what they are going for before even attempting to break in. So unless you have something special to protect, it's unlikely that you will need to worry about them.

There's one more thing to think about, in case you still aren't convinced that it is worth protecting a few bits and pieces which are insured anyway. Once a thief has broken in, his nerves will be on edge. He doesn't know how much time he's got and he is frightened of being disturbed — so he won't be very careful about how he searches. Drawers get ripped out and cupboards are overturned and if he doesn't find anything worth taking, he is quite likely to smash things simply out of spite. This sort of damage is often more upsetting than losing the items which were stolen. Lost items can be replaced, peace of mind can't.

The way in

It pays to be systematic, so as not to miss the obvious. The diagram above shows the danger points to check in your survey. The guide below covers the special points that you should look for.

Obviously, you need some common sense to decide what is reasonable within the limits of what you are prepared to spend. For example, it's generally accepted that an exterior panel door should be at least 45mm thick. But if yours happens to be made from a tough hardwood like oak, you would probably decide not to replace it even at only 42mm.

Doors

Doors are the easiest way into a house, and account for nearly half of all forced entries — there's about the same number through the back door as the front. Don't forget the patio door, as well — a burglar will go for the weakest link — and if you keep anything in sheds, garages or outhouses or if they could give access to the house, check their doors, too.

The commonest way of breaking in is simply to use force. Back doors, particularly, are often quite weak. Even where the locks are of poor quality, it's usually the wood that gives way first, generally at the point where it is weakened by fitting the lock. The strength of the frame and hinges is just as important as the door's.

If the only lock is a nightlatch, and there's a gap around the door, it can be easy to slip the lock from the outside with a slip of thin metal or plastic — using a credit card is the favourite trick. A mortise lock is the most secure type but you can fit a Yale-type lock as well for the convenience of not needing to use the key every time you want to let someone in.

All your locks should be *deadlocking* to prevent them from being forced — to check, open the door and turn the key to throw the bolt.

Bolts will do for doors which aren't the ones you enter and leave by — what security experts call the *final exit door,* — which must be lockable from outside. Concealed mortise bolts are more secure than those fitted on the surface. You may need to fit hinge bolts to any door to prevent it from being forced on the opposite side to the lock.

It's important that you, or your family, don't admit unwanted callers. If you cannot see the area by the main door from inside the house, the door will need either a door viewer or a security chain. Remember that doors can also give away vital clues about your house and your movements. If it's possible to see in through a letterbox or glass panel, are there valuables on view? And will it be possible to tell when the family is away because of the pile of mail behind the letterbox?

Windows
Over a third of burglars get in through a ground floor window at the back of the house. Although entry through other windows is much less common — under a tenth of the total — *all* windows pose some risk because their frames are often weak and glass is easy to break while security glass is prohibitively expensive for any but the most important locations. Don't make the mistake of thinking that wired glass is secure — it's often called 'the burglar's friend' because the wires stop it shattering explosively.

The windows that are most likely to be broken will be out of sight, and will have *small* panes. It's rare for glass to

Alarms in a prominent place may act as a deterrent to burglars

Don't advertise that you are away. Cancel your milk and newspaper deliveries

be broken so that the thief can climb through — difficult and dangerous. He will usually want to open the window by forcing the frame, or by smashing the glass to get at the catch.

Every *openable* window is a potential entry point. The most vulnerable are those which can be reached from the ground, but a ladder or even a handy drainpipe will give access to those higher up. Don't overlook the skylight or roof window, and any windows in the shed or garage. And don't assume that because you couldn't get through a small pane, no one could — many thieves are children.

Think when you last opened each window, or whether it ever needs to be opened. If it does not, then screw it up — it will be one less to worry about — but remember that a window may be your escape route in case of fire.

Even more than in the case of doors, windows are a convenient way for thieves to size up your house. Look out for places where valuables are in full view, and don't rely on net curtains.

Gaining access
Thieves like time to work on breaking in, so the harder it is to get out of sight of the street, the less likely a prospect your house will be.

The best deterrent is a high wall, fence or hedge, which is hard to climb — walls are easier than fences or thick spiky hedges. Look out for any gaps around the garden where someone might be able to get in. Gates should also be high enough to stop climbers, and the same rules apply to strength and locks or bolts as for doors. Check for anything which would help a thief to climb to an entry point — drainpipes, low walls, lean-to roofs or flat-roofed outbuildings, for example.

Concealment
Given somewhere to hide, enough time and the right tools, a thief can probably still get past all your other precautions. Make sure you don't help him. Don't leave tools where he could get at them, and ensure that there are no areas which would give cover.

Make sure that outbuildings, the garage, coal store and so forth are secure. There's not much that you can do about concealed corners of the building, but cut down the risks by cutting back any dense shrubbery near

THINK SECURITY

Going Out?

Make sure that you have:
- Locked *all* doors and windows.
- Set the alarm.
- At night, left a light on — but not the hall or porch light alone.
- Not made it obvious that you are out.

Going on Holiday?

Make sure that you have:
- Locked *all* doors and windows.
- Set the alarm.
- Stopped all deliveries.
- Informed the police.
- Left a key with a trusted friend or neighbour who knows your security arrangements.
- Not made it obvious you are away.
- Put all valuables in safe keeping.

Where to Keep Valuables

- Not in the house, if possible.
- Not on view.
- Keep small valuables in a safe deposit or install your own safe.
- Identify valuable goods with your own marks and keep full, written details.

the windows or doors — especially at the back of the house.

At night, think about illuminating dark areas with outdoor light, or cutting back branches that shade them. You should certainly think about a light by the front door — not to leave on as an advertisement when you are out, but to see who is calling.

Alarms

There are mixed feelings about alarms. Some view them as a deterrent, while others think it means a house with something worth stealing. What is certainly true is that an alarm won't physically keep a thief out. If you want one, opinions are divided about where to site the alarm box — on show, to deter, or concealed, to give an unwelcome surprise.

In a few special cases, the insurance company will insist on an alarm, so you have no choice. But if you do decide to fit one, having it is no good unless you use it properly. And if it's the deterrent value you want, consider fitting one of the dummy alarm boxes available.

Making things difficult

So you are satisfied that your security precautions are likely to keep out unwelcome visitors. But all the locks and alarms in the world are a complete waste of effort unless you use them sensibly and don't invite theft. This is as much a matter of habit as extra security equipment, although there is a good deal you can do to make things hard for anyone who does manage to get in.

Locking up

Use your locks every time you go out — and don't just put on the latch. Many burglaries only take minutes, and insurance companies take a dim view of claimants who let the thief walk in while they popped next door.

Don't keep lots of copies of keys, and make sure that you know who has them all. Don't tag keys with your name and address, and if you lose them together with anything that will identify you, change the locks. Even if you get your keys back, they might have been copied. For the same reason, change the locks when you move into a new house.

Keep your keys on you or in a safe place. Don't leave them lying around,

"I WAS BURGLED"

It shouldn't really have happened to me, because I was only going out for a few minutes to the corner shops. I know I stopped for a bit longer than I meant to, but I did lock the front door when I went out, and in any case, you'd have thought Mrs. Davies next door would have heard something.

They smashed the glass, you see. That's how they got in through the back door. They broke one of the little glass panes to reach the knob of the lock. There are bolts, too, but they're such a bother to use that I hardly ever do.

They couldn't have been in for more than fifteen minutes at the most, but they turned everything over — pulled out all the drawers, and even broke one that we keep locked.

I was so shocked. I didn't think about ringing the police for nearly

an hour. They came round almost at once, and thought it was probably kids.

They didn't think there was much point in taking fingerprints. Anyway, they never caught anyone, and I never got anything back. Of course, no one had seen a thing.

The worst part was all the damage. It took most of a day to clean up, and we had to have a lot of furniture mended. The bit that hurt most was a china ornament that got broken. It wasn't worth much, but it was the only things I had left of my mother's and it was too badly broken to repair. The insurance paid for all the broken and stolen thing, but I don't suppose we got what everything was worth.

The Expert's Report

It's all too easy to slip out for a few minutes without locking up properly. Basically, the house's security was quite good, but it was easy for a

caller to slip round unnoticed to the back door. The neighbours might have heard, but the street is noisy, and the thieves used a piece of sacking to muffle the glass. It was the insecure lock and no bolts that made it easy for them, and, of course, the lack of a side gate.

Once inside, they had the run of the place. They didn't know what they were looking for, so they just looked everywhere. It was sheer luck on their part that they got anything at all.

In cases like this, it's very difficult for the police to do anything, although the sooner they are contacted the better. No one saw the intruders, and they wore gloves.

Insurance can't really compensate for things of sentimental value, but more cover would have helped to minimize the losses from damage to other things. At least, in this case, the family had kept details and receipts for most things.

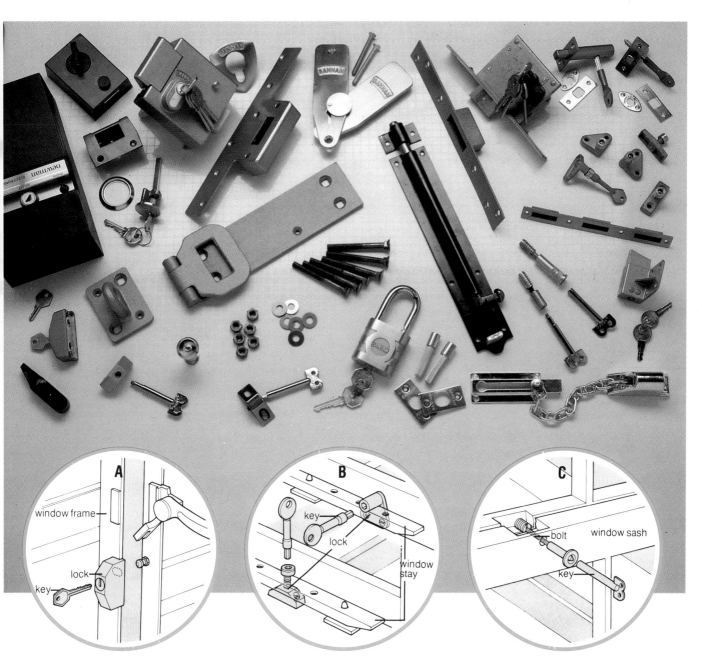

A window frame / lock / key

B key / lock / window stay

C bolt / window sash / key

There are a wide range of devices which will help you tackle almost any home security problem. Window locks (inset), in particular, are designed for specific needs dictated by differing window designs – A used on metal-framed windows; B prevents window stay being lifted; C secures sash windows

and *never* leave them under the mat, in a flowerpot or on a string inside the letterbox — even amateur thieves will know all the hiding places.

When you are in

A surprising number of houses are robbed while there is someone in — often while everyone is watching TV and the burglar is unheard, or when everyone is asleep. So it makes sense to keep the doors and windows locked properly.

When visitors call, you should check who they are before opening the door — with a door viewer or chain, if there is no window. If it's someone you don't know, it's better to be suspicious than sorry — many people have been attacked or robbed in their own homes. A lot of officials have the right to enter your house on business, and there are many you might welcome, but check first. Don't be fooled by a uniform or a printed card: both might be faked.

When you are out

If you keep the doors and windows locked at all times, you won't need to do anything special when you leave for a short time, except to lock the final exit door behind you, and perhaps set the alarm.

The main thing is not to advertise that you are away, so don't leave the curtains drawn in the day, or open at night. At night, it makes sense to leave a light on in a living room. Don't leave notes for callers, saying you are out.

SAFETY AND SECURITY

IF YOU DISCOVER A BURGLAR

● In general, be very wary of tackling him unless you really know what you are doing — he may be armed. If you surprise a casual thief, he will probably bolt, but if he does not see you, try not to alert him.

● As soon as you can, call the police on the emergency number and give them as many details as possible, including all the exits to the house if the thief is still inside.

● Try to remember as much as possible about the thief himself, or any other suspicious circumstances, such as strange parked cars outside.

Deterrence

The casual thief isn't looking for a wealthy household. He is looking for:

● An *easy* way in — the weak door, the unlatched downstairs window.
● An empty house.
● Valuable items on show.
● No witnesses.

These are the things that make it difficult for him:

● Secure doors and windows.
● No access to the back.
● Evidence that the house is occupied.
● Alert neighbours (neighbourhood-watch schemes have proved very effective).
● Nowhere to hide.
● An alarm system (or, sometimes, a noisy dog)!

When you go on holiday

Holidays need a little more preparation. You need to lock up fully, and make sure that you don't advertise an empty house.

It's a good idea to leave some keys with a reliable friend or neighbour in case of emergencies and to check on the house occasionally. Make sure whoever it is knows where all your security devices are — especially if you have an alarm. Tell the police how long you will be away and who is the keyholder.

Stop all the regular deliveries — milk, newspapers and so on — by asking the person who delivers them or calling the office — not by leaving a note. You cannot stop all the unsolicited deliveries, but if you have a good letterbox, they should not be on view, and you can ask your neighbour or friend to see that everything is pushed through.

Indoor plants should be left out of sight unless they are going to be watered regularly, and don't leave cut flowers to wither in a vase. Your caretaker may be prepared to water plants for you, and perhaps wind clocks if they need it. If you are away for a long time, you can ask them to cut the grass, too — but be prepared to repay these favours!

There are several types of security switch and timer which will turn lights on and off either at preset times or when it gets dark, to make it look as if the house is inhabited.

Internal arrangements

If the worst comes to the worst and a thief does get in, in most cases he will be able to work for some time undisturbed. For this reason, it's probably unwise to lock interior doors or cupboards. Even though this might seem a worthwhile delaying tactic, in practice these doors are rarely very strong, and it's more likely that you will come back to find them broken, adding to the mess. Never lock interior doors while people are in, as you might block off an escape route in the event of fire.

Securing your valuables

The general rule is not to keep valuables at home if you don't have to. Keep real valuables in a safe deposit at the bank, or install a wall or floor safe.

To a casual thief, your most valuable possessions probably are not your priceless works of art, which he wouldn't be able to sell, but cash, your cheque book and credit cards. Keep these with you, or hide them. Don't keep more cash than you have to, and don't keep your cheque book and cheque card together.

Keep a list of the serial numbers of your valuable household goods, like the hi-fi, video or bicycles, and note down any identifying marks to give more chance of recovery. You can identify things for yourself by scratching a mark on them, or using a special 'invisible' security marking pen which will only show up under ultra-violet light. Keep your list safe; it will do no good if it is taken, too.

Insure everything against theft for the full replacement value. What's known as a new-for-old policy will

Wilful damage during a break-in can be very distressing

make sure that you get enough back to buy new goods, rather than just getting the second-hand value. The insurance company will want details of specially valuable or high-risk items and may stipulate special security requirements. The *British Insurance Associations* (see page 138) offers insurance advice and publishes a free valuables checklist, which you may be able to get from your own insurance company.

Where to get advice

Although there is a great deal you can do by making your own survey, you may feel that it would help to have a specialist opinion. There are several professional advisers you can contact, and in some cases, it won't even cost you a penny to obtain an expert assessment of your home's vulnerable points and how to strengthen them.

The police

To help to stop crime before it takes place, the police have a number of crime prevention officers (CPOs), who are specially trained in security techniques. You can find out about the local service by contacting your police station — not all of them have a CPO permanently attached, but they can still arrange an appointment. The service is free, and the CPO will inspect your home to point out the risks, If the CPO is local, he or she will probably be able to tell you about specific problems in the area.

The CPO isn't permitted to endorse particular security companies' products, so the advice you will get is impartial. But you can ask the CPO to check your home again after you have done the work.

The insurance company

Although your insurance company wants you to take all reasonable precautions to secure the property which they have insured (and in some cases may refuse to pay out if you haven't), they will not necessarily be prepared to advise you how to go about it, except in general terms such as specifying that you should have a mortise lock on the front door.

It's true that insurance companies employ surveyors to make individual property assessments. But these are relatively few in number and are normally mainly for industrial and high-risk property — which can attract much higher premiums and claims than domestic insurance. So, while it may be worth asking your insurance company if they can recommend a security adviser, it's unlikely that they will be prepared to do the work themselves.

Locksmiths and security companies

There are some firms of independent security consultants, but their surveyors are likely to be very expensive because most of their work is for large companies. You can probably expect to pay at least as much as for a full house-buying survey — *if* you can find a firm that will do it. So for most people, the alternative is to go to a firm specialising in selling or fitting security equipment.

Although locksmiths and security companies will probably give *good* advice, they are interested mainly in selling you their stock, so their advice will not be impartial.

If you don't have a recommendation and are unsure about picking a reputable firm, you can contact the *British Security Industry Association*. For locksmiths, get in touch with the *Master Locksmiths Association* and for alarm systems, the *National Supervisory Council for Intruder Alarms,* (see page 138 for addresses) are the people to ask.

Safety

Although we think of home as a place which is safe and sound, statistics seem to indicate otherwise. In fact, staying indoors is almost as dangerous as driving a car and certainly more dangerous than one's place of work. A staggering six times more people are killed or injured at home than at work. More than 15 people are killed each day due to accidents at home, and thousands are hurt badly enough to require hospital attention.

This isn't just because you spend most of your time at home. The dangers involved on the roads or at work have been recognized for a long time, and it was also realized that most accidents are preventable. So there are many laws designed to protect people — especially the young and elderly who are particularly at risk — in these situations.

By giving the layout of your home and its contents a little thought, accidents can be prevented. Being safety-conscious can be a life-saver. Although no one would want to see their own home life governed by law, there are in fact a number of laws designed to increase your safety at home. For example, a fire-guard is a legal requirement if there are young children at home. But unlike a car there is no requirement for a periodic safety check — which is why it is important to do it yourself. The most

hopeful aspect shown by accident statistics is that most home accidents are preventable with common sense and elementary safety provisions.

Safe as houses?

There are a number of hazardous areas in the home. The kitchen offers the most serious threat to health — burns, scalds, cuts, falls, poisoning and electrocution.

Burns and scalds can be the result of carrying hot plates and bubbling saucepans. Children are at risk by pulling containers full of hot liquid over on to their heads. If you are deep-frying, don't forget that the oil is inflammable.

Electrocution can result from having

Every house has its safety flaws, both inside and out. Simple precautions can quickly overcome any problems before an injury occurs

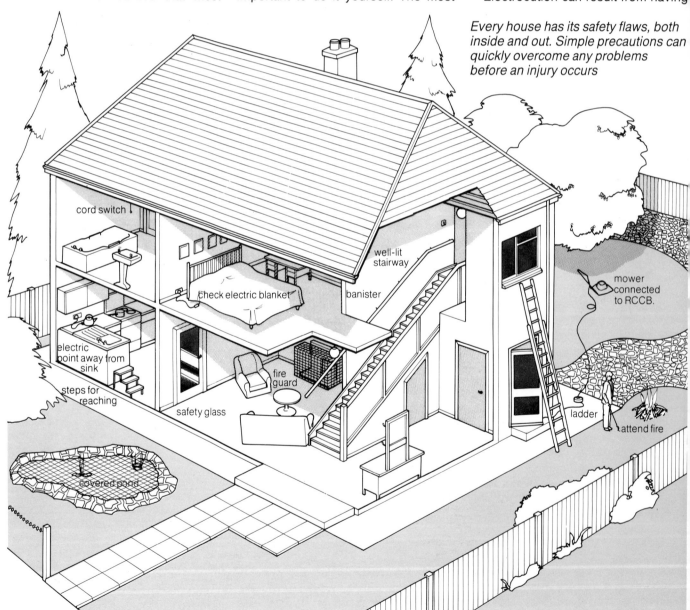

cord switch

well-lit stairway

check electric blanket

banister

electric point away from sink

steps for reaching

fire guard

safety glass

covered pond

mower connected to RCCB.

ladder

attend fire

FIRST AID

The outcome of many accidents in the home is actually more serious than it need be — people are simply unsure of what to do first. Make sure you know some of the basic guidelines in First Aid — it can help save lives.

Falls

● Do not try to pick up the person immediately — check first for injuries.
● If the person is unconscious, check for breathing then place him in the recovery position.
● If the person is neither injured nor unconscious, place a chair nearby and help him to it.
● If there is any sign of injury, or if the person is unconscious, make sure he remains in the recovery position and then call for medical help.

Poisoning

● Call or send for an ambulance immediately, giving details if possible of what the poison is.
● If the person is conscious, make him drink at least two glasses of milk, milk and water or plain water.
● If the person is unconscious place in the recovery position and keep a close watch until the ambulance arrives.
● If the person is not breathing, give artificial respiration until help arrives.

Burns and scalds

● If the person's clothes are on fire, smother them with a cloth or water.
● Immerse the affected area in cold water for at least 10 minutes.
● Cover the burnt area with a clean, dry dressing.
● If the person's throat is scalded, cool quickly with mouthfuls of cold water or by sucking ice.
● DON'T pull away anything that is stuck to the skin.
● DON'T apply any creams or ointments to the burn, until seen by the doctor.

---

too few sockets for the number of electrical appliances. Don't run adapters, or you risk fire or electric shock. Make sure that the sockets can't be splashed with water, and be careful not to operate switches with wet hands.

Falls accounted for nearly half of home accidents, and half the deaths, last year — and there are a number of causes which are easily preventable. Highly polished floors are a hazard throughout the home, but particularly in the kitchen, bathroom, and on stairs and landings. Falls can lead to other injuries if boiling liquids are involved, for example. In particular, beware of loose rugs that have been placed on a shiny floor.

Fire guards are a legal requirement for open fires in homes with children. to minimise the risk of accident

THE RISKS OF FIRE

Fire is the second largest cause of deaths in household accidents. In most cases it isn't the fire that kills, but the fumes given off in burning. Make sure that fire is unlikely to start and that you can get out if it does.
● Keep heat sources away from inflammable material.
● Service heaters and fires regularly.
● Check electrical appliances and wiring regularly to see they are in good order and that any insulation has not perished or chafed through.
● Don't store combustible materials or flammable solvents in the house.
● Avoid foam-filled furniture where possible — if you cannot, only buy furniture which has been treated to increase its fire resistance.
● Polystyrene tiles can be very dangerous as they burn freely, melt and so spread the fire, and give off highly noxious fumes. If you install polystyrene tiles, glue all across the back, don't leave air pockets, and never gloss-paint them. It is better to avoid polystyrene altogether.
● Flammable fumes can travel a long way. Keep solvent or glue well away from heat sources — even a boiler pilot light.
● Keep a fire blanket and perhaps an extinguisher in the kitchen — and know how to use them. Ensure that you can remove the safety cover quickly and easily.
● Keep interior doors shut to prevent fire spreading.
● Smoke detectors may give you advance warning. Fit them in the middle of the ceiling in the hall and landing — not in the kitchen or bathroom where ordinary fumes will cause false alarms.
● Make sure everyone knows the escape routes.

SAFETY AND SECURITY

If your home has old-fashioned, steep stairs you are more at risk than if you have a more modern, shallower design. Although there is nothing you can do to change your stairs, save major structural alterations, there are many ways of making them safer — make sure the stairs are well-lit and that nothing is left on the stairs.

The majority of risks in living rooms and bedrooms come from fires. Sparks may ignite furnishings, or there may be a build-up of combustible soot in the chimney. Fire guards are a legal requirement if you have young children or old people in the house. Regular sweeping will clear the soot.

Gas and electric fires should not present too much of a hazard if they are serviced regularly and used sensibly, but gas build-up and electric shocks can both prove fatal. Cigarettes and badly-maintained electric blankets are two more fire risks.

Young children can be at risk from falling from windows. But if you fit locks, make sure they can be opened in an emergency. Glass in doors and windows can result in horrific cuts, so think very carefully where you are installing this material. Toughened or laminated safety glass will reduce the risk of cuts, but cannot be broken in an emergency as an escape route.

Safety considerations should also apply outdoors — untended bonfires, inflammable materials stored unwisely and incorrectly placed ladders can all

A child has a natural curiosity for things in the kitchen. But it is, in reality, a dangerous room to play in. Far better to be safe and keep children out and away from the danger

Beware when drilling near electrical sockets and light switches. It is easy to penetrate live wires that have been chanelled just beneath the plaster and cause an electric shock

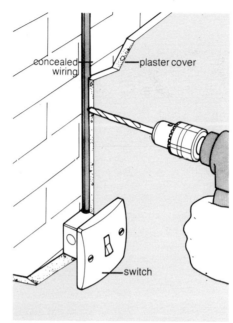

concealed wiring — plaster cover — switch

be dangerous. Deep garden pools pose a threat of drowning to young children if they are not covered.

Feel safer

You house may now seem more like a minefield than a place to live, relax and

GLASS AND INJURIES

Over 50,000 injuries were caused last year by glass being broken. The cost to the National Health Service has hit a staggering £7.5 million, but more than the financial cost, there is the human tragedy of thousands of badly scarred people.

A recent survey at Dudley Road Hospital in Birmingham showed many of the worst accidents to be the result of people walking through transparent glass doors, after failing to notice them. And more than 70 per cent of glass-related injuries occurred in the home – doors and windows caused two-thirds of the injuries.

Members of the Glass and Glazing Federation use the new BS 62/62 Safety Glass, which could save many of these injuries, but legislation does not compel its use. If you are having new windows, it is worth thinking about safety glass.

feel safe. It need not be that way, though. The diagram on page 120 shows how to make individual rooms as safe as possible by a little planning ahead, and installing a few safety products. Safety need not cost money as awareness prevents accidents.

The 1930s Semi

The house you live in has its own personality and its own peculiarities. The style in which it was designed, the materials from which it was built and its location and geographical situation all play a part in its make-up. An understanding of these points is important, whether you are buying, maintaining or simply decorating. The better you know your house, the easier you will find it to repair and adapt. In the first in this series, we take a look at the functional and ever-popular semi-detached house built between the two World Wars.

THE 1930s SEMI

House-building styles have changed dramatically in the last 150 years. Until Victorian times, local customs and locally-made building materials meant that a house in, say, central Wales — probably built of stone with a slate roof — differed considerably from one in east Kent with its brick-and-flint walls and plain tiles. Then came the railways and the canals, and within little more than a generation similar houses built from architect's pattern books in 'foreign' mass-produced materials were springing up all over the country.

As we near the end of the twentieth century the process of standardization is almost complete, and local building customs are in their death throes; only in certain parts of the country do planning authorities seem to make any attempt to keep modern buildings in character with their older neighbours.

The one guarantee that we shall keep some variety in our housing stock is the recent decline in the rate of housebuilding. This ensures that many people will go on living in and looking after houses a lot older than they are.

This chapter is for those people — occupiers and house-hunters alike — who want to know more about the various house types that have developed since the mid-nineteenth century. These fall into several broad groups — Victorian terraces, Edwardian villas, the semis and bungalows of the 1920s and 1930s, the 'modern' detached houses of the 1950s and 1960s, the 'town house' of the 1970s and the 'executive-style' home of the 1980s.

The semi — a social phenomenon

The suburban semi-detached house had a difficult birth, which began at the end of the nineteenth century with the developing concept of 'Garden Cities'. The original plan was to ring several cities, and London in particular, with new towns of about 30,000 people, and to separate them from the existing built-up areas by a 'green belt' of countryside. Private backing enabled building work to start at Letchworth in 1903, and at Welwyn Garden City in 1920.

The principles of country-style living also influenced developments such as Hampstead Garden Suburb, which was begun as the new Hampstead

A typical example of the mock-Tudor style of semi-detached house with elaborate gables over the porch

underground line was extended to Golders Green in 1907, and the London County Council's early garden suburb-style estates at Norbury and Tottenham. The common factor linking private and public building of this type was low density — around 12 properties to the acre in many cases. This presented a stark contrast to the packed urban terrace development of Victorian times.

This major change in housing planning laid the foundation for twentieth-century suburbs to spring up all over the country. On the one hand came the largely unplanned speculative estates, privately built and sold to town-dwellers seeking a semi-rural retreat with all the advantages of a new home; on the other were the rather more modest 'cottage-style' estates, paid for by local councils and rented to their tenants.

The plan was rudely interrupted by World War I — the fact that there was virtually no housebuilding for ten years is the reason why pre-war and post-war styles differ so radically from each other.

The second major change came in the funding of housing development. The Government passed a bill in 1919 giving generous grants to local authorities to build new houses, and in the London area alone some 30,000 houses were built in the next three years (60 per cent of all housing built in that period was council-built, compared with only 6 per cent before 1914). The quality was high too, with most houses having three bedrooms, hot and cold running water, a bathroom and inside toilet, and gardens front and back.

As economic crises came and went through the 1920s in the public housing sector, huge social changes were also affecting the private sector. Before the war very few people owned their own homes; after it the building society movement began to grow significantly, and so did the number of people in the new middle classes to whom house ownership was highly

An older style semi-detached with symmetrical bay windows and distinctive oriel window

gage meant you could have your new house for as little as £5 down and 10 shillings (50 pence) a week.

One of the most significant differences between the public and private sector housing of the period was in architectural style. The actual floor plan of the suburban semi was fairly well standardized, with minor variations between smaller and larger buildings. Public-sector houses were planned and designed by the council architect — extremely well in functional terms, but rather bland and modest in looks, so that estates had a rather dull uniformity once completed.

By contrast the keynote of private developments between the wars was the individuality each builder gave to houses within an estate. Some variations were major — different styles of gable, bay window or porch, the presence of mock-Tudor timbers and so on — and the builder might offer five or six choices on one estate. Other variations were minor — fireplace styles, or different patterns of stained glass in front doors and windows.

This sort of differentiation made each home unique and therefore especially desirable, and reinforced the sense of possession and status so important to home-owners of the period. Even the outbreak of house names added to the impact: here was home, and the owner was 'Dunroamin'.

The evolution of the semi-detached house was not governed purely by social changes; economic factors played a major part too. The move towards low-density housing suggests that the detached house would have been the most natural to build. However, cost factors made this unrealistic, and the semi was the compromise solution adopted. The semi also offered one major cost advantage compared with terraced development; because access to the back garden could be provided by a side path, there was no need for expensive rear service roads.

The back garden itself was at the root of the major house design/layout changes. Its existence was to provide a place for the family's children to play

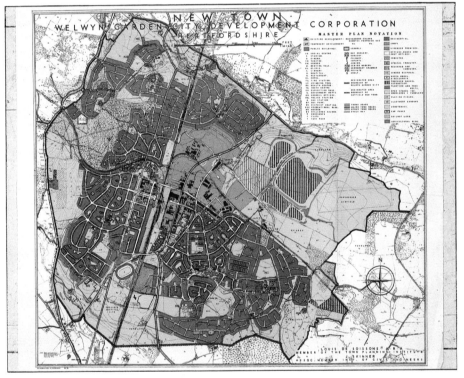

1930s' town planning centred on the semi, and ringing London with New Towns such as Welwyn Garden City

appealing. For this new social group, the age of marriage was falling (as was the size of the family) and domestic servants were out of the question, so the need was for more and more small, convenient and affordable homes.

The private builders grew apace, in league with the building societies in many cases, and 'pools' were developed to enable the estate develop-

ers to underwrite the initial cost to the first-time buyer of acquiring a house. Prices plummeted as competition increased and the costs of raw materials and labour fell during and after the slump. An average semi in the early 1930s could be had for as little as £350, and all sorts of incentives were thrown in by the builders to increase sales — free railway season tickets, fridges and furniture, even a free car in the garage in one celebrated case in Surbiton, Surrey.

Buying on a building society mort-

safely, yet to remain under the parent's watchful eye. The traditional pre-war house had a rear extension, giving the house a depth of three rooms, but cutting off the garden from the rear living room by a narrow back yard. Since purchasers expressed an overwhelming desire for two living rooms (not counting the kitchen), the house depth was fixed at two rooms with the kitchen located at the back alongside the rear living room; both then overlooked the garden.

The hall, with its straight staircase against the outside wall rather than the party wall in most cases, took up the front quarter of an essentially square floor plan. Upstairs, the layout was a virtual repeat, with two main bedrooms above the living rooms, a bathroom above the kitchen (to simplify the plumbing) and the traditional 'box' of a third bedroom over the hall. The same plan is repeated all over suburbia.

Styles

Externally, the semi is unique — a hybrid of many architectural styles from mock-Tudor to 'Arts & Crafts' style cottages. The overwhelming features are the hipped main roof and the symmetrical gabled bay windows, and it is the many different treatments of the gables that distinguish one pair of houses from another. The bay windows may be rectangular, curved or splayed, containing between five and eight separate casements and opening top lights. The face of the bay was frequently tile-hung, with neatly-trimmed lead flashings visible beneath each sill, while the apex of the gable was often 'timbered' in the popular mock-Tudor style.

The gable itself was sometimes a plain triangle the width of the bay, but increasingly in the 1930s the swept gable — descending in an unbroken line to the porch — took its place. With either design the porch was often recessed — another sign of status not enjoyed by the cheaper semi with its simple canopy. Many recessed porches have been fitted with porch doors giving more weather protection.

The profile of the gable was often echoed by an oriel window to the third bedroom or the landing which seemed to satisfy twin longings for the owner — as a display point for treasured ornaments, and as a vantage point for observing the neighbours and the rest of the estate.

One particularly common feature of the semi is the extensive use of pebbledash as a wall finish. This had two major advantages for the builder: it meant he could use cheap ordinary bricks rather than expensive facing ones for the external walls, and could cover up less-than-perfect bricklaying with a treatment that could be applied by comparatively unskilled labour. It appealed to the purchaser too as a surface of natural 'real' stone (perhaps reminiscent of summer holiday beaches) that was permanent and incidentally difficult for the children to chalk on!

The side and rear of the house, by contrast with its public 'front', were given far less attention by the builder. Windows were usually flat and plain — no stained glass here — and the rear or side wall was disfigured by cast iron waste pipes and hoppers and a full-height soil stack.

Internally, the unmodernised semi will reveal more status symbols and attempts to reinforce the 'rural retreat' effect. The hall and stairway often featured woodwork that was stained or brush-grained to make the cheap deal look like oak. Walls were sometimes part-panelled, or decorated below dado level with lincrusta and at picture rail level with a decorative frieze.

In the sitting room, the hearth, with its open fire set in a fireplace of tiles with an oak or mahogany surround, was the centre of attraction. The floor was often of parquet blocks, and wall lights would hang in the recesses beside the chimney breast.

The dining room had a less ostentatious fireplace, and full-length French doors gave an excellent view of the back garden. In the kitchen a built-in dresser stood alongside the latest in modern equipment — an Ideal boiler

A modernist semi of the late 1930s showing the shallower roof slope, green pantiles and smooth rendering so typical of the type. The wooden framed windows of earlier years have been replaced by wide steel framed windows with curved ends. Few interiors survive intact, but an original 1937 magazine picture (left) shows the style of the period, with tiled fireplace, a bay window designed to admit maximum light, and a typical colour scheme. There were no fitted carpets then — rugs were the favoured floor covering

Front and back gardens, and space to the side – often used later for a garage – are part of the attraction of a 1930s semi-detached house.

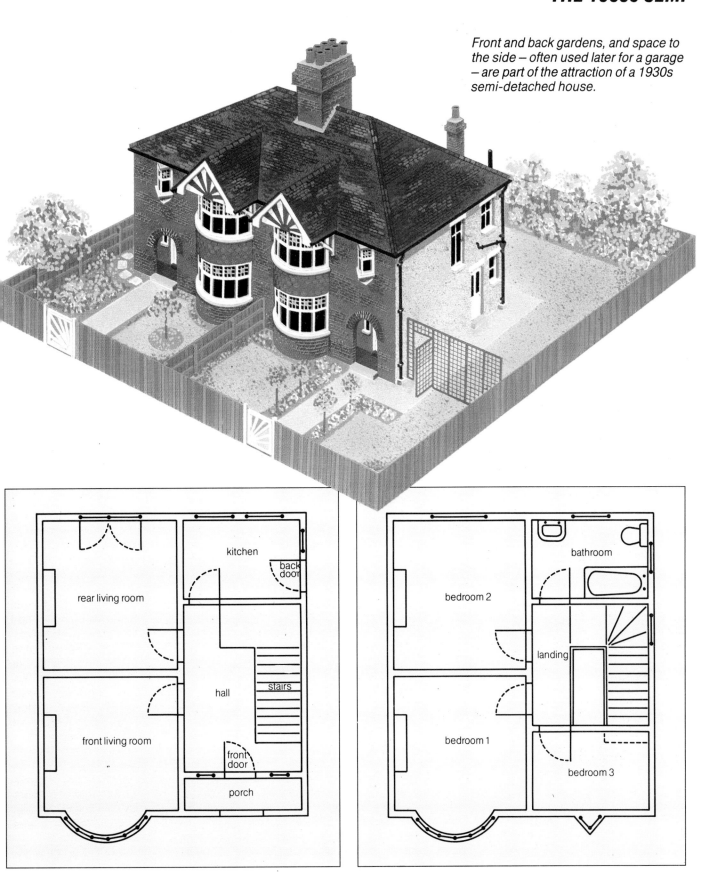

The floor plan of a typical semi-detached. The design was so well-liked that it was repeated all over suburbia with few deviations. Semis have two living rooms on the ground floor, and a kitchen at the rear behind the hall. On the first floor there are two large bedrooms, a box room and a bathroom all leading off a small landing

THE SEMI'S GOOD POINTS

As a building, the semi's main advantages are:

- generally sound construction
- good sound insulating qualities
- reasonably-sized main rooms, with well-planned circulation routes
- structure that is easy to adapt or extend — there is usually plenty of room for side extensions since space will have originally been left for a garage in most cases, even if one was not built, and rear gardens are generous enough for rear extensions to be built on one or two storeys
- situation that is generally pleasant, as trees and shrubs planted after the house was built will have matured over the years, and the original planning of the estate will have ruled out later development between or among existing houses.

As far as geographical and social benefits are concerned, it is more difficult to generalize. Much depends on the subsequent development of the surrounding area; what was once a pleasant semi-rural estate may have been swallowed up by later (and highly intrusive) development, and houses built in ribbon developments along main roads may now suffer seriously from greatly increased traffic volumes. In other areas, estates have acquired a distinct gentility over the years, to the point where they are regarded as a sort of privileged enclave . . . with prices to match their new-found exclusivity.

In the 1970s and 1980s many public-sector (council-owned) houses have passed into private ownership. They may be surrounded by properties still in council ownership, and this may effect the house's future saleability.

for the hot water, a GEC cooker and perhaps even a refrigerator.

The bathroom revealed perhaps the biggest changes from a generation earlier, with tiled walls and floor, a panelled-in bath and a gleaming chrome towel rail. All that was missing (except from the most expensive homes) was central heating.

By the mid-1930s, some of the traditional features of the early semi were being replaced by elements of the modern movement in architecture. Roof slopes became shallower and green pantiles could be seen taking the place of the red and brown plain tiles. The gables (but not the hipped roof) often disappeared, and the bay window developed into a double bay with curved ends and wide steel-framed windows. Gone were the timbering and pebbledashing, to be replaced by smooth rendering or facing brick work. The recessed porch often disappeared too, being replaced by a simple concrete canopy echoing the bay window line, and in came the characteristic sun-ray styled glazed front door. Yet within, the same standard semi floor plan survived.

Construction and materials

The walls of 1920s and 1930s semis are usually of cavity construction, with two leaves of brickwork, (blockwork, usually in breeze concrete blocks, was sometimes used for internal partition walls, but seldom for the inner leaf or cavity walls as is now the case). Solid 230mm (9in) brickwork may occasionally be found early in the period, and can be identified where it is exposed by the bonding pattern of the bricks.

The roof Almost always hipped, and is usually clad in small plain tiles (although pantiles are sometimes found on 1930s semis, especially those built in the 'Spanish' style). Gables are occasionally hipped, while protruding bays and dormers (sometimes found in mansard roofs over the front door) often had bituminous felt flat roofs, or zinc or lead sheet in better quality houses. Lead was almost universally used for flashings, aprons and soakers.

The roof structure is usually trussed, and in good quality construction the rafters may have been boarded before the tiles were added. Cheaper houses often had inadequately-sized timbers, which years later reveal themselves in sagging ridges and hips.

Windows and doors Usually of timber, with frequent use of leaded lights and decorative stained glass panels, although steel windows were widely used for public-sector building (now often owned rather than rented) and in the 'Modernist' semis of the mid-to-late 1930s.

Gutters, downpipes and external plumbing Normally of cast iron, with upstairs waste pipes and some valley gutters between gables discharging into hoppers. Where there is a secondary chimney flue (for a kitchen solid fuel boiler) a metal soot door may be found on the outer face of the flue near ground level.

Foundations Generally the concrete strip type, and unless they were of inadequate thickness or the subsoil has a low bearing capacity, they should still be performing well.

Floors Mainly the suspended timber type, although a shortage of timber in the 1920s led to an increase in solid ground floor construction.

Interior woodwork Generally of softwood, and this may originally have been stained to resemble more expensive hardwood on doors, staircases and picture rails. Many houses have (or had) areas of wood panelling which were usually of plywood rather than solid timber, and were very prone to woodworm.

Plumbing and electrics Likely to have been considerably altered and updated since the house was built. The original pipework was usually lead or iron and hot and cold water storage tanks were almost always of galvanised iron, and any remaining parts are likely to be a serious source of corrosion. The wiring, with lead (1920s) or rubber (1930s) insulation, will be well past the end of its safe life, and the fusebox and circuit provisions are likely to prove totally inadequate for modern needs. Most semis, however, will probably have been rewired.

Drains Usually of ceramic ware except on the best quality developments, where cast iron will have been used. The most distinctive feature of many properties built between the wars is the existence of interceptor chambers at the end of the drain run nearest the sewer. This was an inspection chamber containing a trap that was designed to keep sewer smells (and rats) out of the house drains, and a rodding eye to allow the last section of drain to be cleaned if it became blocked. The chamber is vented to the open air by a low-level ventilator which is a familiar sight in many suburban gardens; its galvanised 'periscope' is now probably rusted or cracked and its metal grille and mica flap damaged or missing.

The simple concept of the suburban semi has spawned a multitude of variations

visible? If it is, check that it is at least 150mm (6in) above paths and flower beds. If it isn't, check skirtings and plaster indoors for signs of damp.

Plumbing Are any galvanised components left? Check the cold tank in the loft and the hot cylinder. Are metal waste pipes still in use? What changes have been made to the system over the years?

Drains Are manholes in good condition? Lift any covers and look for debris build-up in the chambers — especially in interceptor chambers. Check the condition of gullies and hoppers too.

Electrics Look out for any signs of lead or rubber-sheathed cable and out-of-date fuseboxes; the switches and sockets may have been replaced without the house having been re-wired.

Interior woodwork Are there any signs of woodworm? Check especially the underside of the staircase and any surviving plywood panelling for woodworm holes that need treating.

Buying a semi

When you are looking over a semi with a view to buying it, run through the following checklist:

Roof Are there any signs of sagging in the roof structure, caused by undersized timbers? Are all the tiles intact and in position? Are chimney stacks sound — look for crumbling pointing, cracked flaunching round the pots and torn flashings. A pair of binoculars will be useful here.

Eaves Are cast-iron gutters sound, firmly fixed and free from sagging? Look for signs of water stains on the walls. Are fascias and soffits free from rot? Try to check the surface of any flat roofs to first-floor bays and dormers.

Walls Is pebbledash sound? Tap the surface here and there, listening for hollow sounds that indicate a bonding failure, and look for bare patches where the pebbles have become loose. Painting may conceal deterioration and cracks. Is half-timbering intact?

Bays Is tile hanging in good condition? Dropped tiles indicate possible nail sickness or rot in the battens, while cracked tiles are difficult to replace. Are sills free from rot? Probe them discreetly with a penknife blade. Check flashings are intact beneath sills and that drip channels are clean. Are there any signs of cracks where the bay joins the main wall? This could be a sign of inadequate bay foundations.

Windows and doors Is the wood free from rot? Are there problems with opening and closing casements due to sagging, paint build-up or, in metal windows, rust? Is stained glass and leaded work sound and apparently waterproof? Putty in the lead cames is a sign that they have begun to leak.

Damp course Is the damp course

THE SEMI'S BAD POINTS

A semi that was originally well-built and which has subsequently been well-maintained should have little in the way of serious problems. Some points to watch out for have already been detailed (see Buying a Semi). Other points to look out for include:
- shared driveways between properties, which may be a source of dispute between neighbours
- shared drain runs
- missing party walls in the roof space
- poor underfloor ventilation due to blocked air bricks
- condensation on the inside of exterior walls, and from within disused flues
- unsympathetic alterations — the fitting of large picture windows in place of the originals, or the fitting of exterior stone cladding to the walls. Any semi that sticks out like a sore thumb from its neighbours as a result of work of this sort may have undergone adventurous but unorthodox internal alterations too and these may not be to your taste.

Decorating the semi

Externally, the typical semi offers more scope for individual decorative schemes than houses of almost any other period. Pebbledashed and rendered areas can be painted white or in any one of a range of colours, while woodwork — fascias, bargeboards, doors and windows — can all be picked out in a matching or contrasting colour.

Pebbledash originally relied on the colour of the pebbles for its effect, but fifty or sixty years of exposure to the weather and to atmospheric pollution will usually have reduced undecorated surfaces to a drab and ugly condition.

It is, of course, perfectly feasible to strip off the old pebbledash and replace it, and such treatment may be necessary if the existing surface is loose, crumbly or badly cracked. However, there is something distinctly unsympathetic about new pebbledash, especially when seen alongside old pebbledash that has been decorated. So unless both halves of the building are being treated at the same time it is generally more harmonious to decorate the surface. The two semis don't have to have the same colour scheme, but it helps if they are not too dissimilar in appearance.

Painting pebbledash is hard work, however. Modern masonry paints give a very hardwearing finish, but there are two problems to overcome. The first is getting good adhesion; the walls may have been treated with cement paint in the past, and this is probably very chalky now and likely to cause early failure of any future repainting. The answer is to treat painted areas with a stabilizing primer before applying the new paint.

The second problem lies in actually getting good coverage; the nature of pebbledash makes it very awkward to get paint into all the recesses with a brush or roller. The solution in this case is to spray the paint on, using an electric spray gun. You must use the correct type of gun for the paint you intend to apply, since many guns cannot cope with the aggregate or filler used in many modern stone paints.

Exterior woodwork and metalwork generally looks best if painted in contrast to the coloured wall areas, and there is plenty of scope for two-colour schemes — frames and sills in a darker colour, for example, contrasting with white or a pale colour on opening casements and top lights, for example.

The most successful modern additions are those which have been designed to be in keeping with the houses' style

If you are unsure about what colour scheme you fancy, spend an hour touring local roads with notebook in hand, looking at schemes other homeowners have tried.

External plumbing is one feature of the semi best disguised, by the simple expedient of painting it the same colour as the wall surfaces it crosses.

Internally, the sky is the limit as far as decoration is concerned. Few people will want to return to the Thirties' look with its emphasis on dark woodwork and nineteenth century revivalist wallcoverings with their exaggerated floral patterns; instead, plain walls in pastel colours seem to be the popular choice.

Certain period features such as fireplaces and picture rails may remain, and can still be attractive parts of an up-to-date colour scheme. In general, the biggest drawback of the 'traditional' semi (as opposed to the 'sunshine' modernist semi with its curved glass windows) is lack of light. The heavily timbered window styles actually block out a lot of light from rooms, so using colour schemes that make the rooms appear light and airy is probably the most suitable approach.

Converting the semi

As mentioned earlier, the conventional semi offers generally greater scope for adaptation, conversion and extension than most other house types, because of the way the house and its site were laid out.

Within the house, by far the most popular conversion of recent years has been to knock two rooms together by removing one of the partition walls in between. Probably the commonest choice has been to link the two main living rooms, but others include opening up the wall between kitchen and dining room, or even between hall and sitting room.

Since all these walls are likely to be load-bearing, the job is not simply one for brute force and a sledge hammer; the load has to be transferred to a steel

1930s ads trumpeted the merits of the fully-equipped and fashionably-decorated new homes in the suburbs

beam adequately supported at each end on suitable bearings and properly encased for protection in the event of fire. Furthermore, such a major structural alteration must have Building Regulations approval, and so plans of the proposed alterations must be submitted to the local authority before work starts. The local building inspector will advise on the size and positioning of any beams being used, so you or your builder cannot make a potentially costly and dangerous mistake.

Side extensions are another possibility, thanks to the usually generous spacing of the buildings. A single-storey garage can be used as the basis for a two-storey extension with extra

After about 50 years, the exterior of many semis will have deteriorated. The pebbledash sometimes looks dull, and painting it is often the only answer (below). But be careful with more ambitious schemes (left) – inappropriate decoration may hide the semi's distinctive character

THE PRICE OF A SEMI

The price you pay for a semi obviously depends on a host of local factors and of course on the actual condition of the house itself. As a broad guide to house prices, the Halifax Building Society publishes quarterly figures for house prices nationwide. The chart below shows the price changes during 1984 and the first quarter of 1985.

Rateable values depend on local authority rating procedures, and may vary widely across local authority boundaries. When considering a purchase, enquire about the rateable value from the seller and confirm it with the local authority. Check too whether there are any plans for a future rate revaluation in the area which may increase the cost of ownership.

Region	1984				1985
	1st Qtr	2nd Qtr	3rd Qtr	4th Qtr	1st Qtr
Scotland	32,056	33,550	34,988	34,309	30,878
North	23,269	25,658	26,243	27,234	26,560
North-west	24,168	24,477	24,669	25,106	24,973
Humberside	21,413	22,261	22,495	22,979	22,576
East Midlands	21,582	21,421	21,868	21,987	22,215
West Midlands	23,210	23,331	24,130	23,791	24,292
East Anglia	25,750	27,674	29,233	29,712	31,598
South-east	36,768	38,948	39,698	40,871	42,667
London	47,767	50,126	51,766	53,152	55,141
South-west	30,276	31,314	31,603	33,853	32,991
Wales	22,750	24,624	25,650	24,245	24,869
Northern Ireland	21,956	22,160	22,420	22,911	22,226
Average	**28,615**	**29,975**	**30,352**	**30,756**	**30,651**

Sun-ray patterns are found all over the semi, particularly as stained glass windows in front doors (above) and even on gates (above)

rooms over a new enlarged garage, and if efforts are made to extend the hipped roof instead of opting for the uglier alternative of a flat roof, the extension can be made to blend in very well with the rest of the house. Similarly, rear extensions can easily be added, although careful thought has to be given to access for extra rooms upstairs if a two-storey addition is preferred. Both types of extension offer the opportunity of concealing the waste and soil stacks within the new structure.

Loft conversions are usually possible too, since the type of roof construction used can be altered and braced to allow the insertion of dormer or roof windows. Access from the first floor may be difficult to arrange without sacrificing some of the usable space on that level, since a proper staircase must be installed to give access to the new loft rooms. In addition, the ceiling joists will have to be strengthened, and some rerouting of plumbing systems is likely to be involved.

Extensions and loft conversions both require Building Regulations approval, and extensions are likely to need planning permission too unless the work falls within the exempt limits of the Town & Country Planning Acts. Check with your local authority as soon as you have drawn up outline proposals.

Useful Information

However skilled a DIYer you may be, there are times when you want to get in touch with the appropriate specialist organisation or professional body for help or advice. Similarly, you may wish to contact a manufacturer for information about a product. All the names and addresses are listed here, together with details of the services which the specialist bodies can offer. There is also a list of prices to help you to calculate the cost of the tools and materials which you will need for the project you are planning.

Manufacturers & Suppliers

In certain cases, you may find that the retailers in your area do not stock a particular product or model reviewed in the product section of this book. If this happens, try contacting the manufacturers or suppliers listed below to establish where to find what you are looking for.

ABC

3M United Kingdom plc
3M House
PO Box 1
Bracknell
Berkshire

Atkinson-Walker (Saws) Ltd
Bower Street
Sheffield
S3 8RU

B & R Electrical Products Ltd
Temple Fields
Harlow
Essex CM20 2BG

BP Aquaseal Ltd
Kingsnorth Hoo
Rochester
Kent ME3 9ND

Baco Homemaster
British Alcan Consumer
Products Ltd
Raans Road
Amersham
Bucks
HP6 6JY

Bartol Plastics Ltd
Doncaster
Yorkshire

Bay Mills Ltd
Montagu Trading Estate
Montagu Road
London N18 2NQ

Belco
Concord House
241 City Road
London EC1

Black & Decker Power Tools
Cannon Lane
Maidenhead
Berks
SL6 3PD

Robert Bosch Ltd
PO Box 166
Rhodes Way
Watford
Herts

H Burbridge
Whittington Road
Oswestry
Shropshire
SY11 1HZ

Butterley Building Materials
Wellington Street
Ripley
Derby
DE5 3DZ

John Carr Joinery Sales Ltd
7 Albemarle Street
London W1X 4QD

Cementone Beaver Ltd
Cementone Division
Tingewick Road
Buckingham
MK18 1AN

Certes Security Ltd
189 Fulham Palace Road
London W6 8QX

Colt International Ltd
Havant
Hants
PO9 2LY

Copydex plc
1 Torquay Street
London W2 5EL

Gerald Coy Developments Ltd
Unit 2
Broom House
Catton Road,
Off Coppice Road
Arnold
Nottingham
NG5 7JD

Cuprinol Ltd
Adderwell
Frome
Somerset BA11 1NL

DEF

Danfoss Ltd
Perivale Industrial Estate
Horsenden Lane South
Greenford
Middlesex

Dunsley Heating Appliance Co Ltd
Fearnought
Huddersfield Road
Holmfirth
West Yorkshire
HD7 2TU

Dura-Drive Co Ltd
3 Albemarle road
Beckenham
Kent BR3 2HZ

Epsicon Products Ltd
PO Box 12
Thorns Road
Quarry Bank
Brierley Hill
West Midlands

Ever Ready (GB) Ltd
1255 High Road
Whetstone
London N20 0EJ

Frelen Ltd
Byron Avenue
Lowmoor Industrial Estate
Kirkby-in-Ashfield
Nottinghamshire
NG17 7LA

GHI

GKN Fasteners
Woden Road West
Kings Hill
Wednesbury
West Midlands
WS10 7TT

Hansil Ltd
Wintersells Road
Byfleet
Weybridge
Surrey KT14 7LH

Home Automation Ltd
Pindar Road
Hoddeston
Herts EN11 0ET

Homeden Ltd
70 High Street
Teddington
Middlesex
TW11 8JD

IMI Opella
Rotherwas Industrial Estate
Hereford
HR2 6JR

JKL

JEM Marketing
180 Princes Avenue
Palmers Green
London N13 6HL

Langdon (London) Ltd
5 Worminghall Road
Ickford
Aylesbury
Bucks
HP18 9JJ

Liberta Hardware Ltd
Elizabethan Way
Lutterworth
Leicestershire
LE17 4ND

A Levermore & Co Ltd
24 Endeavour Way
Wimbledon Park
London
SW19 8UH

London and Lancashire Rubber Co Ltd
Montague Industrial Estate
Montague Road
London N18 2NQ

MNO

MK Electric Ltd
Shrubbery Road
Edmonton
London N9 0PB

Makita Electric (UK) Ltd
8 Finway
Dallow Road
Luton
Beds
LU1 1TR

J Manger and Son Ltd
Mansfield House
Wollaston Road
Irchester
Northamptonshire
NN9 7DQ

Marley Waterproofing Ltd
PO Box 17
Otford
Sevenoaks
Kent
TN14 5EW

Myson Domestic Products Ltd
Ongar
Essex CM5 9RE

OBO
Douglas Kane Ltd
Carlyon Road
Atherstone
Warwickshire
CV9 1LQ

Onlyway Products Ltd
Aspendale Works
Bridge Street
Church
Accrington
Lancashire

PQR

POB Savident Ltd
Unit P
Craddock Road
Luton
Bedfordshire
LU4 0JF

Peglars Ltd
St Catherine's Avenue
Doncaster
South Yorkshire
DN4 8DF

Peugeot Power Tools
AEG-Telefunken (UK) Ltd
217 Bath Road
Slough
Berkshire
SL1 4AW

Pentabridge Ltd
Pentabridge House
53 Newham Road
Cambridge CB3 9EY

Phillips Lighting
City House
420-430 London Road
Croydon
Surrey CR9 3QR

Piccadilly Products Ltd
199 Piccadilly
London W1

Plasplugs
Sheridan House
Vernon Street
Derby DE1 1FR

Polycell Products Ltd
Broadwater Road
Welwyn Garden City
Herts
AL7 3AZ

Potterton International Ltd
Portobello Works
Emscote Road
Warwick
CV34 5QU

The Rawlplug Co Ltd
Rawlplug House
London Road
Kingston-upon-Thames
Surrey
KT2 6NR

Readymix Drypack Ltd
The Sion
Crown Glass Place
Nailsea
Avon
BS19 2XY

Rentokil Ltd
Felcourt
East Grinstead
West Sussex
RH19 2JY

Ryton's Ventilation Equipment Ltd
58-60 Roundhill Road
Kettering
Northants
NN15 6BG

STU

Sandhill (Bullion) Ltd
Security Division
Sandhill House
Templar Place
Leeds
LS2 7NX

Sandvik UK Ltd
Hereward Rise
Halesowen
West Midlands

Seaboard International Ltd
British Columbia House
3 Regent Street
London
W1Y 4NY

Semiconductor Supplies International Ltd
Dawson House
128/130 Carshalton Road
Sutton
Surrey
SM1 4RS

Shop-Vac Ltd
Thorp Arch
 Trading Estate
Wetherby
Yorkshire
LS23 7EA

Skarsten Manufacturing Co Ltd
1 Cronin Courtyard
Corby
Northants
NN18 8AG

Skilten Electronics Ltd
30 London Road
Woolmer Green
Knebworth
Herts
SG3 6JP

Smiths Industries Environmental Controls Co Ltd
Waterloo Road
Cricklewood
London
NW2 7UR

Spiralux Handtools Ltd
Gillingham
Kent

Steinel UK Ltd
17 Reddicap
 Trading Estate
Sutton Coldfield
West Midlands
B75 7BU

Sterling Roncraft
Chapeltown
Sheffield
S. Yorkshire
S30 4YP

Superswitch Electric Appliances Ltd
Station Trading Estate
Blackwater
Camberley
Surrey
GU17 9AH

Swan Houseware Ltd
Midland House
New Road
Halesowen
West Midlands
B63 3HY

Swish Products Ltd
Lichfield Road
 Industrial Estate
Tamworth
Staffordshire
B79 7TW

Thorn EMI Ltd
Thorn House
Upper St Martin's Lane
London
WC2H 9ED

Thorsman (UK) Ltd
Thor House
Yarrow Mill
Chorley
Lancs
PR6 0LP

Tobylec Marketing Ltd
Park Bridge Mill
Grimshaw Park
Blackburn
Lancashire
BB2 3AG

Uni-Tubes Ltd
189 Bath Road
Slough
Berkshire
SL1 4AR

VWXYZ

Vitrex Tools Division
Florin Ltd
457-463 Caledonian Road
London
N7 9BB

Vencil Resil Ltd
Arndale House
Arndale Centre
Dartford
Kent
DA1 2HT

Willan Building Services
2 Brooklands Road
Sale
Cheshire
M33 3SS

Wolfcraft
PTS Tool Spec Ltd
PO Box 224
Henley Street
Camp Hill
Birmingham

These addresses are correct at the time of going to press. But the list of addresses will change from year to year. If you are unable to contact the manufacturer you require, please check the addresses with Directory Enquiries or look in the Yellow Pages for the most up to date information.

Where to get advice

There will always be a time when you need advice, help or even a specialist in a particular field. This chapter should ease the difficulty of finding who to turn to, giving the names and addresses of associations, authorities and councils who can offer advice on how best to tackle your particular problem.

ARCHITECTS & SURVEYORS
Incorporated Association of Architects & Surveyors
Jubilee House
Billing Brook Road
Weston Favell
Northamptonshire NN3 4NW
Tel: Northampton 404121
Will provide lists of IAAS members in your area.

Royal Institute of British Architects
Clients Advisory Service
66 Portland Place
London W1N 4AD
Tel: 01-323 0687
Will provide lists of RIBA members in your area, plus standard form of contract for building work and cost scales.

Royal Institution of Chartered Surveyors
12 Great George Street
London SW1P 3AD
Tel: 01-222 7000
Will provide lists of building surveyors in your area

BUILDERS
Building Employers Confederation
82 New Cavendish Street
London W1M 8AD
Tel: 01-580 5588
Will provide lists of BEC-registered builders in your area.

Federation of Master Builders
33 John Street
London WC1N 2BB
Tel: 01-242 7583
Will provide lists of FMB builders in your area, plus those on their register of warranted builders.

National Home Enlargement Bureau
PO Box 67
High Wycombe
Buckinghamshire HP15 6XP
Tel: High Wycombe 711649
Will provide lists of builders in your area specialising in home extension work.

National House Building Council
58 Portland Place
London W1N 4BU
Tel: 01-637 1248
Operates 10-year protection scheme on new houses and flats, will arbitrate in case of disputes.

Society of Self Builders
Chelston House
Flower Lane
Amesbury
Wiltshire SP4 7HE
Tel: Amesbury 22933
Offers detailed advice on building your own home.

DAMP, WOODWORM & ROT
British Chemical Dampcourse Association
PO Box 105
Reading
Berkshire RG3 6NG
Tel: Reading 24911
Will provide lists of members in your area (who must obey a code of practice) and publishes useful leaflets.

British Wood Preserving Association
Premier House
150 Southampton Row
London WC1B 5AL
Tel: 01-837 8217
Will provide lists of member firms in your area (who must obey a code of practice) and will deal with complaints; publishes many useful leaflets.

Timber Research & Development Association
Stocking Lane
Hughenden Valley
High Wycombe
Buckinghamshire HP14 4ND
Tel: (Naphill) 3091
Will provide names of independent consultants who can arbitrate in cases of dispute over wood treatment; publishes much useful technical literature.

DECORATING MATERIALS
British Floorcovering Manufacturers Association
125 Queens Road
Brighton
Sussex BN1 3YW
Tel: Brighton 33322
Will provide manufacturers' literature and background information.

Paintmakers Association of Great Britain
Alembic House
93 Albert Embankment
London SE1 7TY
Tel: 01-582 1185
Will provide fact sheets and technical information.

DECORATORS
British Decorators Federation
6 Haywra Street
Harrogate
North Yorkshire HG1 5BL
Tel: Harrogate 67292
Will provide lists of members in your area (who must obey a code of practice).

British Institute of Interior Design
Lenton Lodge
Wollaton Hall Drive
Nottingham
Nottinghamshire NG8 1AP
Tel: Nottingham 701205
Will provide lists of members in your area and background information.

Scottish Decorators Association
249 West George Street
Glasgow G2 4RB
Tel: 041-221 7090
Will provide lists of members in your area.

ELECTRICIANS
Electrical Contractors Association (ECA)
Esca House
34 Palace Court
London W2 4HY
Tel: 01-229 1266
Will provide lists of members in your area; operates Guarantee of Work scheme

Electrical Contractors Association of Scotland
23 Heriot Row
Edinburgh EH3 6EW
Tel: 031-225 7221
Will provide lists of members in your area; operates Guarantee of Work scheme

National Inspection Council for Electrical Installation Contracting (NICEIC)
237 Kennington Lane
London SE11 5QJ
Tel: 01-582 7746
Maintains a roll of approved contractors; will investigate complaints against members

BUILDING & BUILDING MATERIALS
Asbestos Information Centre
Sackville House
40 Piccadilly
London W1V 9PA
Tel: 01-439 9231
Advice on working with materials containing asbestos and on disposing of them safely.

Brick Development Association
Woodside House
Winkfield
Windsor
Berkshire SL4 2DX
Tel: Winkfield Row 885651
Will give technical advice on building with bricks.

British Board of Agrément
PO Box 195
Bucknalls Lane
Garston
Watford
Hertfordshire WD2 7NG
Tel: Watford 670844
Publishes lists of building

products and installers holding Agrément certificates of approval.

Building Centre Group
26 Store Street
London WC1E 7BT
Tel: 01-637 1022
Also in Birmingham, Bristol, Cambridge, Glasgow, Liverpool, Manchester, Nottingham and Southampton. Mounts displays of building products and equipment, offers extensive manufacturers' literature and book shop facilities.

Building Research Station
Bucknalls Green
Garston
Watford
Hertfordshire WD2 7JR
Offers an advisory service and extensive publications on building materials, practices and problems.

ELECTRICITY
Build Electric Bureau
26 Store Street
London WC1E 7BT
Tel: 01-580 4986
Publishes information on electric heating and equipment, gives advice and answers queries.

Decorative Lighting Association
Bishops Castle
Shropshire SY9 5LE
Tel: Bishops Castle 4658
Will supply lists of manufacturers of light fittings.

Electrical Association for Women
25 Fouberts Place
London W1V 2AL
Tel: 01-437 5212
Publishes literature, gives advice and answers queries.

Electricity Council
30 Millbank
London SW1 4RD
Tel: 01-834 4444
Publishes useful leaflets and books.

Institution of Electrical Engineers (IEE)
Savoy Place
London WC2R OBL
Tel: 01-240 1871
Publishes the IEE Wiring

Regulations and more intelligible guides to understanding them. Can be contacted for advice and guidelines on installation of appliances.

FIXTURES & FITTINGS
British Security Industry Association
68 St James Street
London SW1A 1PH
Tel: 01-493 6634
Will provide lists of firms making locks, burglar alarms and other home security equipment.

Council of British Ceramic Sanitaryware Manufacturers
Federation House
Station Road
Stoke-on-Trent
Staffordshire ST4 2RU
Tel: Stoke-on-Trent 48675
Will give advice and answer queries on ceramic bathroom fittings, and provide literature and names and addresses of manufacturers.

Kitchen Specialists Association
31 Bois Lane
Chesham Bois
Amersham
Buckinghamshire NP6 6BO
Tel: Amersham 22287
Will provide a list of members (who are bound by a code of practice) and will investigate complaints; offers a consumer protection scheme for customers buying from members.

Master Locksmiths Association
13 Parkfield Road
Northolt
Middlesex UB5 5NN
Tel: 01-845 1676
Will provide lists of members in your area.

National Supervisory Council for Intruder Alarms
St Ives House
St Ives Road
Maidenhead
Berkshire SL6 1RD
Tel: Maidenhead 37512
Will provide a list of approved installers of burglar alarms meeting British Standard BS 4737. Will advise on choice of alarm.

HEATING AND VENTILATION
Air Conditioning Advisory Bureau
30 Millbank
London SW1 4RD
Tel: 01-834 4444
Gives advice and answers queries.

Confederation for the Registration of Gas Installers (CORGI)
St Martins House
140 Tottenham Court Road
London W1P 9LN
Tel: 01-387 9185
Will provide a list of registered installers of gas equipment of all types (list also available at local Gas Board showroom).

Heating & Ventilating Contractors Association (HVCA)
Esca House
34 Palace Court
London W2 4JG
Tel:01-229 5543
Publishes literature, gives advice and operates consumer protection scheme for people using HVCA members.

National Association of Chimney Sweeps
PO Box 35
Stoke-on-Trent
Staffordshire ST4 7NU
Tel: Stoke-on-Trent 44311
Will provide lists of member firms (who must obey a code of practice).

National Fireplace Council
PO Box 35
Stoke-on-Trent
Staffordshire ST4 7NU
Tel: Stoke-on-Trent 44311
Publishes fact sheets and leaflets and distributes manufacturers' literature.

National Heating Consultancy
PO Box 370
London SE9
Tel 01-859 5543
Will give advice on all aspects of central heating products and systems.

Solar Trade Association
19 Albemarle Street
London W1X 3HA
Tel: 01-629 7459
Publishes useful literature and will provide a list of member

firms (who are bound by a code of practice).

Solid Fuel Advisory Service
Hobart House
Grosvenor Place
London SW1X 7AE
Tel: 01-235 2020 and branches nationwide.
Offers advice on solid fuels and equipment, and publishes useful leaflets.

Ventilation Advisory Bureau
PO Box 16
Poole
Dorset
Tel: Poole 735222
Will provide lists of member firms who will install ventilation equipment in your area.

Wood & Solid Fuel Association of Retailers and Manufacturers
33 Alfred Place
London WC1E 7EN
Tel: 01-508 3344
Publishes literature on wood-burning and other solid fuel heating equipment.

INSULATION & DRAUGHTPROOFING
Association of British Manufacturers of Mineral Insulating Fibres (eurisol-UK)
St Pauls House
Edison Road
Bromley
Kent BR2 OEP
Tel: 01-466 6719
Publishes useful leaflets on insulation materials, techniques and statistics.

Association of Noise Consultants
6 Long Lane
London EC1A 9DP
Tel: 01-606 1461
Will give advice on noise problems, and provide names of specialist noise reduction consultants.

British Standards Institution
Quality Assurance Division
Maylands Avenue
Hemel Hempstead
Hertfordshire HP2 4SQ
Tel: Hemel Hempstead 3111
Will provide a list of registered installers of approved types of cavity foam insulation in your locality.

WHERE TO GET ADVICE

Cavity Foam Bureau
9-11 The Hayes
Cardiff CF1 1NU
Tel: Cardiff 388621
Will provide a list of firms
installing in your area.

**Draughtproofing Advisory
Association
External Wall Insulation
Association
National Association of Loft
Insulating Contractors
National Cavity Insulation
Association**
PO Box 12
Haslemere
Surrey GU27 3AN
Tel: Haslemere 54011
Gives advice, answers queries
and provides lists of member
companies, plus consumer
protection scheme.

PLUMBING
Institute of Plumbing
Scottish Mutual House
North Street
Hornchurch
Essex RM11 1RV
Tel: Hornchurch 72791
Will provide names from its
register of plumbers or firms
working in your area; does not
guarantee members' work, but
will investigate complaints.

**National Association of
Plumbing, Heating and
Mechanical Services
Contractors**
6 Gate Street
London WC2A 3HX
Tel: 01-405 2678
Will give names of members
working in your area.

PROPERTY
**Incorporated Society of
Valuers and Auctioneers**
3 Cadogan Gate
London SW1X 0AS
Tel: 01-235 2282

**National Association of
Conveyancers**
2-4 Chichester Rents
Chancery Lane
London WC2A 1EJ

**National Institute of
Conveyancing Agents**
41a Prospect Hill
Swindon
Wiltshire
SN1 3JS
Tel: (0793) 6952570

**National Association of
Estate Agents**
Arbon House
21 Jury Street
Warwick CV34 4EG
Tel: (0926) 496800

**The Housing Enquiry
Service**
8 Manchester Square
London W1M 6AJ

ROOFING
**Bituminous Roofing
Council**
PO Box 125
32a The Broadway
Haywards Heath
West Sussex RH16 3TJ
Tel: Haywards Heath 416681
Will give advice and answer
queries, and publishes fact
sheets and leaflets.

**National Federation of
Roofing Contractors**
15 Soho Square
London W1V 5FB
Tel: 01-439 1753
Will provide lists of member
firms, operates a complaints
procedure but does not give
an overall guarantee of
members' work.

**National Society of Master
Thatchers**
25 Little Lane
Yardley Hastings
Northamptonshire
Tel: Yardley Hastings 280
Will provide a list of members
working in your area, and also
publishes useful leaflets.

SOLICITORS
The Law Society
113 Chancery Lane
London WC2A 1PL
Tel: 01-242 1222

The Law Society of Scotland
PO Box 79
26 Drumsheugh Gardens
Edinburgh EH3 7YT.

SAFETY & SECURITY
**British Insurance
Association**
Aldermary House
Queen Street
London EC4N 1TU

**British Security Industry
Association**
68 St James Street
London SW1A 1PH

**National Supervisory
Council for Intruder Alarms**
St Ives House
St Ives Road
Maidenhead
Berks SL6 1RD

WINDOWS & DOUBLE GLAZING
**Aluminium Window
Association (AWA)
Steel Window Association
(SWA)**
26 Store Street
London WC1E 7BT
Tel: 01-637 3578 (AWA),
01-637 3571 (SWA)
Publishes leaflets and
distributes manufacturers'
literature.

Glass & Glazing Federation
6 Mount Row
London W1Y 6DY
Tel: 01-409 0545
Will give advice and answer
queries, publishes useful
literature on glass and double
glazing, and will provide lists of
registered members carrying
out installation work in your
area.

WOOD
**British Woodworking
Federation**
82 New Cavendish Street
London W1M 8AD
Tel: 01-580 5588
Will give advice on timber
frame housing, wood windows
and doors, and provides lists
of registered installers working
in your area.

**Chipboard Promotion
Association**
50 Station Road
Marlow
Buckinghamshire SL7 1NN
Tel: Marlow 3266
Gives advice, answers
queries, publishes fact sheets
and further information.

**Fibre Building Board
Development Organisation
(FIDOR)**
1 Hanworth Road
Feltham
Middlesex TW13 5AF
Tel: 01-751 6107
Gives advice on hardboards
and other fibre building
boards, publishes useful
leaflets. Will recommend
best applications for
particular boards.

Blocked Drains
Contact local authority
environmental health
department if no local private
firm can help.

Carpet Cleaning
Carpet Cleaners Association
Ventnor House
97 Knighton Fields Road West
Leicester
Tel: Leicester 836065

Electrical Emergencies
Contact local electricity board,
emergency number — in
telephone book under
ELECTRICITY.

Fire Safety
Fire Prevention Information
and Publications Service
Aldermary House
Queen Street
London EC4N 1TU
Tel: 01-248 4477

Gas Emergencies
Contact local gas board
emergency number
immediately — in telephone
book under GAS.

Junk Removal
Hire a skip, or contact local
authority for details of public
dumps in your area.

Locked Out?
Contact local police station if no
locksmith can help.

Pests
British Pest Control
Association
Alembic House
93 Albert Embankment
London SE1 7TU
Tel: 01-582 8268
or contact local authority
environmental health
department.

Removals
British Association of
Removers
279 Grays Inn Road
London WC1X 8SY
Tel: 01-837 3088/9

Uphholsterers
Association of Master
Upholsterers
348 Neasden Lane
London NW10 0EP
Tel: 01-205 0465

Tools, materials, prices

Most DIY jobs start with a shopping list for the tools and materials needed for the job. In this section, we give some of the answers to your questions on what you need, what quantities you need and just how much it's going to cost you. But shop around — our prices are only a guideline.

CUTTING TOOLS

	Use	Price £
Panel saw	good general-purpose saw for cutting	from 10.00
Tenon saw	useful saw for accurate cutting	from 10.00
Power jig saw	primarily for curved cuts	from 22.00
Hacksaw	for cutting metal	from 5.00

MEASURING AND MARKING TOOLS

	Use	Price £
Flexible metal tape	useful pocket rule to carry around	3.25
Folding rule	portable rule for woodworking	3.00
Mitre block	guide for cutting small timber at an angle of 45° or 90°	4.50
Spirit level	for checking horizontals and verticals	from 8.00 for 24 in
Try square	for marking and checking right angles	8.00

SCREWDRIVERS

	Use	Price £
Slotted-head screwdriver	for driving slotted-head screws	from 2.30
Cross-head screwdriver	for driving cross-head screws; there are two types — Phillips and Pozidriv	from 2.00
Ratchet screwdriver	for driving screws without having to alter your grip on the handle	from 3.75

ELECTRICIAN'S TOOLS

	Use	Price £
Wire strippers	for removing insulation from cable or flex	4.50
Long-nosed pliers	for cutting and bending conductors	from 4.50
Mains tester	for tightening terminal screws; also warns when wires are live	1.30 for 6in screwdriver

HOW MANY TILES?

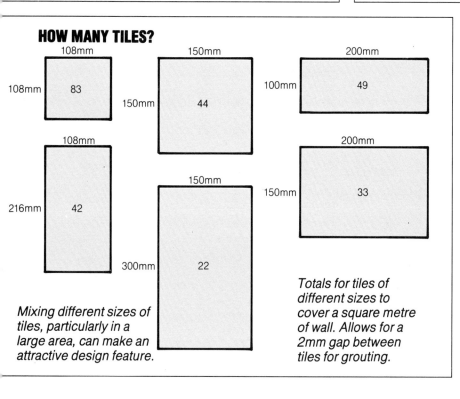

Mixing different sizes of tiles, particularly in a large area, can make an attractive design feature.

Totals for tiles of different sizes to cover a square metre of wall. Allows for a 2mm gap between tiles for grouting.

HOW MANY BRICKS?

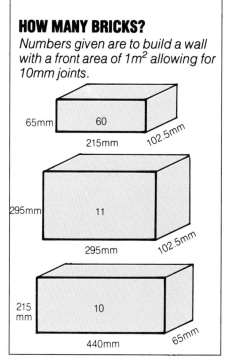

Numbers given are to build a wall with a front area of 1m² allowing for 10mm joints.

TOOLS, MATERIALS & PRICES

TOOLS FOR HOLDING THINGS

	Use	Price £
G-clamp	general-purpose clamps in many sizes for holding and clamping	from 3.00
Frame clamp	for making up four-cornered frames	about 2.00
Woodworker's vice	for gripping wood while it is worked on	from 10.00
Workbench-cum-vice	for supporting and gripping things	around 35.00

PLUMBING TOOLS

	Use	Price £
Plunger	for unblocking the waste pipes of sinks and basins	from 1.20
Pipe bending spring	to support the walls of copper pipe as it is bent to shape	from 1.70
Pipe cutter	to cut squarely through pipe	around 5.00
Adjustable wrench	for holding and turning nuts	from 4.50
Basin spanner	for undoing nuts in tight spots	3.50

BUILDING TOOLS

	Use	Price £
Brick trowel	flat triangular trowel for bricklaying	from 12.25
Pointing trowel	smaller version of the brick trowel	from 4.25
Club hammer	for driving a bolster chisel	from 7.00
Bolster chisel	chisel for cutting bricks and blocks	from 3.00
Plasterer's trowel	rectangular tool for applying plaster	from 6.00
Putty knife	for smoothing putty to the right angle	1.50

DECORATING TOOLS

	Use	Price £
Paint brushes	for applying paint to most surfaces	from 0.90
Paint scraper	for scraping off paint	from 1.75
Filling knife	for pushing filler into holes	around 1.90
Tile cutter	for cutting ceramic tiles	from 17.00
Hot air stripper	for softening paint to be removed	from 15.00

CONCRETE AND MORTAR

These are both mixed from cement, sand or aggregate and water in varying proportions.

	Size	Price £
Cement	50 kg	2.80
Sand	40 kg	1.40
Aggregate	40 kg	1.40

ELECTRICAL HARDWARE

	Use	Price £
13 amp plug	connecting appliances to socket outlets	from 0.40
Socket outlet	providing power to appliances	5.25
Socket outlet box	metal: for sinking into the plaster	1.10
	plastic: for surface mounting	1.70
Ceiling rose	for 'loop-in' lighting circuits	1.00
Pull-cord switch	for use in bathrooms	3.25
Fused connection unit	provides permanent connection for appliances	4.25

CABLE AND FLEX

Cable is thick plastic covered wire used for fixed wiring; flex is flexible cable for connecting electrical equipment to the fixed wiring. Choose the size of cable to match the job. The size of flex depends on the current rating of the appliance.

	Use	Price £/metre
CABLE		
$1.0mm^2$ two-core and earth	most lighting circuits	0.22
$1.5mm^2$ two-core and earth	lighting circuits with more than ten lighting points	0.35
$2.5mm^2$ two-core and earth	ring circuits, 20 amp radial circuits	0.45
$1.0mm^2$ three-core and earth	wiring between two-way light switches	0.50
FLEX		
Double insulated two-core	has no earth so can be used only with double-insulated equipment	0.50
Double insulated three-core	most general purposes	0.80
Unkinkable three-core	for irons	1.46

PAINTS

	Use	Coverage sq.m/litre	Price £/litre
Primer	To seal a bare surface and make it ready for the next coat	15	3.75
Undercoat	Between primer and topcoat when painting over a dark colour	15	3.75
Liquid gloss	Topcoat for wood or metal	15-17	3.00
Non-drip gloss	Topcoat for wood or metal	12-14	3.00
Emulsion paint	For walls and ceilings indoors; usually sold as vinyl matt or vinyl silk	7	1.60
Masonry paint	For walls outside; available smooth or sand textured	6	1.80

PIPES AND FITTINGS

The size of pipe you use is determined by the job: 15mm for supplies to sinks and basins; 22mm for showers and baths.

PIPES

	Use	Size mm	Price £/metre
Copper	all plumbing jobs	15	0.70
		22	1.50
cPVC	hot and cold water supplies (indoors only)	15	0.70
		22	1.15
Polybutylene	hot and cold water supplies indoors and outdoors	15	0.70
		22	1.33
Rigid plastic	waste pipes for all sorts of fittings	32	0.90
		38	1.15

FITTINGS

	Use	Price £ 15mm equal tee
Capillary	with copper or polybutylene pipes	0.55
Compression	with copper or polybutylene pipes	1.00
Push-fit	with copper or polybutylene supply	1.30
Solvent-weld supply	with cPVC supply pipe	1.72
Push-fit waste	with rigid plastic waste pipe — price for 38mm size	1.70

HIRE COSTS

Always allow yourself plenty of time when you hire an appliance, then you won't need to rush the job in order to get it back to the hire shop on time.

	£ per day	£ per week
Wallpaper stripper	7.50	13.50
Ladder 8m	6.50	10.25
Roof ladder	2.00	2.50
Platform tower	12.50	20.00
Floor sander	17.50	33.00
Pipe bender	3.50	5.00
Chain saw	25.00	48.00

MAN-MADE TIMBER BOARDS

Man-made boards are cheaper than timber straight from the tree and come in larger sheets which are easy to work with.

Board Thickness	Typical use	Size length × width	Price £
8mm Chipboard	cabinets, flooring, shelving	2.4m × 1.2m	7.00
18mm Melamine-faced chipboard	cupboards in kitchens and bathrooms; shelving	1.8m × 150mm	0.95
3.2mm Plywood	backing furniture, drawers and shelves	1.8m × 600mm	8.25
3.2mm Hardboard	cover floorboards before carpeting; drawer bases	2.4m × 1.2m	3.50
18mm Blockboard	heavy-duty shelving, table tops	1.8m × 600mm	9.00

NAILS

Nailing is a quick and easy way to join things together. Loose nails by the kg are generally cheaper than pre-packs.

	Use	Size	No in kg	Price £
Panel pin	for fixing thin wood and moulding; reinforcing glued joints	25mm	1540	¼kg from 75p
Hardboard pin	for fixing hardboard	20mm	1980	¼kg from 90p
Oval wire nail	general-purpose to avoid wood splitting	50mm	235	½kg from 1.20
Round wire nail	for rough work	50mm	170	½kg from 1.20
Masonry nail	fixing into masonry	51mm	—	50 from 60p

Glossary

New technology means new products, new materials, new tools and new techniques — and this means new words. The aim of this glossary is to keep the language of DIY abreast of new technology and also to give clear meanings to those words which have been constantly misused over the years.

Electricity

Bonding The linking of metalwork to the main earth of the electrical system. Metal service pipes should be bonded as near as possible to where they enter the house. Other metalwork should be bonded locally.

Cable The thick, plastic-covered wire used for permanent wiring.

Cartridge fuse A factory-made fuse which simply slots in its holder in the house fusebox. Smaller ones are used in square-pin plugs.

Conductors The solid or stranded copper wires inside cable or flex.

Earthing The main protection against shock if faults develop in an electrical system. Each circuit has an earth conductor which is connected to the house earth terminal.

Earth leakage circuit breaker (ELCB) Also known as a residual current circuit breaker (RCCB). These special circuit breakers can be lifesavers. They work by sensing when current is escaping from a circuit — if someone gets an electric shock, for example — and cutting off the electricity to the appliance being used.

Fuse A deliberate weak link in an electrical circuit, which is designed to 'blow' if a fault causes the circuit to carry too much current.

Miniature circuit breaker Used instead of a fuse in the main fuse box, this serves the same function as a fuse but is quicker-acting, more reliable, and can be simply reset if a fault causes it to trip.

Protected socket A socket protected by an ELCB. Sockets used to supply electrical equipment used out of doors — such as a lawnmower — should be protected with a high-sensitivity ELCB.

Radial circuit An electrical circuit which goes out from the fuse box but does not loop back. It is generally used for wiring fixed equipment which needs its own circuit, but can also supply sockets.

Residual current circuit breakers (RCCB)/residual current device (RCD) See earth leakage circuit breaker.

Ring circuit An electrical circuit which is formed as a large loop of cable going from a 30amp fuse and back again. Sockets are usually installed on a ring circuit.

Spur A branch of cable off a ring circuit. It can serve only one socket outlet or fixed appliance.

Plumbing

Airlock A pocket of air trapped in the pipe which can cause the water to splutter or cease to run: it is more common in hot water pipes than in cold.

Ballvalve A valve operated by an arm with a ball float on it which rises with the water level to close the valve when the water in a tank or cistern reaches a certain level.

Ceramic disc tap A tap which has long lasting ceramic discs instead of conventional washers.

Dead leg A long branch of hot water pipe where the water will cool down before it reaches the tap.

Direct system A water supply system in which all the taps and plumbed-in appliances are connected directly to the pipe bringing water into the house.

Gatevalve A valve installed in a supply pipe to shut off the flow of water.

Indirect system A water supply system in which the drinking water tap in the kitchen is connected directly to the pipe bringing water into the house, but all other taps and plumbed-in appliances are supplied from a cold water storage cistern.

Sewer An underground drain pipe.

Soakaway A hole below ground which is filled with rubble to make a place where water draining from the house roof or from paving can literally soak away into the ground.

Soil pipe The large pipe into which the house waste goes. It eventually flows underground to the sewer.

Stopvalve A valve, also called a stopcock, which can control or shut off the flow of water through a pipe.

Trap A bend in the waste pipe from a fitting which always stays full of water to stop smells rising from the drains.

Tube Another name for copper pipe.

Unvented system A direct water supply system in which hot water is stored under pressure with safety valves instead of vent pipe: existing water byelaws do not permit them in this country, but the byelaws are under review.

Vent pipe The pipe from the top of a hot water cylinder which leads back to the cold water cistern: its function is to allow steam to escape should the water in the cylinder overheat.

Warning pipe The pipe from a cold water cistern or WC which carries the overflow if the ballvalve sticks and the cistern overfill

Water hammer Knocking noises in the pipes, usually caused by a faulty valve or tap.

Water meter A meter to measure your consumption of water. You can elect to have your water metered and pay for the quantity you actually use rather than a flat rate calculated as a percentage of your house rates.

Heating

Corrosion inhibitor A liquid which is added to the water circulating in the boiler and radiators to reduce rusting.

Cylinder thermostat A sensor used to regulate the temperature of the hot water the cylinder. If it is set to below 60°C, it wi save money on heating bills and ensure that the hot water never reaches scalding point.

Combined boiler A central heating boiler which heats the water to circulate through the radiators and also works as an instantaneous water heater.

Feed-and-Expansion cistern A small water storage cistern, usually in the roof space, which is used to supply the water circulating through the radiators and also cope with any overflow.

Kickspace heater A convector radiator with an electric fan which is only about 100mm tall and can be fitted in the 'kickspace' beneath kitchen units.

Microbore Copper pipe with a small diameter which can be used for central heating systems.

Motorised valve A valve used to control the flow of water round a central heating system. The motor opens or closes the valve according to a signal received from a programmer or temperature control.

R value The measure of the effectiveness of an insulating material. The higher the R value, the more resistant it is to the passage of heat and the less quickly heat will pass through.

Room thermostat A sensor used to regulate room temperature. When the air in the room reaches the set temperature the thermostat turns off the central heating, usually by shutting down the boiler.

Thermostatic radiator valve An air temperature sensing valve which replaces the ordinary on/off valve of a radiator. When the air in the room reaches the set temperature, the valve closes to turn off the radiator. Each radiator is controlled individually.

U value The measure of the rate at which heat passes through part of the house — a wall, say. The lower the U value, the more slowly the heat will pass through. Adding insulation lowers the U value.

Indoor Features

Architrave The wooden moulding around a door which covers and neatens the join between the door frame and the wall.

Cornice Ornate plaster moulding which covers the angle between wall and ceiling.

Coving Similar to a cornice, but less ornate and sometimes in polystyrene.

Dado A moulding fitted to the wall at approximately waist height: there is sometimes wood panelling on the wall below.

Reveal The area of wall space around a window which is set back into the wall with a deep sill on the inside.

Winder A wedge-shaped stair which is used to turn a staircase round a corner without a half landing.

Outdoor features

Bargeboard The wooden board fitted at the gable end of the house to protect the roof timbers exposed there. It is often quite ornate.

Fascia The wooden board nailed to the ends of the rafters, partly for neatness but also for protection.

Flashing A sheet of lead or zinc used to seal the junction between the roof and anything which rises above it — a chimney or an adjoining wall, for instance.

Gully An open drain at ground level into which downpipes and waste pipes drain.

Gutter The channel fitted at the bottom of the roof slope to collect water draining off the roof and feed it to a downpipe and thence to a drain.

Header A brick used end on in a wall.

Hopper head The collection trough at the top of a soil pipe into which the waste pipes from first, and higher, floors drain.

Plinth A slightly thickened section of walling sometimes seen at the base of a house wall.

Stretcher A brick used side on in a wall.

Soffit A board fitted to the underside of the ends of the rafters, to box in the eaves of a house.

Valley gutter A special lining of lead sheet fitted where two parts of a sloping roof meet.

Lighting

Architrave box A narrow metal box intended for use with narrow wall switches, such as bell pushes, but useful for enclosing the connections to wall-mounted lights.

BESA box A round conduit box used to enclose the connections to ceiling-mounted fittings where a ceiling rose is not used. It can also be used with wall-mounted lights.

Dimmer An electronic control which can be used to alter the brightness of a light. Most replace the ordinary wall-mounted light switch, but you can get plug-in dimmers and ones to wire in the flex to a table lamp.

Fluorescent lamps Lamps which give out light from glowing (or fluorescing) particles used to coat the inside of the glass. Fluorescent tubes were once the only type, but there are now 'compact' fluorescent lamps which can be used in the same light fittings as tungsten lamps.

Lamp The correct collective name for light bulbs, spotlights and fluorescent tubes.

Lumens The units used to measure the amount a light, a lamp emits — a 100W tungsten lamp gives out roughly twice as many lumens as a 60W one. To compare the light output of a tungsten lamp with a fluorescent one, you need to know the outputs in lumens.

Photocell A light-sensitive control which can be used to make a light come on at dusk and go off at dawn.

Timeswitch A time control which can be set to make a light go on an off at different times. These are very useful for porch and security lights.

Two-way lights Lights which can be switched on and off from two different switches. Although mostly used for the top and bottom of stairs, they can be used in many other places — in a bedroom, for instance, the main light can be switched off both from the bed and by the door.

Tungsten lamps Lamps which emit light from a heated wire. The ordinary light bulb is most common; lamps such as spots are also tungsten. They cost much more to run than fluorescent lamps.

Tungsten halogen lamps Special tungsten lamps which run hotter and give out a brighter, whiter light.

Damp and rot

Dampproof course A band, usually of bitumen felt, which is laid in a mortar course between bricks at least 150mm above the ground to stop moisture from the ground rising up the wall.

Dampproof membrane (dpm) A sheet, usually of plastic, incorporated into a concrete floor to stop moisture rising from the ground below.

Dry rot Serious fungal decay which, although it principally attacks timber, can spread through brick and plaster. Once discovered it must be eradicated by stripping back the affected plaster, removing infected timbers and treating the whole area with a fungicidal solution.

Moisture meter An instrument used by damp surveyors to detect moisture in a wall. It does not give an exact measure of the amount of damp, but can be used to discover the 'pattern' of dampness which will give a clue to its cause.

Solid floor A ground floor made of concrete laid over hardcore resting directly on to the ground.

Suspended timber floor A wooden floor at ground level or on higher floors of a house which is constructed from boards laid over supporting timber joists.

Vapour check A membrane, usually a plastic sheet, which is intended to stop moisture vapour from inside the house escaping into the fabric of the house where it could condense and cause rot. It is needed, for instance, where insulation is installed on the inside of a wall.

Wallplates Lengths of timber fitted on top of the dwarf walls which support the joists for a suspended timber ground floor.

Wet rot Rot caused by fungi that attack wet wood. If the source of dampness is removed, the rot will cease, although badly damaged wood may need to be removed. Timber treated with modern wood preservative shouldn't rot and should last indefinitely.

Index

Simply look up the subject you wish to know about under the appropriate letter in the A-Z index. Should you not find it there, think of a broader subject area. For instance, if you wanted to know how to make a bathroom cabinet, you could look under *Cabinet* or *Bathroom*.